Steeped in History

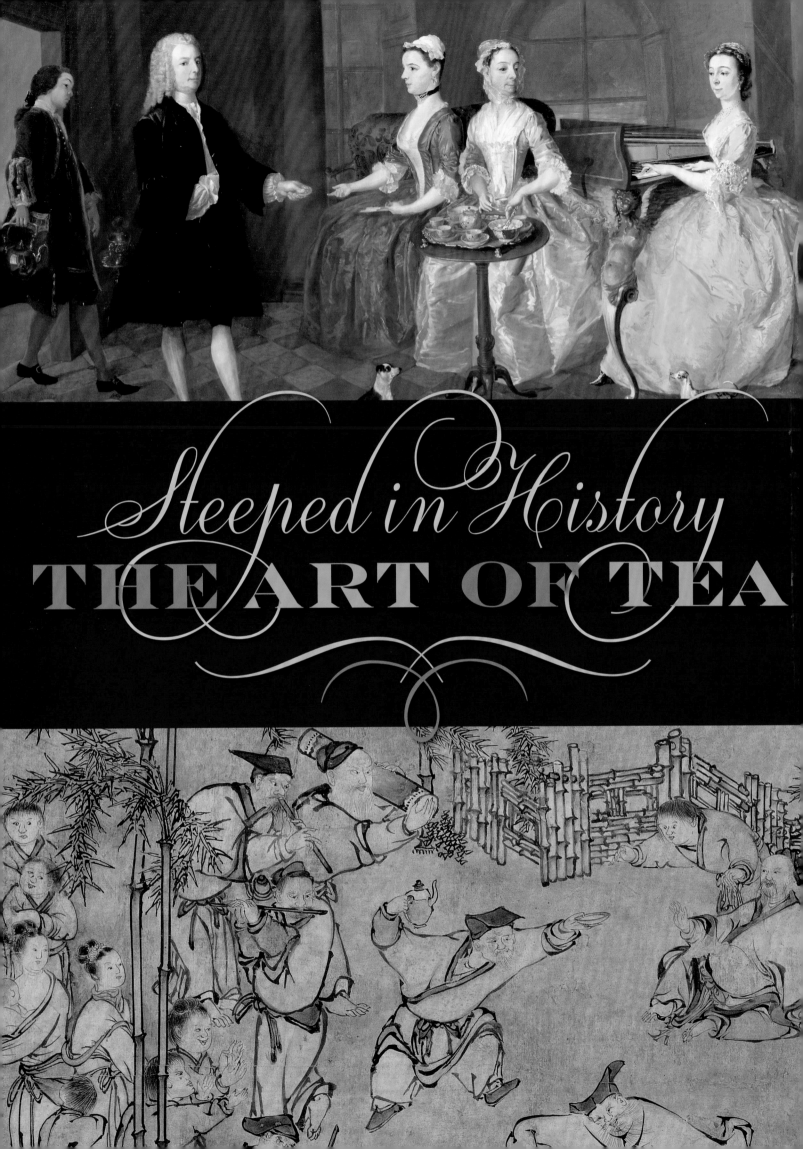

Steeped in History
THE ART OF TEA

Beatrice Hohenegger, Editor

With essays by

Terese Tse Bartholomew
Barbara G. Carson
Patricia J. Graham
Dennis Hirota
Elizabeth Kolsky
Jane T. Merritt

Steven D. Owyoung
Woodruff D. Smith
Reiko Tanimura
Angus Trumble
John E. Wills Jr.

Fowler Museum at UCLA
LOS ANGELES

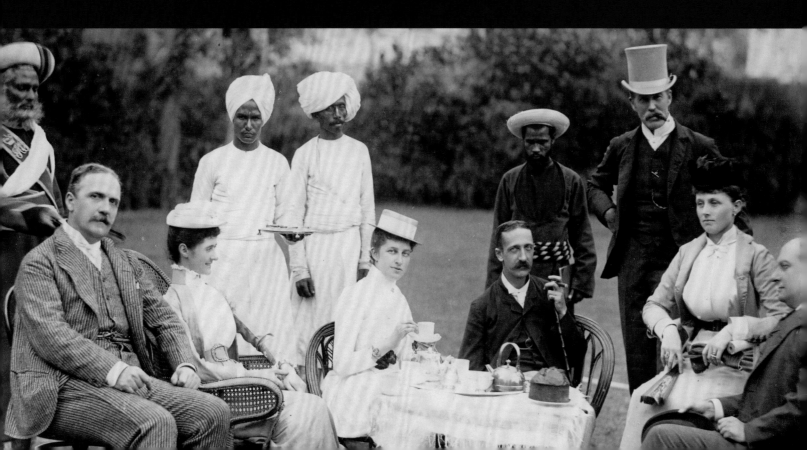

Major support for the exhibition is provided by the Henry Luce Foundation. Mr. Lloyd Cotsen, in memory of Bob Ahmanson, generously contributed to the publication.

Steeped in History: The Art of Tea is presented by The Coffee Bean & Tea Leaf

Additional support is provided by Patsy and Robert Sung, The Edna and Yu-Shan Han Charitable Foundation. The accompanying programs are made possible through the Yvonne Lenart Public Programs Fund, the UCLA Asia Institute, and Manus, the support group of the Fowler Museum.

In-kind support was provided by Hotel Angeleno

The Fowler Museum is part of UCLA's
School of the Arts and Architecture

Lynne Kostman, *Managing Editor*
Gassia Armenian, *Editorial Assistant*
Danny Brauer, *Designer and Production Manager*
Don Cole, *Principal Photographer*

Fowler Museum at UCLA
Box 951549
Los Angeles, California 90095-1549

Requests for permission to reproduce material from this volume should be sent to the Fowler Museum Publications Department at the above address.

Printed and bound in Hong Kong by Great Wall Printing Company, Limited.

Library of Congress Cataloging-in-Publication Data
Steeped in history: the art of tea / Beatrice Hohenegger, editor.
   p. cm.
  Includes bibliographical references and index.
  ISBN 978-0-9778344-1-9 (pbk.)
  1. Tea—Social aspects. 2. Tea—History. I. Hohenegger, Beatrice.
  GT2905.S84 2009
  394.1'2—dc22

                2009022926

LENDERS TO THE EXHIBITION

Asian Art Museum, San Francisco, California

Assistance League of Long Beach, California

Ayervais Collection

S. Baba and Jim Keck

Nicholas Cahill

Charles E. Young Research Library, UCLA, Los Angeles, California

Chicago History Museum, Illinois

Colonial Williamsburg Foundation, Virginia

Fowler Museum at UCLA, Los Angeles, California

Japanese American Cultural & Community Center, Los Angeles, California

J. Paul Getty Museum, Los Angeles, California

Gloria and Sonny Kamm

Kelton Foundation

Lewis Walpole Library, Yale University, Connecticut

Library of Congress, Washington, D.C.

Los Angeles County Museum of Art, California

Louise M. Darling Biomedical Library, UCLA, Los Angeles, California

Maryland Commission on Artistic Property, Maryland State Archives, Annapolis

Robert W. Moore

National Gallery of Art, Washington, D.C.

The Newark Museum, New Jersey

Pacific Asia Museum, Pasadena, California

Peabody Essex Museum, Salem, Massachusetts

Private Collections

Qin Xuan Collection, San Francisco, California

Rena Bransten Gallery, San Francisco, California

Robert E. Gross Collection of Rare Books in Economics and Business, Rosenfeld Management Library, UCLA, Los Angeles, California

Saint Louis Art Museum, Missouri

Scripps College, Claremont, California

Richard R. Silverman

Jose J. Terz

UCLA Grunwald Center for the Graphic Arts, Hammer Museum, Los Angeles, California

CONTENTS

南方炎帝之君

FOREWORD

THIS BOOK AND THE EXHIBITION IT ACCOMPANIES have been "brewing" for a number of years. Guest curator Beatrice Hohenegger first approached the Fowler Museum about a collaboration in the early stages of work on her previous book, *Liquid Jade: The Story of Tea from East to West* (St. Martin's Press, 2006). We immediately agreed with Beatrice that telling the fascinating story of tea through an exhibition of related works of art was an exciting proposition and one eminently suited to the Fowler Museum's mission and characteristic exhibition strategies. Gradually, the lengthy process of developing the exhibition got underway. In the course of its evolution, we determined to publish a new book that would meaningfully and specifically unite the history of tea with the history of art, from east to west. We asked Beatrice to help us identify a number of scholars who could contribute to the volume, writing from their own fields of expertise based upon their most recent research. We are extremely grateful for the participation of the distinguished group of scholars that Beatrice assembled, all of them eager to tell a part of this multifaceted global story of tea.

The astonishing growth of the market for quality teas in the United States in the past few years has been matched, it seems, by a similar increase in the quantity and quality of scholarship on the subject. This book is one of several that have been published from a wide variety of perspectives in recent years. There have been exhibitions, symposia, tastings, and even entire museums dedicated to tea, among them the Flagstaff House Museum of Tea Ware in Hong Kong. What we hope to add to this mix is a serious telling of the history of tea, which is by no means always light reading—consider for example the "tea parties" of revolutionary America or the ruthless system of indentured labor on nineteenth-century Indian tea plantations. At the same time we seek to readily engage the reader and the visiting public with the compelling presence of the many beautiful and fascinating tea-related works of art featured in this volume and its accompanying exhibition.

Like previous Fowler Museum efforts, such as *Mami Wata: Arts for Water Spirits in Africa and Its Diasporas* (2008) or *The Art of Rice: Spirit and Sustenance in Asia* (2003), this exhibition draws its power from the thematic arrangement of a highly diverse and eclectic selection of artworks—ranging in this case from ancient Chinese ceramics to French tapestries, from deeply philosophical Japanese Zen paintings to satirical political posters of Tony Blair's England. The scope of tea's history, dating as far back as the Zhou dynasty (1046–256 BCE) in China and crisscrossing the globe up to the present moment, has required the project's curator to locate and identify a vast array of objects. With her comprehensive knowledge and boundless dedication to her subject, Beatrice Hohenegger has included in her selection a number of important European and American paintings from lenders unusual for the Fowler Museum. *Steeped in History: The Art of Tea* includes works borrowed from more than thirty institutions and private parties, from both near and far—all of them listed in the front of the book. We warmly thank our colleagues, too many to be named individually, at all of the lending institutions for their attentiveness and cooperation. We also acknowledge especially the individual private lenders who allowed their prized possessions to enrich this exhibition. The Museum is also pleased to have included seven beautiful examples from its notable Fowler Family Silver Collection.

Nambang Yeomje ([Nanfang Yendi] *Lord of the Southern Quadrant, the Fiery Emperor, Shen Nong*), Korea, Joseon dynasty, 18th century
Ink and color on hemp or ramie
100.9 x 73.7 cm
LOS ANGELES COUNTY MUSEUM OF ART,
PURCHASED WITH MUSEUM FUNDS, NO. M.2000.15.10
PHOTOGRAPH ©2009 MUSEUM ASSOCIATES/LACMA

In this Korean depiction, probably one of an original set of five, the emperor Shen Nong is portrayed as Lord of the Southern Quadrant (the other four paintings would have shown the lords of the north, east, and west quadrants in addition to a central figure). The five figures were early Daoist deities that were later incorporated into Buddhist cosmology.

We thank Beatrice Hohenegger for weaving the diverse threads of tea's history into a compelling and coherent story. She has not only brought her superb and innovative writing and organizational skills to the project, she has consistently been a pleasure to work with and has retained her sense of humor and flexibility through all the challenges that a large and complex exhibition project inevitably entails.

Steeped in History was made possible by a generous grant from the Henry Luce Foundation and is presented by The Coffee Bean & Tea Leaf. Lloyd Cotsen, in memory of Bob Ahmanson, provided critical assistance for the production of this volume. Additional support came from Patsy and Robert Sung, The Edna and Yu-Shan Han Charitable Foundation. Associated programming has been funded by the Yvonne Lenart Public Programs Fund, UCLA Asia Institute, and Manus, the support group of the Fowler Museum.

The effort required to mount a major exhibition of this complexity demands great teamwork and the participation of every member of the Fowler Museum staff, and *Steeped in History: The Art of Tea* is no exception. A complete staff list appears at the end of the volume, and I extend my thanks and admiration to everyone involved. Roy Hamilton, the Museum's Senior Curator of Asian and Pacific Collections, served as the project manager and main liaison with the guest curator. The editing of this multiauthor book engaged the consummate skills of the Museum's Managing Editor, Lynne Kostman. Danny Brauer, Director of Publications, created a remarkably imaginative and elegant book design, and Don Cole, Photographer, has once again produced striking images for the text.

As you set off on the global journey of discovery and enlightenment that awaits you in this volume, we wish you bon voyage. We further suggest that you savor your trip with your favorite cuppa!

Marla C. Berns
SHIRLEY AND RALPH SHAPIRO DIRECTOR
FOWLER MUSEUM AT UCLA

ACKNOWLEDGMENTS

MY FASCINATION WITH TEA COMMENCED a dozen or so years ago when I discovered the disturbing historical connection between tea and opium. Intrigued, I undertook further research, traveled to Europe and India, interviewed experts, collected images, and wrote a book on the history and culture of tea, *Liquid Jade: The Story of Tea from East to West* (St. Martin's Press, 2006). In addition to telling the story with words, however, I felt all along the need to expand my research in a more visual direction, taking advantage of the many magnificent, and also sometimes controversial, objects and images relating to tea that are held in public and private collections. The vastness of the topic also inevitably called for a more in-depth treatment of numerous cross-cultural themes by experts in varying disciplines. Thus began the long and arduous process of selecting objects for the exhibition as well as determining topics and contributors for the present volume—enormous tasks that have proven tremendously rewarding.

I have learned so much while preparing *Steeped in History: The Art of Tea*. I am profoundly grateful to each and every person I have encountered in the process for so generously sharing insights and expertise with me—learning is the best part of every project. An army of curators, researchers, historians, agricultural and botanical specialists, and academics in various disciplines in the United States, Europe, and Asia has made it possible for me to understand, sort, and compile knowledge about tea and tea-related art. These knowledgeable individuals helped me choose one object over another, suggested sources or images I did not know existed, put me in touch with private lenders, corrected misperceptions, and explained shapes and iconography. I cannot name you all; I hope I shall be forgiven for that and for any errors I may have committed in interpreting your knowledge.

Thanks are due also to the authors represented in this volume for generously sharing the results of their research, and special thanks must go to Steven D. Owyoung for always being there to answer my many questions and help wherever necessary. Many thanks to the institutional and private lenders to the exhibition, both for being willing to part with their precious objects and for sharing their knowledge about them. My gratitude goes as well to the tea purveyors who donated rare and costly teas to the exhibition and who contributed their expertise in describing them.

Marla Berns, the director of the Fowler Museum, has been a great source of encouragement through all phases of exhibition and publication development, and I am very grateful for her continued support and friendship. I must also add a special thank you to Roy Hamilton, Curator of Asian and Pacific Collections, for expertly guiding me through the object selection process and for his unflinching commitment to quality. Thanks are due as well to former Fowler director Doran H. Ross for his valuable help in the preparation of my exhibition proposal. Let me also join Marla Berns in expressing my appreciation for the hard work of the Fowler Museum staff, without whose tireless efforts nothing would be possible: from fundraising (in a depressed economy!) to building shelves; from creating the look of the exhibition to providing administrative support; from photographing objects to maintaining the building; from securing loans and dealing with endless registration issues to designing and editing this volume; from managing budgets to creating educational programs and reviewing wall text. You are the true pillars of culture. My heartfelt thanks to you all for your professionalism, enthusiasm, and good humor.

In the personal arena, my gratitude goes to Gretel Hohenegger for keeping me going in low moments and to Lenny, Sofie, and Martin Isenberg for their patience and unstinting support over the years.

And last, a wish: while the publication of this volume has provided the opportunity to deepen tea research in several areas, and while I have no doubt that the groundbreaking essays contained here will be used as a valuable reference for a long time to come, my hope is that they will also function as an inspiration for ongoing future scholarship as well as a foundation for a more interdisciplinary discourse. May the enrichment brought about by cross-cultural and historical knowledge have an active role in increasing social awareness and improving sustainability for our people and our planet.

Beatrice Hohenegger

Beatrice Hohenegger

TEATIME

An Introduction

THE QUESTION "DO YOU TAKE SALT IN YOUR TEA?" was not uttered, as one might guess, by an absentminded hostess in an Oscar Wilde play, but it certainly could have been posed in earnest about fifteen hundred years ago in China. At that time, adding salt to tea was a common practice. Inquiring as to whether one took onions in one's tea would have been equally plausible, as tea was boiled and consumed soup-like with the addition of ingredients that we in the West might consider quite extraneous, among them ginger, spices, and orange peel—some of which remain in use today. The lengthy story of tea is rife with similar details and replete with intriguing anecdotes.

For the Chinese, tea is recognized as one of the seven daily necessities of life, along with fuel, rice, oil, salt, soy sauce, and vinegar. For the Irish, the tea mug is also an essential element of quotidian existence, and good tea "should be served strong enough for a mouse to trot on." For the Japanese tea is a ritual element in the search for enlightenment, while for Americans it is a symbol of independence. Nomadic North African peoples use tea to welcome travelers to their tents, and in England afternoon tea has long been an established routine. Tibetans, maintaining the age-old tradition of tea soup, add *tsampa* (barley flour) and yak butter to their tea. In Thailand and Burma (Myanmar) tea can also be eaten: the leaves chewed or made into chips.

Some like tea hot, some like it iced, some with milk, some with lemon. Some prefer black tea, some green, and some oolong. Some seek out whole leaves, while others prefer a tea brick or tea bags. Whatever form it may take, enjoying a cup of this familiar beverage is an act performed at least three billion times a day all around our planet. According to the Food and Agriculture Organization (FAO 2008, 5), world tea production has reached an all-time high of 3.64 million metric tons[1] (one metric ton being equal to 1,000 kg or 2,200 lbs). Indeed, with the exception of water, more people drink tea than any other beverage worldwide. Over the last few years, tea has experienced a powerful resurgence, not only in Europe and the United States but also in several Asian countries where

1   *The China Tea Trade*, China, 1790–1800
Oil on canvas
143 x 205 cm
PEABODY ESSEX MUSEUM, NO. M25,794

This rare painting illustrates the stages of tea cultivation and production. At the top left, the lush green bushes are tended; in the center the tea is processed; at the bottom near the water's edge, workers pack the tea in preparation for shipping. British ships can be seen waiting for their cargo in the bay. This painting was executed at a time when China was the sole provider of tea to the world, with England importing millions and millions of pounds of tea each year.

ancient traditions are being brought back to life with renewed passion. In its latest incarnation, tea is being discovered in the West as a versatile and powerful health remedy, coming full circle from its beginnings in China, where it has long been recognized and appreciated as such.

It is truly remarkable that all of the fantastic varieties of tea and their related traditions and activities have their source in a single plant (figs. 3a,b). The *Camellia sinensis*, a shrubby or tree-like native of southeastern Asia, now supports a sixty-six billion dollar global industry[2] and is responsible for the livelihood of several million workers in Asia (fig. 2), Africa, and, more recently, South America. Strictly speaking, the term "tea" refers only to the beverage produced with leaves from the *Camellia sinensis*, whether it is black, green, oolong, yellow, red, or white tea and whether it is loose-leaf, compressed, powdered, or CTC (cut-tear-curl). The differences in color and shape are due to the manufacturing process and the varying levels of oxidation to which the tea leaves are exposed—black teas are fully oxidized, oolongs are semioxidized, and green and white teas are nonoxidized. Chamomile, rooibos, mint, and the like, which are derived from other plants, are herbal infusions, not teas.

2   Workers pluck tea leaves on the Khongea tea plantation in Assam, India. They select only the young shoots at the top of the bush, which are often referred to as the "two-leaves-and-a-bud" used to produce good-quality tea. PHOTOGRAPH BY BEATRICE HOHENEGGER, 2006.

3a,b   John Coakley Lettsom
(b. Virgin Islands, 1744; d. London 1815)
Green Tea (right); *Bohea Tea* (p. 14), from *The Natural History of the Tea-Tree: With Observations on the Medical Qualities of Tea and on the Effects of Tea Drinking*, London, 1799
Hand-colored engravings
Each sheet: 30 x 24 cm
HISTORY & SPECIAL COLLECTIONS FOR THE SCIENCES,
LOUISE M. DARLING BIOMEDICAL LIBRARY, UCLA

John Coakley Lettsom was a Quaker and advocate of social reform as well as a plant collector. When his book on tea first appeared in 1769, Europeans still believed that green tea and black tea (known as "bohea tea" at the time, referring to the region where it originated in China) came from two different plants despite their extreme botanical similarity. The classification of genus and species of the tea plant was not unequivocally determined until the International Botanical Congress of 1905, two hundred and fifty years after tea arrived in Europe.

Green Tea.

Painted & Engrav'd by J. Miller.

Publish'd according to Act of Parliament Dec.10th 1771.

BOHEA TEA.

3b

Today two main varieties of the tea plant are recognized. One is *Camellia sinensis* var. *sinensis*, the Chinese multiple-stem shrub with small leaves, which is long-lived and can withstand cold weather. The other is *Camellia sinensis* var. *assamica*, the Indian single-stem plant with larger, softer leaves—more like a tree if left unpruned—which is more delicate, shorter-lived, and best grown in subtropical and rainy regions. Although the local populations have always recognized this distinction, the existence of the two varieties was not discovered by the British until the nineteenth century, a fact that would become enormously significant, as we will discover later in this volume.

In terms of the history of tea-drinking practices, we can distinguish three main phases: boiled, whisked, and steeped. The earliest form of tea drinking, still practiced today in Central Asia and Tibet, is boiled tea, usually made with compressed tea that is shaved off a brick or broken off a cake and allowed to boil with the water for a while, sometimes along with other ingredients. Indian chai is also made in this fashion,

but not with compressed tea. By the tenth century—during the Song dynasty (960–1279)—whisked tea became popular in China. This is the tea that traveled to Japan and was incorporated into ceremonial practices. Tea leaves are ground into a fine powder and whipped with bamboo whisks and hot water in individual bowls. It was only during the Ming dynasty (1368–1644) that steeped tea—tea leaves allowed to steep in the teapot—became common practice in China. This is the tea that maritime traders, the Portuguese and the Dutch, first brought to Europe during the seventeenth century. At this point in time, the Chinese had already been drinking tea for thousands of years.

While various teas have been prepared in an assortment of ways and have played parts in countless culinary practices, it is also important to note that tea is and nearly always has been a highly important commodity. As such, it has triggered major historical events, provoked international conflicts, and led to profound spiritual insights. Beginning in China (fig. 1),

spreading to Japan, traveling over the centuries to Europe and America, and then returning to Asia—this time India—tea has played a variety of striking roles. It has been viewed as a promoter of longevity; incorporated in diverse cultural and religious practices; proven valuable and contentious in the context of history, labor, politics, and international trade; and appeared as a wide-ranging theme in fine and decorative arts. Tea thus represents a rich and truly interdisciplinary subject of observation and study, engaging historians, anthropologists, agricultural researchers, medical doctors, philosophers, poets, spiritual practitioners, museum curators, private collectors, and countless artists (figs. 4, 5)—each one of these varied investigators, if I may use an oft-quoted metaphor, examining one part of the "elephant."

The *Chajing*—the first book on tea—appeared in China in 780 CE, authored by the Daoist Lu Yü, and ever since that time, much has continued to be written about the ubiquitous beverage from many different perspectives. At various times,

4 Ralph Bacerra
   (b. Garden Grove, California 1938; d. Los Angeles, 2008)
   Untitled (teapot), 2000
   Earthenware, glaze
   H (assembled): 45.7 cm
   COLLECTION OF GLORIA AND SONNY KAMM,
   COURTESY OF THE KAMM TEAPOT FOUNDATION

Ralph Bacerra was a highly influential ceramic artist and teacher who merged complex Asian techniques with his own unique contemporary style. He was also known for his meticulous attention to detail. Bacerra's teapots illustrate the creativity with which modern artists have approached the form.

5 Ralph Bacerra
   (b. Garden Grove, California 1938; d. Los Angeles, 2008)
   Untitled (teapot), 2001
   Earthenware, glaze
   H (assembled): 52.1 cm
   COLLECTION OF GLORIA AND SONNY KAMM,
   COURTESY OF THE KAMM TEAPOT FOUNDATION

6   New Vithanakande Superior, single estate black.
     Vithanakande Estate, Ratnapura region, Sri Lanka

7   Mokalbari TGFOP. Mokalbari Estate, Assam, India

8   Assam CTC PF. Assam, India

tea has been celebrated, damned, romanticized, and analyzed as a phenomenon in books, essays, treatises, instructional manuals, and poetry. In complementing this vast literature, it has been one of my main objectives to bring together, for the first time, disparate voices in a cross-cultural approach at the highest level of scholarship—to offer, so to speak, a view of "the whole elephant."

In selecting the topics to be addressed in *Steeped in History: The Art of Tea*—and in the exhibition that accompanies it—I was also motivated to confront lesser-known themes surrounding tea, for example, the prerevolutionary tea-related activities that took place in colonial America in addition to the Boston Tea Party; to discuss issues that are too often forgotten in history books but that involve the lives of millions of people, such as life and labor conditions on tea plantations; and, finally, to provide a forum for new scholarship in under-researched areas, such as the seemingly contrasting roles of women in Japanese tea culture. I wanted as well to celebrate the art of tea by illustrating and displaying works that attest to the richness and variety of the cultural practices associated with it both in Asia and the West. Numerous photographs and other documentary materials have also been included in the book and the exhibition to serve as witnesses to the darker side of the history of tea.

With these objectives as the driving forces in its development, *Steeped in History: The Art of Tea* takes us on a journey of discovery beginning with the mythical origins of tea in the hills of South China and the subsequent development of the fine art of tea throughout the country, while also exploring the significance of tea to Daoist thought. From there we move to Japanese Buddhist monasteries, where tea had a place in meditative rituals that evolved over the centuries into the rich aesthetics and profound meanings of *chanoyu*, the Japanese tea ceremony, as well as the lesser-known, but not less significant, *sencha* tea practice with its strong links to Chinese culture. The evolving position of women in both spiritual and secular Japanese tea practices is also given close examination. The third part of the volume focuses on the encounter of Eastern cultures with early Western maritime traders and the tea craze in England during the seventeenth and eighteenth centuries, during which tea became an essential element of social rituals as well as a valuable commodity that was frequently smuggled and adulterated to increase profits. America's colonial love affair with tea and the famous, and not so famous, historical events leading up to the American Revolution are investigated. In the last section the clash of cultures and economic interests between East and West, which culminated in the Opium Wars, is examined as well as the development of tea in colonial India and Ceylon, which caused mass migrations of unskilled labor and profound socioeconomic inequities, with results still visible today. We also explore the present-day world of tea, illustrating life on tea plantations and the emerging organic and fair trade movements in support of indigenous populations in the producing countries.

The story of tea provides an unusual but apt metaphor for the contradictions of human nature: capable of the most profound spirituality but triggering the excess of imperialism; regaling us with exquisite elegance and beauty in the arts and inflicting treachery for material advantage. Reading the essays in this book and marveling at Japanese folding screens, Victorian fans or satirical illustrations, paintings of American clipper ships, Chinese tea bowls, or Sèvres porcelains, readers of this volume and visitors to the exhibition alike will discover adventure and conflict, beauty and humor, spirituality and greed, and also little-known facts and surprising connections. *Steeped in History: The Art of Tea* offers an experience that is at the same time pure aesthetic enjoyment and a learning opportunity, in an effort toward achieving a more balanced perspective in the dialogue between East and West.

9   Glendale Artisan (handcrafted). Nilgiri (Blue Mountains) region, south India

10   Yunnan Black Needle. Yunnan, southwest China

11   Keemun 1254. Huangshan City, Anhui Province, China

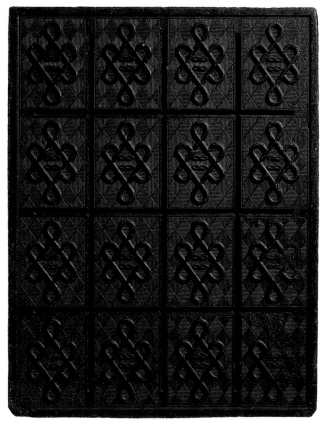

12a,b Brick made from powdered black tea, China. In the past such bricks were used as currency, especially in Central Asia and the Himalayan region. The scoring on the brick (fig. 12b) was used to break off pieces and "make change."

13 Organic Tieguanyin. Anxi, Fujian Province, China

14 *Matcha*. Near Kyoto, Japan

15 *Sencha*. Shizuoka Prefecture, between Tokyo and Kyoto, Japan

16 *Puer* cake, 2004. Yi Wu, southern Yunnan Province, China

17 Horse brick *puer*, 2002. Yunnan Province, China

18 Dragonwell Superior WTE. Hangzhou, Zhejiang Province, China

19 Gunpowder 3505. Zhejiang Province, China

20 Green Pearl. Fujian Province, China

21 Left to right: You Zi Cha, 1997, Yunnan Province, *puer* tea compressed inside the skin of a pomelo that has been turned inside out; You Zi Cha, early 1990s, Guangdong Province, *puer* tea in a larger pomelo; Jiu Zi Cha, 2003, Yunnan Province, *puer* tea in a wild orange; basket containing *puer* tea, 1999, Anhui Province. All of these *puer* tea objects are Chinese.

Figures 6–11 are examples of black teas. Figure 13 is an oolong tea. Figures 14, 15, 18–20, 22, and 23 are green teas. Figures 24, 26, and 27 are white teas. Figure 28 is a blended/scented tea, a black tea with orange peel, rose petal, cinnamon, papaya, and other ingredients. All illustrated loose-leaf teas are Qtrade Teas and Herbs, courtesy of Manik Jayakumar, and were selected and described by Ron Eng of Kopius Teas. The *puer* teas illustrated are from The Phoenix Collection, courtesy of David Lee Hoffman.

25   Tea chest, Japan, 20th century
      Wood, exterior paper decoration, tin
      H: 35 cm
      PRIVATE COLLECTION

This tin-lined wooden chest was used to promote the sale of Japanese green tea in the United States during the late nineteenth and early twentieth centuries. Decorating its exterior and interior lid are colorfully lithographed scenes of a tea plantation situated at the foot of Mount Fuji in Shizuoka Prefecture in central Japan. The finest green tea is traditionally harvested by hand beginning on the eighty-eighth day after Lunar New Year and continuing for a period of twenty days.

part 1

CHINA
Cradle of Tea Culture

Beatrice Hohenegger

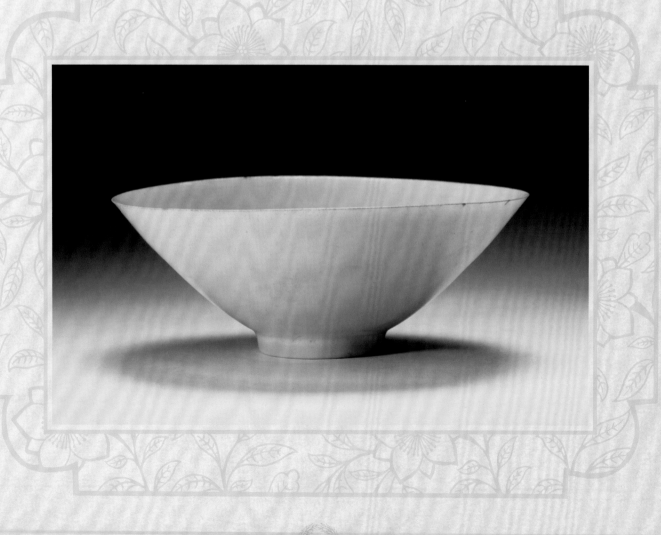

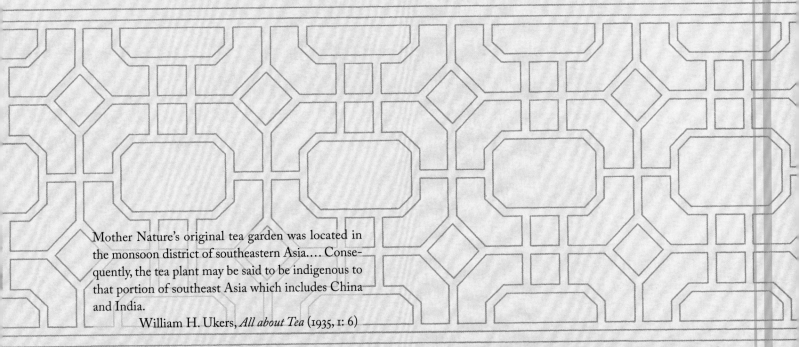

IT WAS IN CHINA over the course of thousands of years that the most ingenious, inventive, infinitely varied, and exquisite teas were created; that the aesthetics of the material culture of tea flourished (figs. 1.1–1.4); and that the literary and spiritual practices that grew to surround tea came to form the bases of traditions that would endure for centuries. Historically, and in all its aspects, tea has been so much a part of Chinese culture that it is not an overstatement to say that virtually everything related to tea today—anywhere in the world—originated in China in one way or another.

In his essay in this section of the volume, art historian Steven D. Owyoung takes us on a fascinating journey through Chinese tea history, one replete with accounts of poets and emperors, priests and painters, nomads and libationers. He illuminates the transformations of tea over the ages, focusing upon varied and changing practices while giving voice to the deep significance that tea held in the lives of Chinese peoples dating as far back as the Zhou dynasty (1046–256 BCE). He guides us in placing tea in the appropriate cultural and spiritual contexts, focusing especially on its relationship to Daoist thought. In the course of his analysis, we discover, for example, that white tea is not a recent addition to our grocers' shelves but a thousand-year-old imperial delicacy; we learn how the tea trade engendered a system of credit known as "flying money"; and we observe that protests surrounding tea and taxes took place in Tang China (618–907), long before the Boston Tea Party.

We come to appreciate as well the differing uses of tea over time: from whole leaves compressed into bricks of various shapes and then shaved and boiled in a cauldron—often along with other ingredients—during the Tang period and earlier; followed, in the Song era (960–1279), by the development of powdered tea, in which the tea leaves were ground (fig. 1.5) and formed into a cake or used as a powder and whisked into a bowl (the form in which tea traveled to Japan and is still in use there today, a thousand years later); and on to the steeped tea most familiar in the West, which came into mainstream use in China only during the Ming (1368–1644), bringing with it the development of that beloved kitchen staple: the teapot.

1.1   Tea bowl, Qingbai ware, China, Northern Song dynasty,
1050–1100 CE
Porcelain, blue-green glaze
H: 7.6 cm
ASIAN ART MUSEUM, THE AVERY BRUNDAGE COLLECTION, NO. B60P1420

The delicate character of this porcelain bowl is accentuated by the thin, blue-green glaze that appears to deepen in color in the carved floral patterns. Made at the kilns of Jingdezhen, it provided a southern counterpoint in celadon to the plain white Ding wares of the north. The pale Qingbai ware enhanced the color of fine tea that was whisked to a light-colored froth in the bowl.

1.2 Tea bowl (one of a set of four), China, early Tang dynasty, 8th–9th century
Porcelain, grayish-white glaze
H: 7 cm
ASIAN ART MUSEUM, THE AVERY BRUNDAGE COLLECTION, NO. B60P219

The austere shape of this Tang bowl is complemented by a plain, gray-white glaze in a style reminiscent of the simplicity and elegance of earlier Sui dynasty (581–618) ceramics. The severe but beautiful profile of the bowl adheres to an aesthetic derived from the Gupta style of India, which was embraced during the Sui along with Buddhism. The straight sides of the bowl result in a "mouth and lip that are not everted," a feature particularly admired in tea bowls by Lu Yü (733–804), the author of the first book on tea, the Tang dynasty *Chajing* (*Book of Tea*).

1.3 Shallow tea bowl, Cizhou ware, China, Song dynasty (960–1279)
Porcelain, Henan type
H: 5.1 cm
ASIAN ART MUSEUM, THE AVERY BRUNDAGE COLLECTION, NO. B62P66

The striking black and russet glazes of this bowl provided a dramatic background for the pale froth of Song tea. Northern black and brown wares competed with the famous Jian wares of Fujian that were the favorite tea bowls of the imperial court at Kaifeng—especially among aficionados of tea competitions. Such wide bowls were used on warm days or in summer when the tea readily gave up its heat through their thin bodies.

1.4 Tea bowl with incurving rim, Jun ware, Henan Province, China, Jin or Yuan dynasty, circa 12th–13th century
Stoneware with grayish blue glaze and purplish splash
H: 8.9 cm
ASIAN ART MUSEUM, THE AVERY BRUNDAGE COLLECTION, NO. B60P107

Jun ware, which is usually classed with celadons, utilized some of the most spectacular copper-based glazes in the ceramic repertoire. Gaudy purple splashes often vied with subtle transmutations of red, blue, and green—all in the same exquisitely shaped bowl. Thickly potted, Jun bowls like this example were favored on cold days or in winter when the heat of the tea was retained by their heavy bodies and unctuous glazes.

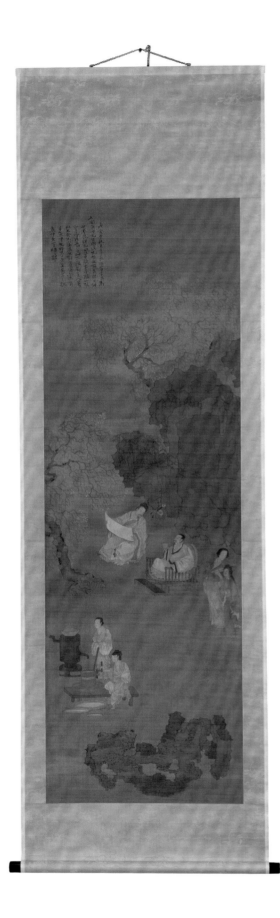

1.5 Cui Zizhong (China, d. 1644)
The Gathering in the Apricot Garden, 1638
Hanging scroll; ink and color on silk
154 x 52 cm
COLLECTION OF NICHOLAS CAHILL

This rare painting depicts a tea-grinding machine, used to make powdered tea (see lower left). According to art historian Judy Andrews, the two seated figures in the middle are the artist and his patron (who commissioned the painting and waited patiently while the artist procrastinated). They enjoy a farewell cup of tea together in the patron's apricot garden.

Tea scholars are generally in agreement that teapot design is the result of adapting the lidded wine ewer to the new requirements of steeped tea. As a result, some early teapots resemble more a tall, narrow jug than the low, paunchy vessels we know today. The first teapots designed and produced for the specific use of brewing loose-leaf tea came into being in the 1500s. They were the unglazed pots from Yixing, coveted by collectors worldwide and considered by many tea connoisseurs the ideal vessel to enhance the experience of tea. Art historian Terese Tse Bartholomew, an international authority on Yixing ware, contributes an insightful essay to this section of the volume relating her experiences in Yixing and considering the lengthy history of its remarkable tea wares.

Loose-leaf tea and teapots are what sixteenth-century Portuguese, Dutch, and English traders encountered when they first arrived in China. Initially, tea was imported to Europe as a secondary item, along with the much sought-after spices and silks that had lured traders to eastern shores. The dried-up, shriveled tea leaves were an unknown entity, and stories abound featuring puzzled Europeans cooking them as vegetables, eating the leaves, and throwing away the "water." Teapots and related pottery were also secondary items of import. They ended up on Western tables primarily as a result of the practical thinking of trading officials and captains of the East Indiamen (the cargo ships sent to Asia from Holland and England). Sturdy Chinese pottery functioned very well as ballast in these large European ships, and unlike deadweight ballast, it could be sold for a profit upon arrival. Soon the demand for tea and chinaware increased, and along with it, a passion for all things Chinese, known as the chinoiserie phenomenon, which spread all over Europe during the second half of the seventeenth century. This, in turn, increased production in China, not only of tea and pottery (fig. 1.6) and any related art (fig. 1.7) but also of Chinese export art in general. Some magnificent examples of this may be seen in the essay by John Wills that appears in part 4 of this volume (see figs. 8.2–8.4).

1.6 Pair of tea caddies, China, Qing dynasty (1644–1912)
Porcelain, glaze
H (of each): 29.2 cm
PACIFIC ASIA MUSEUM COLLECTION, GIFT OF MR. AND MRS. HENRY THOMSON, NO. 1985.21.IAB

Tea caddies were used to store loose-leaf tea. The word "caddy" derives from the Malay-Chinese word *kati*, which designates a weight of a little more than a pound. Caddies were often placed on the tea table and were therefore decorated in a variety of styles. While the preferred medium for caddies was porcelain, other materials used included pottery, lacquerware, metal (silver, pewter), tortoiseshell, and papier-mâché. These tea caddies, however, are unusually large and probably meant for kitchen storage rather than as part of the table setting.

I.7   Painting from an album of twenty-three images,
Guangzhou, China, 1780–1790
Watercolor and ink on paper
33 x 33 cm
©V&A IMAGES/VICTORIA AND ALBERT MUSEUM,
LONDON, NO. D.1074-1898

The album of twenty-three pictures, from which this watercolor is drawn,
illustrates the cultivation and processing of tea. Albums of this type depicting the production of Chinese commodities were created to satisfy the
curiosity of Western buyers but actually revealed very little detailed information. This particular scene shows men and women carrying picked tea
leaves in their baskets.

During this period of intense trading, China rapidly became the sole provider of tea to the world. In the years between 1713 and 1720, the English East India Company imported a total of 2.1 million pounds of tea. Less than forty years later, in the decade between 1751 and 1760, that amount grew to 37.3 million pounds (Chaudhuri 1978, 388). By 1834, 32 million pounds were imported in a single year (Ukers 1935, 1: 77). A year before that, however, the English East India Company had lost the monopoly of the China trade as a result of the passage by Parliament of the Charter Act of 1833. The discovery of tea growing wild in India had, however, captured the attention of the EIC in the 1820s. The title of world's main tea provider was soon stripped from China with the aggressive development of Indian tea by the British Empire. This all but obliterated Chinese tea from the trading scene during the 1800s. Although

1.8   Making Tea in a Rich Native's Home, Peking, China, late 19th–early 20th century
Photographic print on stereopticon card
17.8 x 8.9 cm
KEYSTONE-MAST COLLECTION, UCR/CALIFORNIA MUSEUM OF PHOTOGRAPHY, UNIVERSITY OF CALIFORNIA RIVERSIDE

1.9   Manchurian Ladies at Tea and Cards, Peking, China, late 19th–early 20th century
Photographic print on stereopticon card
17.8 x 8.9 cm
KEYSTONE-MAST COLLECTION, UCR/CALIFORNIA MUSEUM OF PHOTOGRAPHY, UNIVERSITY OF CALIFORNIA RIVERSIDE

Chinese Cat Merchants

Les vendeurs de chats et marchands de thé à Tong-tcheou
[De Pays de Pé-king]

Katzenhändler und Theehändler zu Tongtchon
[Gebiet von Pé-king]

THE LONDON PRINTING AND PUBLISHING COMPANY, LIMITED.

Chinese tea continued to be an integral part of daily life in China (figs. 1.8–1.10), by 1900 it represented only seven percent of the amount imported to Europe (Appleton's 1903, 313) with the remainder being supplied by India and Ceylon.

Until 2005, India remained the largest tea producer and consumer in the world. Today, however, nearly two centuries after dramatic historical events had relegated Chinese tea to near oblivion on the global stage, China is again the world's largest tea producer with an estimated output of 1.15 million metric tons in 2007 against India's 0.95 million metric tons, according to the latest (still unpublished) Food and Agriculture Organization figures. Chinese tea also circulates throughout the world a great deal more than Indian tea: 80 percent of the latter is consumed domestically, while only about 34 percent of the former remains at home. ☙

1.10 Thomas Allom (Britain, 1804–1872)
Cat Merchants and Tea Dealers
From G. N. (George Newenham) Wright, *The Chinese Empire—Historical and Descriptive*, London, 1843
Engraving
H (of book): 32 cm
DEPARTMENT OF SPECIAL COLLECTIONS, CHARLES E. YOUNG RESEARCH LIBRARY, UCLA, DS707.A44

Thomas Allom was a British architect and a much-admired illustrator. This engraving, one of the illustrations that Allom prepared for a history of China, depicts a tea seller and cat vendors, who peddle their respective wares next to each other.

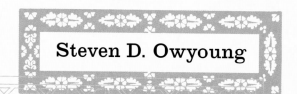

Steven D. Owyoung

TEA IN CHINA

From Its Mythological Origins to the Qing Dynasty

Tea is from a splendid tree of the south.
Lu Yü, *Book of Tea*

MORE THAN TWELVE CENTURIES AGO, the first words of the *Chajing*, or *Book of Tea*, portrayed a stately evergreen deep within the primeval forest as the progenitor of all tea.[1] Tea was native to the ancient kingdom of Shu, located in a remote and distant land known as Sichuan, or "four rivers." A continental basin isolated and ringed from the world by high mountains, narrow defiles, and steep, tortuous gorges, Sichuan incubated the distinctive Shu culture and a unique subtropical flora and fauna. The region was rich and fertile with abundant grain, minerals, timber, and plants. Tea was cultivated for thousands of years within Shu and the neighboring kingdom of Ba to the east, but it remained long unknown beyond their borders.

Legend described the tea tree as "luxuriant," and early lexicons compared its lush foliage to the shiny, vivid leaves of the gardenia. In early spring the profusion of buds and sprouts were picked from tea plants by hand. This first plucking stimulated a second growth and produced a harvest of even finer sprouts and buds. The regenerative powers of the tea plant echoed the rebirth and the renewal associated with spring by both humans and gods. On feast days, tea was offered to heaven and the ancestral spirits in ceremony and ritual. In return, heaven bestowed an abundance of tea. In the wild, tea grew in majestic arboreal form. Such great trees were blessed by nature, growing for a thousand years to attain remarkable height and girth, their beauty attracting gods and sages.

Tea and Myth

Revered since the Neolithic, Shen Nong, the "Divine Cultivator," was also the "Sovereign of the Earth," the patron of agriculture (fig. 1.1; see also p. 6). He roamed the wilds, searching for plants beneficial as medicine and food, and he examined the nutritional and pharmacological properties of each new discovery. His catalog thus became the first *materia medica* in apothecary lore (Karlgren 1946).

1.1   Sculpture of Shen Nong, the "Divine Cultivator," China,
ca. 1850–1900
Ceramic
51 cm
SCIENCE MUSEUM, LONDON, NO. A658077

This depiction of Shen Nong, wearing a shirt and skirt composed of leaves, emphasizes his roles as herbalist and husbandman. According to myth, it was Shen Nong, the "Divine Cultivator," who first discovered tea, researched its properties, and extolled its health benefits. Compare this representation to a depiction in a Korean painting, page 6.

Myth relates that Shen Nong discovered tea while sitting in contemplation beneath a tall tree. A sprite descended from heaven in the guise of a gust of wind and blew into the branches, sending a shower of leaves into the Divine Cultivator's open cauldron of gently boiling water. Attracted by the pleasant fragrance rising from the steaming brew, the sage sipped the tea. He found its flavor pleasantly bitter with a lingering, sweet aftertaste; its effects were soothing and refreshing. Shen Nong gave his imprimatur to the plant and to its use as a beverage.

As Shen Nong required proper names and characters to distinguish one plant from another in his records, he engaged the scribe of the Yellow Emperor, Cang Jie, the legendary inventor of writing. With an extraordinary set of four eyes, Cang closely examined everything in nature, naming all that he saw, inspired by the movements of stars and planets and the patterns of trees, rocks, and animals. On seeing the plant that Shen Nong presented him, Cang Jie bestowed the first name and character for tea (Needham 1986, 196–97, figs. 32, 33). Since the time of Cang Jie, however, tea has been called *tu, jia, she, ming,* and *chuan,* reflecting differences in dialect, as well as the quality and character of the tea in question (Lu Yü [1273] 1985, ch. 1, pt. 1, 1a).

Zhou

According to the *Record of the Southern Realms beyond Mount Hua*, tribute was exchanged between the Zhou dynasty, centered in Henan, and its allies to the south in Sichuan. The first Zhou sovereign, King Wu (r. 1049/1045–1043 BCE), sent palace concubines to Shu and Ba, binding Sichuan rulers through marriage to the Zhou aristocracy. In return, Sichuan sent tribute north to the Zhou in the form of copper, iron, salt, cinnabar, animals, preserved fish, timber, vermillion lacquer, hemp, honey, and herbs. Tea was sent from the "backwaters of Ba" and from Shu, "good tea" from the mountains of Shifang and "rare tea" from Nan'an and Wuyang (Chen Binfan 1999, 4).

During the Zhou, tea was used as an herb and beverage. Tea had been highly regarded within the medical, culinary, and alchemical arts since ancient times. As a medicinal plant, it was long employed as a stimulant to promote positive moods; it calmed and clarified the mind, sharpening mental acuity, while relaxing smooth muscle. A diuretic and antitoxin, tea flushed the body of poisons and harmful wastes. It was also a mild disinfectant and an efficacious rinse that soothed strained, tired eyes and relieved skin ailments. When swished in the mouth, tea cleansed the palate and promoted dental health with trace minerals such as fluoride. Furthermore, vitamins contained in tea sustained overall physical well being.

The connection between tea and Daoism (see box, next page) is long-standing and significant. Among Daoists, tea was thought to possess miraculous properties that promoted health and longevity. It was in fact viewed as the portal to enlightenment and the fabled herb of everlasting life. The impressive preventative and curative powers of tea also led to its prescription by apothecaries and physicians as tonic and remedy. Royalty and the aristocracy, ever in pursuit of health and long life, sought out Daoist healers for their palace courts. Recommending tea as a medicinal herb, beverage, and food, physicians worked closely with the master chefs of noble households, combining prescriptions of tea in nutritious recipes and savory dishes for the table. In the kitchen, tea was a bitter herb and vegetable used by cooks as one of the five flavors: bitter, salty, sour, hot, and sweet. Tea took many forms: fresh leaves, pulp, pastes, and gels in season, dried loose leaves or "bricks" of compressed leaves, and "wafers" and "cakes" of dried paste. Tea leaves flavored stews and soups and were eaten as vegetables. At meals, brewed tea freshened the palate and aided digestion; drunk as a beverage, tea was a custom and habit.

By the eighth century BCE, the Zhou kingdom had fragmented into independent, ducal states, but tea as a commodity continued to be sent north as far as Linzi, the capital of the state of Qi (located in present-day Shandong). There, Yan Ying (d. 500 BCE), the chief minister to Duke Qing (r. 547–490 BCE) of Qi, chided his wayward lord for indulging in rich banquet fare. In the *Spring and Autumn Annuals of Master Yan*, a primer on moral rule, the minister urged his sovereign to be more virtuous in deed if not in thought. Yan Ying was himself the model of frugality and simplicity, wearing plain cloth and taking "only coarse grain, five eggs, and the tender leaves of tea and herbs" for his daily meal (Chen Binfan 1999, 3).

Far to the south, tea spread from Shu and Ba eastward along the Yangzi. In the principality of Zeng at the northern marches of the state of Chu, tea was found in the elaborate tomb of Marquis Yi (479–ca. 433 BCE). The body lay in two nested lacquered coffins, and at the foot of the inner casket, a silk packet contained plant seeds (Wenwu 1989, 1: 452)—water caltrop, Sichuan pepper, cocklebur, and apricot—all used in the herbal tradition to treat respiratory and stomach ailments (Hsu et al. 1986, 253–54, 382–83, 363–64, 705–6, respectively). Tea—as whole seeds and husks—was included to complete the ancient prescription for persistent coughing and painfully labored breathing (Hsu et al. 1986, 279–80, 496).

The expanded use of tea as medicine and food coincided with the imperial ambitions of Qin, an autocratic state in Shaanxi destined to unify the country into an empire. In 325 BCE, the ducal heir declared himself King Hui of Qin (r. 324–311 BCE) and in the brilliant gambit of 316 BCE invaded Sichuan to tap its abundant resources. For more than a hundred years, the Qin treasury overflowed with tribute from Shu and Ba. The vast wealth funded the statecraft, intrigue, and naked aggression required to conquer the rival states of the central plains and the southern kingdom of Chu (Sage 1992, 114–56; Kleeman 1998, 24–25, 36, 39–41). Though short-lived, the Qin (221–207 BCE) unity created by the First Emperor established Sichuan and the south as integral to the empire and broadened the dispersal of tea.

Han

The cultivation of tea also spread rapidly beyond Shu and Ba and eastward along the middle reaches of the Yangzi and south into Chu. Dissemination was aided by the long association of the Han imperial family with the tea regions of Sichuan and Hunan. After the fall of the Qin, the rebel general Liu Pang (r. 206–195 BCE) was made King of Han and of Shu and Ba. Later, as the founding emperor of the Han dynasty (206 BCE–220 CE), Liu Pang appointed his younger brother to govern Hunan as Prince of Chu (Watson 1961, 109–10); thereafter, many generations of imperial princes ruled from the provincial capital of Changsha in Hunan. In the second century BCE, a place known as Tuling was a Han marquisate ruled by Marquis Xin, grandson of Emperor Jingdi (r. 157–141 BCE) and the son of Ding, prince of Chu (Nunome 2001, 279). During the expansion of the empire and the ensuing peace, the fertile lands of Chu produced a southern tea industry, and Tuling (Tea Hill) was "named for the hills and valleys there that produce tea."[2]

As in the past, tea continued to have an important role as tribute and an offering to the dead. On the death of a sovereign or noble, tea was offered at the ancestral altar and at the tomb as a sacrament and a contribution to the material goods placed in the grave. A small case of tea was found in the tomb of Xizui (d. ca. 168–164 BCE). A Chu aristocrat, she had been

DAOISM

THE LEGENDARY FOUNDER OF DAOISM (also known as Taoism) was Laozi, the author of the *Daode jing* (*The Book of the Dao and the De*), who was supposed to have lived during the Zhou. *Dao* means "way" or "path," a concept that refers to an underlying oneness, which is the original state of the universe and the point from which all things emanate and to which they eventually return. In myth, Laozi is often referred to as being the embodiment of the Dao itself. De, another crucial Daoist concept, is used to describe the energy and power of the Dao. It explains the endless variation in and changing nature of things before they ultimately return to the Dao.

Early in its history, Daoism focused on harmony with others and with nature in sharp contrast to the aggression and political disharmony that characterized the time. It advocated *wuwei*, or "not doing," which meant refusal to participate in aggressive or unkind behavior, the pursuit of status or dominance, or the adherence to rigid hierarchies and regulations. Daoism placed emphasis instead on meditation, fasting, and health as means to realign the individual with the Dao.

Like other religions and philosophies, Daoism changed over time. In 142 CE, Zhang Daoling (34–156) established the Way of the Celestial Masters, which is the first known instance of an organized Daoist religious system. Daoism gained widespread popularity from this time through the fourteenth century. At various points in its long history, it has stressed the prolongation of life and the search for immortality through magic: exploring charms, amulets, and various substances that

could be used in elixirs to further these goals. Among these highly valued substances were gold, cinnabar, and tea. Daoism also incorporated belief in deities, some of which were borrowed from Chinese folklore and others of which bore resemblance to Buddhist counterparts introduced from India in the first century CE.

In the Tang (618–907), Daoism became the official religion of the imperial court. This was also a period in which Daoists increasingly engaged in monastic life, often taking vows of abstention and celibacy and living in seclusion. The Daoist Way of Complete Perfection, which focused on refining human energies through breathing and meditation with the goal of prolongation of life and possible immortality, was founded by Wang Zhe (1113–1170) during the Song. This period also witnessed attempts to syncretize Daoism, Buddhism, and Confucianism, which flourished through the Yuan.

The goal of achieving harmony among the three religious traditions did not, however, survive into the Ming dynasty when differences between Buddhists and Daoists became acute. Daoism flourished despite this, however, and in the Qing its ideas and practices made even further gains in acceptance into popular religious culture. Although the advent of Western colonial powers and later the effects of the Cultural Revolution were devastating to Daoism and other religious practices, today the study and practice of this long-standing religious tradition is once more growing in China and throughout the world.

---

consort to Li Cang (d. 186 BCE), the marquis and hereditary ruler of Dai and chief minister to the prince of Chu. Xizui, Lady Dai, was buried in an elaborate, timbered tomb containing chambered stores of food in covered bamboo baskets, ceramic jars, and sacks. One sealed basket bore a wooden label that read "*jiasi*, case of tea," a provision verified by the tomb's inventory that recorded "*jia yisi*, tea-one case" (Wenwu 1974, 45: Zhou 1979, 65: Yü 1987, 10–11; Zhou 1992, 200–203). The finest tea came from Sichuan, but as Tea Hill lay just southeast of Changsha, the tea in Lady Dai's tomb may well have been grown in the nearby "hills and valleys" of Tuling.

Regarding sources of tea, the great Han poet Wang Bao (active ca. 61–59 BCE), a native of Shu, considered the select tea from Wuyang, Sichuan, to be the finest. In 59 BCE, Wang wrote *Contract for a Youth*, a humorous tale about the onerous labors that he imposed as punishment upon a querulous and stubborn servant, who refused to fetch a jar of wine. Among

the long list of the servant's chores was the instruction that while in nearby "Wuyang, he shall buy tea" and "when there are guests in the house, he shall…boil tea and fill the bowls."[3] From this passage we learn that tea was not merely exchanged among the aristocracy at this time but was also sold in the market to commoners. The poet also revealed that tea had a role in the formal welcome and honor of visitors. Also significant, brewed tea was boiled by a servant and served in bowls. Doubtless, tea had ceremonial aspects at elegant court receptions and banquets during the Han dynasty, especially among conservative officials whose Confucian sensibilities dictated formality at every turn. Yet, Wang Bao, a distinguished and cultured official, described tea preparation and service so elementary that his servant could carry it out.

By the first century BCE, choice tea was grown along the lower Yangzi. In the late Han, the name Tuling slowly gave way to Chaling, the new pronunciation of Tea Hill. *Tu* was an ancient name for tea, but about the third century BCE, the character *tu* was altered by the deletion of a single brushstroke to produce the derivative ideograph *cha*. The new character *cha* as well as the character *ming*, meaning specifically "the young, tender buds and sprouts of *tu*," were formally introduced in 121 CE in the great dictionary *Commentary on Literature and the Explanation of Words*.[4] The distinction between teas made of *cha* and *ming* leaves revealed the growing sophistication of tea production and tea drinking that continued throughout the latter Han period.

The medicinal efficacy of tea inspired *Dietary Proscriptions*, a book written by Hu Gong (active ca. 25–220), "Master of the Gourd," a mysterious healer of the Western Han, who made the claim that "bitter tea taken for a long time bestows immortality" with the caveat that it should not be used with chives, an herb that negated longevity (Lu Yü [1273] 1985, ch. 3, pt. 7, 6a). Such teachings of everlasting life were part of a Daoist religious movement known as the Way of the Celestial Masters that taught the primacy of health and longevity through hygiene and diet. The cult was founded in Sichuan by Zhang Daoling (34–156) who envisioned a utopian society free of poverty, sickness, and disease. The social order of the Celestial Masters was maintained by libationers, who presided over sacrificial rites before festivals and banquets and who enforced the prohibition on wine (Kleeman 1998, 66–72). In lieu of alcoholic beverages, tea was promoted among the Daoist faithful as a healthy alternative that offered longevity and even life without end. As a drug, tea aided meditation and helped achieve states of spiritual transcendence. In the practice of alchemy, tea prepared and fortified the body for the physical rigors of the laboratory and the ingestion of elixirs of immortality.

Three Kingdoms

In 230, the scholar Zhang Yi (active ca. 227–230) compiled *Expanded Elegance*, a lexicon that described preserved pulped tea shaped in the form of "cakes" using rice paste as a binder. To make tea, he wrote that a tea "cake is first toasted until lightly browned" and next "ground into powder," then using a ceramic bowl, "hot water is poured over the tea until all the powder is covered" (Lu Yü [1273] 1985, ch. 3, pt. 7, 4a). In some quarters, the spread of tea as a custom and habit displaced wine as a beverage and offering.

Clearly, however, this was not the case in the court of Sun Hao (r. 264–280), the despotic, debauched king of the southern state of Wu, who was known for deliberately inebriating his officials by insisting they drink seven pints of wine at daily court banquets. At the court, the official Wei Yao (204–273), who could not hold his liquor, was known for being "direct and outspoken" (Sima 1965, 2: 390). He frequently voiced blunt, critical remarks before his ruthless, ill-tempered lord, endangering everyone, including himself. In an uncharacteristic act of compassion, however, Sun Hao "secretly bestowed on him tea instead of wine"[5] so that whatever criticisms Wei Yao uttered were, at the very least, spoken with a clear mind and

a sober, if not quite temperate, tongue. The king's sympathy, however, was short-lived, and in the end, the fickle Sun Hao executed the hapless Wei Yao.

Jin

In the third century, tea was commonly sold throughout the empire—as a beverage and a commodity—in the marketplace. The high censor Fu Xian (239–294) received intelligence of a raid on the stall of an old woman from Shu who sold tea porridge and tea cakes (Lu Yü [1273] 1985, ch. 3, pt. 7, 5a). Similar reports of petty officials harassing tea sellers suggested an increase in local oversight and greater corruption spurred by competition in the tea market (Lu Yü [1273] 1985, ch. 3, pt. 7, 7a).

The northern scholar Zhang Zai (active ca. 280–289) elevated tea to a sacred libation in his poetry, declaring that "fragrant, beautiful tea is the crown of the Six Purities; its overflowing flavor spreads to the Nine Regions" (Ding 1969, 1: 389–90). Zhang Zai composed these lines around 280 during a sojourn in Sichuan. Moved by his experience of tea, he noted its lovely scent, an aesthetic aspect described in literature for the first time. Zhang Zai also confirmed the use of tea throughout the archaic Nine Regions, that is to say, the entire country. Using literary license, he heretically exalted tea above the Six Purities—the four wines, water, and sauce—used as ceremonial and ritual offerings to the ancestral spirits.

Tea was also praised in the *Ode to Tea* by the poet Du Yü (d. 316): "On the peaks of Mount Ling, a wondrous thing is gathered: It is tea. Every valley and hill is luxuriously covered with this wealth of the Earth, blessed with the sweet spirit of Heaven." The ode described a "perfect" tea of "thick froth, afloat with the splendor of the brew: lustrous like piling snow, resplendent like the spring florescence." He instructed the adept to "take water from the flowing river Min" of Sichuan and "choose ceramics produced from Eastern Ou," the fine porcelaneous celadons of the southeastern kilns. Du Yü further advised serving tea with a ladle made of gourd—typically used for offerings—in emulation of the ritual gravity and dignity of ancient nobility.[6] Tea was itself admired and praised, its brewed, flowery foam and banks of froth likened to driven snow, showing pale and pure against finely glazed bowls of jade green. No longer restricted to the kitchen, making tea was a performative, ceremonial, and aesthetic event in which masters, adepts, and skilled servants artfully employed the tasteful display and elegant use of beautiful implements and wares.

As an aesthetic endeavor, the art of tea was a matter of philosophical discourse. The learned Prince Yü (320–372), ruler of the southern marquisate of Kuaiji, presided over a literary salon of Daoists and Buddhists of which Liu Tan (active ca. 335–345) was a prominent member. Liu Tan was chief minister to the prince and an eminent scholar of Daoism. He was also a master of the art of tea. As Liu Tan made tea before his lord, Prince Yü remarked "Verily, Liu Tan and his tea possess the Truth" (Liu 1972, 13a). Moved by the moment, the prince reflected on tea as beyond mundane ritual and worldly beauty.

Transcendent and ethereal, tea was in harmony with the Dao and the embodiment of the fundamental principles within nature: the Universal Truth.

As a medicinal plant, tea was part of the Daoist herbal tradition as far west as the Silk Road. A Daoist and native of the caravan town Dunhuang, Shan Daokai (active fourth century) was known to swallow several small stones as part of his daily health regimen. In addition to these, he took "preventative" pills containing "the essences of pine, honey, ginger, cassia, and fungus," which he downed with "two pints of a brew made from tea and minty perilla." He traveled east to Nanjing and in 359 headed far south for Nanhai where he entered the Daoist sanctuary on Mount Lofu. When he died at more than one hundred years of age, his remains were sealed in a cave. When the tomb was later opened, it was recorded that his body appeared as it was when he was alive (Fang 1974, 8: ch. 95, *lieh* ch. 65, 2491–92). Such tales of healthy longevity and incorruptibility continued to encourage Daoist alchemists to use tea to fortify their bodies for the rigors of meditation and the ingestion of elixirs (Owyoung 2008b, 232–52).

Meanwhile, the literati of the time began to examine the social and spiritual import of tea. The famous encounter in which Commandant Lu Na (d. 395) greeted General Xie An (320–385) by serving tea is illustrative. Xie An, who had lived a life of leisure during his first forty years, later became the epitome of the scholarly recluse. When he finally accepted a government post, he was highly regarded for his detached and disinterested air, considered a manifestation of his true Daoist heart. On a trip to the southern town of Wuxing, Xie An visited Lu Na, a member of the illustrious Lu clan and a man of supreme cultivation. When seated, Xie An was served "only tea and fruit" with little ceremony. The paltry offering to so distinguished a guest flew in the face of custom and protocol, yet Xie An and Lu Na understood each other perfectly. Suddenly, however, Lu Na's nephew set out costly food and drink in precious vessels, enough for ten people, to repair his uncle's apparent lack of respect for an eminent guest. After Xie An departed, Lu Na cried out to his nephew in outrage, "You have never been able to bring honor to me. Why do you now disgrace my simple ways?"[7] Fettered by petty conventions, the nephew was blind to the virtues of simplicity and temperance that his uncle embraced. Xie An, however, knew instantly from the utter purity of his repast that Lu Na was a superior man and a kindred spirit in the Dao.

Southern and Northern Dynasties

At the fall of the Jin, the south fragmented into a number of small states with short histories, their rulers all claiming the title of emperor. The golden era of wise Emperor Wen (r. 424–453) of the Liu Sung dynasty (420–479) witnessed the establishment of the first imperial tea gardens. The *Record of Wuxing* noted that six miles from the county seat of Huchou near the shores of Lake Tai was "Mount Wen that produces imperial tea."[8] To celebrate the tribute harvest, the governor of neighboring tea gardens at Changxing and Kunling held an annual "tea picking" banquet under a pavilion.[9] In 491 and 493, Emperor Wu (r. 483–493) of the Southern Qi dynasty (479–502) altered imperial ancestral rites by incorporating tea as an offering.[10] During the Southern Liang dynasty (502–557) the emperor bestowed an annual gift, "gathered from the rarest things in the kingdom," which was then distributed to the noble houses of the principalities in the form of eight imperial provisions, including tribute tea.[11]

In the north, the Northern Wei dynasty (386–581) was ruled by the Xianbei Toba, formerly nomads of the steppes who were highly sinicized and employed many Chinese officials at their court. Cultured and sophisticated, the Toba elite served tea as a point of courtesy, but they did not drink it. In fact, the Toba harbored a visceral dislike for tea, associating it with the effete manners of the decadent south. They sarcastically called tea drinking "drowning,"[12] and constantly mocked prominent southerners for their fondness of the drink while excoriating any Toba daring to consume it. Their favorite target was the minister Wang Su (464–501), a southerner who enlisted with the Northern Wei and rose to become president of the Department of State Affairs. Although esteemed by the Toba emperor, Gaozu (r. 471–499), Wang Su was the butt of jokes among the Toba aristocracy. His addiction to tea was so extreme, and he so incontinent as a result, that he was given the nickname "Leaky Goblet." After many years in the north, however, Wang Su attended a palace banquet and, to the surprise of the Toba, he ate mutton and drank copious amounts of koumiss, fermented mare's milk—a nomadic fare that he previously could not abide. Curious about this change, the emperor asked, "Among you of Chinese taste, how does mutton compare with fish stew, and tea with fermented milk?" Tipsy from the fermented milk, Wang Su earnestly replied, "Sire, lamb is the best of land produce, while fish leads among seafood…. Only tea is no match; tea is a slave to koumiss" (*Loyang qielan ji gouchen* 1969, 116–17). The Toba princes gleefully repeated the phrase, and tea was thereafter disdainfully known as the "slave to fermented milk." Caught in his cups, Wang Su unwittingly furthered the denigration of his beloved tea. With the reunification of the empire, however, the northern revulsion to tea eventually waned.

Tang

The Tang high censor Feng Yan (active ca. 755–794) noted that "southerners are fond of drinking [tea], but northerners drank little at first." He credited Buddhist clerics of the Zen sect for "changing the minds of the northerners."[13] Zen Buddhism had been established by the Indian monk Bodhidarma (ca. 440–528) in Loyang, the Toba capital and a major center of Buddhism. In legend, Bodhidarma drank stimulating tea as a meditational aid and thus began a Buddhist tradition of tea. The seventh Zen patriarch Bao Tang Wuzhu (714–774) promoted tea to the laity as "a catalyst for entering the Path"[14] and leading to enlightenment so that believers "embraced the habit, everywhere boiling and drinking tea" (Feng, cited in Chen and Zhu 1981, 211).

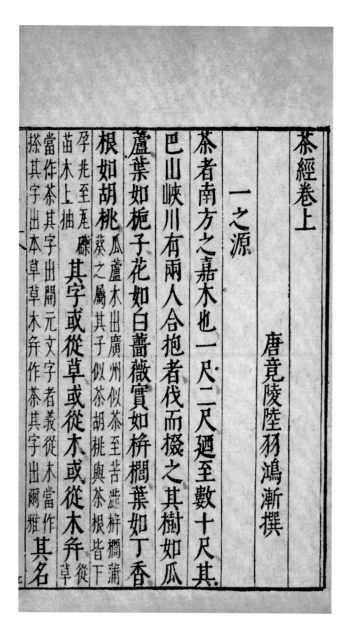

I.2 Lu Yü (China, 733–804)
Chajing (Book of Tea), Ming dynasty (1368–1644) edition
Woodblock print
REPRODUCED FROM SHIH (1999, 26)

The *Chajing*, or *Book of Tea*, was first published in 780, but the earliest extant copy was published in 1273 in the compendium of scholarly works known as the Baichuan xüehai. Subsequent editions were published in the Ming dynasty. The later publications perpetuated the influence of the *Chajing* on tea through the centuries.

On the northern steppes, the expanding use of tea among nomads remained inexplicable. On seeing northern foreigners buy tea, Feng Yan expressed his amazement: "In recent years, the Uighur have come to court, driving their great horses to trade for tea, then returning to their homeland. How truly strange!" (Feng, cited in Chen and Zhu 1981, 211). Gathered in sprawling yurt-cities on the steppes of Mongolia, the cultured Turkic Uighur maintained vast herds of horses and a mighty cavalry to protect their substantial interests in trade along the Silk Road. Allied to the Tang, the Uighur often came to

the aid of the court. With the collapse of the Tibetan tribute treaties, the Tang imperial army lost an important source of equine mounts. The Uighur offered their herds, taking advantage of the Tang court to extort imperial princesses, silk, and fine tea. For nomads, tea was no mere luxury but an important supplement to their meat and dairy diet. Moreover, as an herbal medicine, it relieved many common ills. The great Tang physician Meng Shen (ca. 621–ca. 713) noted that among many things "tea is beneficial to the large intestine…it clears blockage."[15] The Uighur thirst for the beverage neatly aligned with their trade interests; as caravaned purveyors, these nomads carried tea farther west to Central Asia and beyond. The Uighur were not, however, the only foreign traders and drinkers of tea. Before the break in Sino-Tibetan relations, the Tang sent diplomatic missions to Tibet. While entertaining the Tibetan chieftain Canbu, the Tang emissary, one Chang Lu, brewed tea to serve him. Curious about what herb was being used, Canbu asked, "What is this?" "It is tea," Chang replied. Canbu then said, "I too have this" and called for his stores of tea—acquired through tribute and trade—to be brought out, identifying each one by place name, as would any southern connoisseur.[16]

Writing in *Records of Things Heard and Seen*, Feng Yan observed the tea practices of his time, noting that "the art of tea has become a great movement. Of princes, nobles, and courtiers, there are none who do not drink it.… Beginning in the heartland, tea has spread beyond the northern frontier." Indeed, tea had traveled north and west and even to Korea and Japan, where it was imported by diplomats and clergy during the eighth and ninth centuries. Domestically, tea drinking had become common throughout society. Used in the palace, court, bureaucracy, monastery, market, and home, tea was even sold by the bowl on street corners in cities and towns.

Feng Yan judged the tea phenomenon with a critical eye. Noting that "the ancients just drank tea," he recalled the aforementioned story of Lu Na who "prepared nothing, only tea and fruit" as an expression of the Dao. The simple yet refined drinking of tea, however, contrasted exceedingly with what Feng Yan condemned as "the severe addiction of people now: incessant, all day and through the night, a veritable epidemic." As for the practice of tea, Feng Yan remarked that "every household keeps a case of tea implements." He attributed the fashion to the southern tea master Lu Yü (733–804) who "speaks eloquently and profoundly of tea" (cited in Chen and Zhu 1981, 211–12).

A foundling raised in a Buddhist monastery, the precocious and brilliant Lu Yü was educated in scripture as well as literary and Daoist works. In 780, he published the *Book of Tea* (fig. 1.2). The first work completely devoted to the subject, it circulated widely to much acclaim and had considerable impact on the practice and appreciation of tea. It also garnered its author great fame in his lifetime. The formal style of tea advocated by the book was extremely particular, full of rules, measures, procedures, and a requisite set of "twenty-four tea implements," all kept in an "elegant case." Lu Yü's elaborate

A DAOIST TALE
FROM THE BOOK OF TEA

THE APOCRYPHAL DAOIST TALE of the tea master Yü Hong[·] and the immortal Danqiu zi appears to have been especially significant for Lu Yü as he alluded to it twice in the *Book of Tea*. Yü Hong is initially introduced in the course of Lu Yü's discussion of tea utensils, specifically the archaic ladle, which was associated with the making of offerings:

> The ladle or *p'iao* is also called *hsi-shao*, sacrificial ladle. Split a gourd to make it.… The Chin retainer Tu Yü wrote in his *Ode to Tea*, "Pour tea using the bottle gourd. Its mouth is wide, its neck is thin, and its handle is short." Once during the Yongjia period, a man from Yüyao by the name of Yü Hong went up into Mount Baobu to pick tea. He happened to meet a Daoist who said, "I am Danqiu zi, 'Master Cinnabar Hill'…I pray you, Master, make daily sacrifices to me and I beg you, share with me the bounty of your tea bowl and sacrificial ladle."

The second mention of Yü Hong, which repeats and expands upon this encounter, occurs in part 7 of Lu Yü's treatise, where he discusses the history of tea. In this section, Lu Yü freely mixed actual incidents and people with myths, orthodox and apocryphal Daoist tales, and fictional characters. He treated both Yü Hong and Danqiu zi as historical personages, assigning the former to the Yongjia period of Emperor Huai (r. 307–312) and the latter to the Han dynasty.

> Yü Hong from Yüyao went into the mountains to pick tea and happened to meet a Daoist leading three black oxen. The Daoist guided Yü Hong to Mount Baobu and said, "I am Danqiu zi. I have heard that you, Master, are superb at preparation and service in the art of tea, and I have long thought to call on you. Within the mountains is a place where supreme tea grows, a tea that I will present to you. In return, Master, I pray you make daily sacrifices to me and beg you share with me the bounty of your tea bowl and sacrificial ladle." Thereafter, having established sacral libations of tea to the Daoist, Yü Hong and his family could enter the mountain to gather *daming*, the rare tea.

Ancient masters often roamed hidden mountains and valleys looking for the finest tea, which was believed to grow wild. Carried out alone in rugged country, this search became a time of communion between man and nature. In the heart of the tea master, it was also a spiritual quest, and the tea symbolized universal harmony. Mountain tea was "blessed by the sweet spirit of Heaven" and watched over by the immortals protecting the "pure, high places." On Mount Baobu, part of the remote and mystical Tiantai range—favored by Daoist spirits and hermits—Danqiu zi offered Yü Hong *daming*, the rarest and finest leaf, a gift that allowed him to perfect the art of tea.

Danqiu means "mound of cinnabar," an ancient term that first appeared in the Han dynasty song "Distant Journey" in which a world-weary mortal casts off his material body and travels as an astral projection to an unearthly place: "I departed, and swiftly prepared to start off on my journey. / I met the Feathered Men on the Hill of Cinnabar; / I tarried in the ancient land of Immortality" (Hawkes 1985, 196).

Cinnabar was a potent and indispensable ingredient used in Daoist elixirs of immortality. The precious mineral came from the mines of Sichuan and its deep vermillion color was intimately associated with the distinctive shamanistic cultures of the south: Shu, Ba, and Chu. It was believed that by feeding on the large, dark ruby crystals of the mineral, mere mortals became feathered transcendents, gathering on high mounds of cinnabar and winging forever between the material and immaterial worlds. The Daoist superior of the avian beings was the same Master Cinnabar Hill who traversed time and space to meet Yü Hong and share in the tea master's quest.

The mortal Yü Hong sought supreme tea in material form, whereas the immortal Danqiu zi required the same tea in its most sacred and immaterial form. The gift of tea allowed Yü Hong to perfect the art of tea. For Master Cinnabar Hill only the extraordinary tea prepared by Yü Hong using his bowl and ladle would suffice as an offering. Yü Hong's tea offering was special because he had selected the leaves with his own hands from Danqiu zi's trees. The story points to the relationships between mortal and immortal, material and spiritual, art and devotion, and the importance of tea in effecting them.

[·]From the *Record of the Supernatural and Strange*, written circa 312 by the Daoist libationer Wang Fou (active ca. 290–312).

methods were hardly the simplicity of "just drinking tea" championed by Feng Yan. The broad popularity of the tea master's style and his influence at court, however, precluded any criticism Feng Yan might express for Lu Yü except through the irony of faint praise: "Near and far, everyone imitates him" (cited in Chen and Zhu 1981, 211–12). Not only did Lu Yü explain in detail the proper preparation and brewing of tea, he also subverted the then-prevailing notion of tea as Buddhist by revealing its true origins in Daoism.

Lu Yü explained the nature of tea with reference to its botanical, culinary, medicinal, dietary, and alchemical aspects. The vast majority of his sources and quotations were drawn from the works of Daoist sages, poets, physicians, apothecaries, and masters of esoterica, all illustrated with stories drawn from the Daoist apocrypha (see box, previous page). As for the art and practice of tea, Lu Yü combined the techniques of haute cuisine with the requisites of the gourmand to satisfy the demands of social custom and connoisseurship. Among Daoist adepts, however, prescriptive doses preserved tea as a stimulant and a meditational aid with the potency to produce transcendent states of mind. To inspire ritual gravity and solemnity, Lu Yü chose key equipage and utensils modeled on ancient ritual implements: the bronze tripod brazier and the gourd serving ladle. The brazier in particular had strong alchemical significance. As the furnace and fire for brewing tea, the brazier symbolized the creation of the Daoist elixir of immortality just as tea symbolized the herb of life (Owyoung 2008b, 232–52).

In the Tang, brewed tea was a "decoction," meaning that the essences of the leaf were extracted in water by either steeping, mixing, or boiling. Tea, whole leaves or powder, was steeped in a covered jar. Mixing was accomplished by pouring a stream of boiled water from a ewer over tea powder in a bowl.[17] These informal methods were common in the household and marketplace. In a ceremonial context, however, Lu Yü boiled tea made from a tea cake that was first toasted, milled, and sifted to a very fine powder. Water was salted to improve flavor. The powdered tea was thrown into a cauldron of rapidly boiling water, the brew was then tempered with a measure of warm water and allowed to simmer and spume. Floating on the steaming tea, a fine, light foam appeared as "lustrous as drifting snow." Ladled into bowls, the tea was served with ample helpings of froth, the "floreate essence of tea" (fig. 1.3; Lu Yü [1273] 1985, ch. 3, pt. 5, 2a).

As already noted, tea masters had extolled the beauty of tea froth since the fourth century CE. Continuing the tradition, Lu Yü wrote poetically that the foamy efflorescence resembled "blooming duckweed whirling along the bank of a deep pond" or "chrysanthemum flowers fallen into an ancient ritual bronze" (Lu Yü [1273] 1985, ch. 3, pt. 5, 2a). In the Tang, fine tea was made from pale buds that were highly processed. Steamed, pressed, and pulped, the even paler tea paste was then dried into cakes. When ground into powder, caked tea produced a very pale beverage and a pale foam. The idea of the "white" hue of frothy tea set against a green, glazed bowl

prompted Lu Yü to favor fine celadons from the kilns of Yüe in the southeast. During the Tang, there were several centers of ceramic production, among the most important was Xing, which made exceptional white wares. Lu Yü, however, took umbrage at any judgment that Xing was superior to Yüe: "This is certainly not so. If Xing is like silver, then Yüe is like jade.... If Xing is like snow, then Yüe is like ice." This was a matter of aesthetics, for celadon provided a greater contrast to snowy froth. Moreover, "Yüe ware is celadon, and thus the color of tea appears greenish"(Lu Yü [1273] 1985, ch. 2, pt. 4, 4b–5a).

The comprehensive character of the *Book of Tea* had broad appeal. Lu Yü covered the origins and sources of tea, its history and personages, production and manufacture, tools and implements, equipage and wares, and brewing and drinking methods. After his death in 804, tea merchants throughout the country came to regard Lu Yü as the "Sage of Tea," and his book as scripture. From the pottery kilns that supplied tea wares and implements, merchants commissioned miniature glazed ceramic tea sets to give to favored customers. The set came complete with a small statue of Lu Yü wearing a Daoist tricorne miter and reading from the *Book of Tea*. Among the aristocracy, as well as the wealthy and socially aspiring, the book became a primer on tea, codifying the art of tea and its aesthetic values for many generations.

As the influence of the *Book of Tea* broadened, the Daoist tradition of tea deepened through the spiritual activities of Lu Tong (775–835), a reclusive poet and connoisseur. Intimately connected to the highest levels of the Tang court, Lu Tong received gifts of rare tea from admiring patrons. On one occasion, he was presented with Yangxian, the priceless imperial tribute tea, in a case containing three hundred of the "moon-shaped tea cakes." Surprised and humbled by the gift, Lu Tong shut himself away and donned his robes and cap; then he calmly prepared the rare tea and drank. Bowl after bowl, he sensed the tea transform him until he felt as though he had become an immortal spirit. Lu Tong memorialized the event in the "Song of Tea" with its famous seven lines:

> The first bowl moistens my lips and throat.
> The second bowl banishes my loneliness
>   and melancholy.
> The third bowl penetrates my withered entrails,
>   finding nothing except a literary core of
>   five thousand scrolls.
> The fourth bowl raises a slight perspiration.
> The fifth bowl purifies my flesh and bones.
> The sixth bowl makes me one with the immortal,
>   feathered spirits.
> The seventh bowl I need not drink, feeling only
>   a pure wind rushing beneath my wings.[18]

Buoyed by the elevated Daoist sentiments resident within the "Song of Tea" and the *Book of Tea*, merchandising, fashion, and cachet all combined to propel tea to even greater popularity. In the eighth century, the general population stood at

fifty million, and the annual amount of tea consumed was prodigious, especially in cities and capitals where trends were rarely embraced in moderation. Far-flung and ever-expanding, the appetite for tea was satisfied by a relatively stable industry, increasing production, and growing market volume. The estate at Mengding alone produced thirteen million pounds of tea per year. By the late eighth century, tea was the single most important trade commodity (Twitchett 1963, 72), and by any economic standard, it was just begging to be taxed.

In 782, the first ever tax on tea was imposed by imperial order. The levy was set at a rate of ten percent of the average market price and had to be paid in cash. The steep rate and cash payment signaled that tea was an essential commodity with a high value, like lacquer, timber, or bamboo. Originally intended as a temporary source of disaster relief funds, tea revenues were diverted to general government expenditures. In 783 the emperor was faced with breakaway provinces and rebellion. Desperate for funds, the court forced the tea tax—one of many ad hoc duties—on the imperial capital of Chang'an. In light of the oppressive taxes already in force, the tea levy set the half-starved citizens of Chang'an rioting and joining the advancing rebel armies. The emperor was forced to flee the city. The imperial Act of Grace of 784 offered amnesties and pardons for the emperor's return to Chang'an. It also rescinded and abolished the state monopolies on wine and salt and other duties, including the tax on tea (Twitchett 1963, 62; Chiu-Duke 2000, 129). Eight years later, disastrous floods devastated forty prefectures killing twenty thousand people. Once again, a tea tax was imposed as an emergency measure, but just as before, the duty and revenues were later made permanent and channeled to government coffers.

The booming tea market had prompted merchants and provinces to devise a system of monetary transfer known as

1.3   Attributed to Yan Liben (China, d. 673)
Xiao Yi Stealing the Orchid Pavilion Preface,
Tang dynasty (618–907)
Handscroll; ink and color on silk
27.4 x 64.7 cm
NATIONAL PALACE MUSEUM, TAIWAN, REPUBLIC OF CHINA

The tea master and servant at the far left of this scroll prepare tea in the Tang manner using a brazier, cauldron, and ladle. The scroll depicts the visit of the imperial agent Xiao Yi to the Buddhist monk Pan Cai who possessed the Orchid Pavilion Preface, a famous example of calligraphy coveted by the throne. According to the story, Xiao Yi later stole the calligraphy and took it to the emperor.

"flying money." On selling his tea and paying his taxes, a merchant in Chang'an deposited the profits in a chancellery maintained in the capital by his home province. The chancellery issued a receipt to the merchant, and a record of confirmation was sent south to the provincial pay officer. Returning home, the merchant submitted the receipt to the pay officer and was given the cash equivalent deposited at the chancellery in the capital. The system of "flying money" relieved the merchant from the danger of traveling with large amounts of heavy coin; saved the province from carting tax monies to the capital; and transferred tea taxes directly to the central government. The transfers of credit were forbidden by the state in 811, however, in a move to wrest financial control from the provincial governments. The following year the state allowed merchants to transfer credit through the provincial offices of the central government: Finance, Public Revenue, and the Salt and Iron Commission, thereby directly controlling monetary transfers (Twitchett 1963, 72; Gernet 1996, 265).

In 835 the first state tea monopoly was established by the chief minister Wang Ya (ca. 760–835), who sought to concentrate economic power in his own hands. The monopoly

1.4   Tea bowl, China, Tang dynasty, 9th century CE
       Stoneware with glaze
       FAMENSI TEMPLE, XI'AN, SHAANXI

Prized for its blue-green hue, "secret color" ware was a superior form of ceramic known for its celadon glaze. Although the existence of "secret color" ware had been long recorded, no examples were known to exist until the discovery of a cache of tea objects under the pagoda at Famensi Temple.

1.5   Covered Box with geese decor, China, Tang dynasty,
       9th century CE
       Gilt silver
       17.8 cm
       FAMENSI TEMPLE, XI'AN, SHAANXI

This ornate box was used to store tea and illustrates the extravagant style of tea equipage among the aristocracy and wealthy of the late Tang.

1.7 Tea bowl and stand, China, Tang dynasty, 9th century CE
Glass
Diam (bowl): 12.7 cm; diam (stand): 13.8 cm
FAMENSI TEMPLE, XI'AN, SHAANXI

This bowl and stand are among the rarest tea objects known. During the Tang, glass was imported from Persia, but the uniqueness of these works—their medium, shape, and function—suggests that they might have been made in China or were perhaps an import commissioned by the imperial palace.

1.6 Tea Mortar, China, Tang dynasty, inscribed 869 CE
Gilt silver
27.5 cm
FAMENSI TEMPLE, XI'AN, SHAANXI

Elaborate mortars of gold and silver, such as this dated imperial example, were used by tea masters of the nobility to grind caked tea into powder, which was then sifted and stored in an ornate container.

abolished private growing, processing, and selling of tea and ordered the transplantation of all tea bushes to state plantations and the destruction of commercial stocks of processed tea. Opposition to the monopoly was so violent that to quell the protests, it was said that the throne would have to "exterminate the population, or force them into resistance in the hills." Within months, the tea monopoly was rescinded (Twitchett 1963, 64; Chen and Zhu 1981, 460–61, 462–63; Twitchett and Fairbank 1979, 2: 685).

The late Tang palace, the courts of the nobility, and the wealthy held the art of tea in highest esteem, sparing no expense for fine tea or costly equipage. The emperor possessed the rarest teas. In 770, an imperial tea estate was established near Lake Tai, west of Shanghai, and by the mid-ninth century, thirty thousand peasants harvested the garden's annual crop with a thousand more people processing tea into cakes[19] that were packaged in fine paper, silk, and lacquered cases.

The opulent palace style was exemplified by the cache of tea utensils discovered beneath the twelve-story pagoda of the Famensi Monastery near Chang'an. Famensi was the repository of the finger bone of Buddha, a sacred relic that attracted patronage from many generations of the Tang imperial family. In 873, Emperor Yizong (r. 860–873) presented the temple with an offering of precious tea wares, which was augmented by a second gift of tea utensils in the following year by Xizong (r. 873–888), the succeeding emperor (Karetzky 1995, 59, 182–84, 191–92). The majority of the tea utensils were gilt silver with repoussé, stamped, engraved, woven, and openwork designs, but among the tea ceramics was "secret color" ware, a rare celadon of extraordinary blue-green hue (fig. 1.4). Caked tea was kept in a covered basket of woven silver wire (fig. 1.5); salt used in tea water was kept in a covered cellar of gilt silver that took the form of a lotus petal. A mortar and pestle of gilt silver (fig. 1.6), dated by inscription to 869, were used to grind caked tea into powder that was sifted in a fine-mesh gilded-silver casket and stored in a gilt-silver covered caddy in the shape of a tortoise. A silver spoon decorated with gilt flying geese measured tea powder into a rare, clear-glass tea bowl atop a matching stand (fig. 1.7). The absence of a cauldron and brazier marked the late Tang change to brewing tea with a ewer. Boiled water was poured from a spouted silver ewer into the bowl to mix the powder into tea (Niigata Prefectural Museum of Modern Art 1999). The technique was widely adopted for its convenience by all tea drinkers.

Liao, Xi Xia, and Jin

The northern cultures—Qidan, Tangut, and Jurchen—of the steppes also made tea with a ewer. After the fall of the Tang dynasty, the north was ruled by a succession of sinicized groups. The highly cultured Qidan established the Liao dynasty (916–1125) with southern borders and settlements that reached beyond the Great Wall into Hebei Province. In the Qidan tombs of the Zhang family at Xuanhua, a wall painting depicted servants grinding tea into powder, heating a ewer of water on a brazier, and carrying cup stands and bowls of tea

(fig. 1.8). To the west in the Ordos Desert within and beyond the great loop of the Yellow River, the Tangut founded the Xi Xia dynasty (1038–1227). From the eastern forests of Manchuria, the Jurchen declared themselves the Jin dynasty (1115–1234). More than thirty thousand pounds of tea were sent annually to the Tangut alone (Gernet 1996, 355), and the Jurchen established tea gardens at the northern limits of the growing range—Shaanxi, Henan, and Shandong—in an effort to stem the flow of silver from the Jin treasury to the south. Despite state measures, however, imported tea accounted for the steep Jin trade deficit, and illegal tea smuggled into Jin across the border was not uncommon (Mote 1999, 286–87).

Song

At the end of the Tang, pretenders to the throne in the south founded the Southern Tang (937–975) and reigned briefly over a vast tea-growing region that included the great Yangzi watershed from Hunan and reached as far south as Guangdong. At Nanjing, the Southern Tang rulers presided over a court of poetry and painting. The last emperor Li Yü (r. 961–978) was himself an important poet and calligrapher. During his refined and sophisticated reign, tea processing reached an apogee, especially in Fujian, which set the standard for imperial tribute tea.

In the north, the newly established Song dynasty (960–1279) gazed covetously southward across the Yangzi at the Southern Tang's great wealth in silk, ceramics, and fine tea. Within its own borders, the Song government monopolized virtually all tea, yet the most superior varieties lay beyond its grasp to the south. Marshaling his forces in 975, the Song emperor Taizu (r. 960–976) put an end to the Southern Tang with the capture of Li Yü. Taking possession of the tea gardens in Fujian, Taizu ordered the continuation of imperial tribute, conveying the tea north to the capital at Kaifeng. By 977 the Song emperor Taizong (r. 976–997) had established North Garden of Fujian, the foremost tea estate of the Northern Song (Liao 1996, 12, 19).

Located at the foot of Phoenix Mountain, North Garden was an official complex of forty-six plantations that grew, harvested, and manufactured "imperially fired" tea. This took the form of wafers or small cakes known as "molded tea." These were specially decorated with a dragon and phoenix. The rigorous refining process took as long as two weeks. On the first day, "small buds," the finest and tiniest tea leaves were carefully picked from the gardens; four hundred thousand buds were required to make a single wafer of the finest tea. The plucked leaves were selected and graded, washed and rinsed four times, and then steamed over vats of boiling water. Excess water was expressed from the leaves in a small press; a larger, heavier press extracted juices and oils overnight. The next day, the leaves were ground by hand in a ceramic mortar with a wooden pestle with added measures of water to make a smooth, pale

1.8   Mural, China, Liao dynasty, 10th century CE
           Tomb of Zhang Kuangzheng, Zhang Family Tombs
           Plaster with ink and colors
           Xuanhua, Hebei
           REPRODUCED FROM TSAO (2000, 24)

Here servants are depicted as engaged in various steps of tea preparation. The seated servant boy grinds tea into powder, the kneeling youth and standing male attend the brazier and water ewer, while two women hold tea bowls and cup stands.

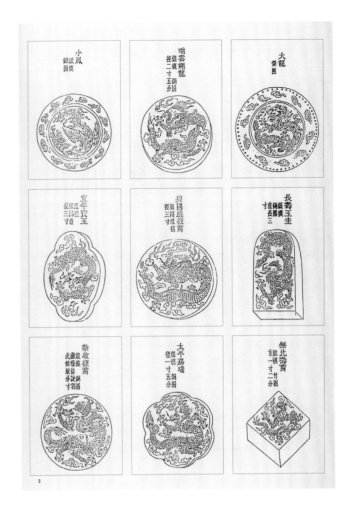

1.9   Illustrations of caked tea from the *Record of North Garden Tribute Tea of the Xüanhe Reign Period* (1121–1125), China, Song dynasty, 1158 (detail)
           Woodblock print
           REPRODUCED FROM SHIH (1999, 35)

The rarest forms of Song tea were created to celebrate the reigns of individual emperors. Caked tea from the imperial estates of North Garden in Fujian were covered with molded decorations, the most famous of which employed dragons and phoenixes. The varied shapes and designs of these tea cakes were made during the reign of Emperor Huizong.

paste. The tea paste was put into molds and heated over a very hot fire, then alternately roasted and immersed in boiling water three separate times. Next, the cakes were slowly dried over a low fire overnight. The following morning, the wafers underwent a cure by light smoking and low heat for as many as fifteen days; the length of time depended on the thickness of the cakes. At the end of curing, the hardened, dry cakes were passed over boiling water to bring out their color, placed in a closed room, and vigorously fanned until their surfaces appeared glossy. The beautifully colored wafers were known as "wax tea," their dark, rich luster resembling the finest lacquer.[20] According to the *Song shi* (*History of the Song Dynasty*), the imperial estates in Fujian and Sichuan were the only places allowed to use this process in the manufacture of caked tea (cited in Liao 1996, 17).

Some caked tea was commonly scented with a variety of fragrances: spices, floral essences, and musk. In the *Record of Tea*, Cai Xiang (1012–1067), a native of Fujian, tea connoisseur, and intendant of the imperial tea estates, noted that one of the peppery fragrances was Borneo camphor, an expensive import known as "dragon brain."[21] Aromatic teas came in the shapes of squares, rounds, and flowers colored red, green, yellow, and black. The cake surfaces were elaborately decorated. The smallest cakes measured about three and one-half centimeters; the largest, about ten centimeters. The names of the teas were auspicious and ornamental, often suggesting preciousness and

long life: Gold Coin, Jade Leaf of the Long Spring, Inch of Gold, Longevity Buds without Compare, Silver Leaf of Ten Thousand Springs, Jade Tablet of Longevity, and Dragon Buds of Ten Thousand Longevities (fig. 1.9).[22] Each cake was set in a protective surround of fine bamboo, bronze, or silver and was wrapped in silk; broad, green bamboo leaves; and then more silk. Sealed in vermillion by officials, the tea was enclosed in a red-lacquered casket with a gilt lock and sent in fine, silk-lined, bamboo satchels by express to the emperor. The first tea cakes of the season were known as "new tea for examination from North Garden" and were so rare that even the throne was initially presented with only one hundred small squares. The emperor shared a cake or two of the precious tea with members of the imperial family, the distribution determined by rank and lineage.[23]

In addition to caked tea, very fine whole, dry, loose-leaf teas had been produced since the Tang by the famous gardens in Sichuan, Jiangsu, Zhejiang, and Fujian. Song loose tea of the eleventh and twelfth centuries included Forged in the Sun, Twin Wells, Sleeping Dragon, and Precious Cloud varieties. Twin Wells was particularly esteemed by the literati and often mentioned in the writings of poets of the Northern Song. Named after the village of Shuangjing, near Hongzhou in Jiangsi Province, Twin Wells was developed in the mid-eleventh century on only a few acres of land by the family of the great Song calligrapher Huang Tingjian (1045–1105). Described as a white tea, Twin Wells was made from very small leaf buds that were shaped like tiny, pointed hooks covered with a fine white fuzz. The picked leaves were selected and graded, washed and rinsed, and steamed. Then the tea was thoroughly and gently dried in small amounts in a warm metal pan to retain the distinctive hook-shape of the tiny leaves. Twin Wells was best stored in a small, fine stone jar, but it was also kept lightly compressed in a pouch of thin red or blue silk, the colors chosen to contrast with the leaves. Huang Tingjian was naturally fond of Twin Wells and gave it as a gift to his friends among the literati, who poetically referred to it as Eagle's Talons and Eagle's Grasping Claws for its sharp, hooked leaves. Singing its praises in their poetry, Huang Tingjian and other famous poets made Twin Wells the most highly regarded loose-leaf tea of the time (Zhu 1985, 129; Chen Zongmou 1997, 125, 183–84; Liao 1996, 24–25).

For more than a century, the central government monopolized all tea production in the south with the exception of Sichuan, a region that remained geographically isolated and administratively semiautonomous. The situation changed dramatically in 1074 under the New Policies implemented by the minister Wang Anshi (1021–1086) to promote the state's share in the empire's growing economy and to build the military. Sichuan tea proved critical to the success of these reforms. Under increasing pressure from Tangut forces of Xi Xia, the Song formed an alliance with the Tibetans, who would serve as a military buffer in the northwest and a major source of much-needed horses: royal mounts, as well as war, post, and work animals. The Tibetan horse traders, who came in great numbers, were primarily interested in bartering for tea, prompting government reformers to purchase tea from Sichuan, ship it to the northern outposts, and sell it in exchange for horses. The tea was presented in the form of compressed "blocks" and "bricks" of leaves. Tibetans preferred the rich, dark color and earthy character of "aged" teas.

The mutually beneficial commercial arrangement between the traders and the Song fostered the development of the Sichuan Tea and Horse Agency, the most powerful state institution in the northwest. As a consequence, however, the Sichuan tea industry—an insular, local, high-quality tea producer—was transformed into a government bulk processor of low-quality tea for distant transport. With the emphasis on quantity rather than quality, gardens were planted with more tea bushes, the intensive cultivation incorporating "waste" and marginal hill land. Harvesting began early in the late winter flush, nearly stripping the plants of leaves, stems, and twigs to force a second budding in early spring. Third and fourth harvests later in the year produced even more leaves, but summer and autumn harvests were declared illegal by the government in an attempt at quality control. In order to meet quotas and increase profit, the processors resorted to ways of increasing the gross weight of manufactured tea. Cuts in processing saved costs in labor and in fuel for firing, and they reduced the drying time, the latter allowing greater water retention in the leaves and adding weight to the tea at the risk of mold and rot. Government tea

inspectors, rewarded for meeting and exceeding quotas, were punished for passing "mixed, ersatz, coarse, or rotten" and "old autumn-leaf" tea. In reaction to corrupt practices and low-quality tea, the horse traders retaliated by selling herds of old, diseased, and stunted mounts at higher prices (Paul Smith 1991, 12–47, 76, 119, 225–27, 260, 277–84). The folly of light-fingered bureaucrats and wily merchants, however, hardly touched the palace courts of the aristocracy or the elegant salons of the literati.

By the eleventh century, the Song had established an inspired variation on the Tang art of tea. Although the basic concerns of color, fragrance, and taste remained constant, the preparation, service, and aesthetics evolved to an extraordinary state. In the Song art of tea, the beverage was prepared by wrapping the hard tea cake in fine, clean paper. The wrapped cake was set in a pounding device and broken with a mallet. The bits and pieces of cake were ground to a powder in a small hand-mill. The tea was then sifted to an extremely fine dust with the powdery consistency of rice flour. Fine loose teas like Twin Wells were pulverized using the same implements and techniques. A measure of tea powder was spooned into a warm bowl. Then a small, precise amount of hot water was poured into the bowl in a thin, forceful stream from a narrow-spouted ewer. This technique, known as "pointing," mixed and liquefied the tea to a creamy, milky consistency. Next, the remaining measure of hot water was poured streaming from the ewer, and the tea was then briskly whipped to a froth with a bamboo whisk. The tea master presented the bowl to the guest who drank the tea in a few foamy sips.[24]

Froth remained the key to a good bowl of tea. Producing a thick spume of tea became a game of skill popular with all tea drinkers but particularly the literati and aristocrats (fig. 1.10). Known as the "tea contest" and the "tea war," the game began as a way to examine the quality of tea from the spring harvest. In the Tang dynasty, the poet Bo Juyi (742–846) revealed that officials of the imperial estates at Huzhou and Changzhou "argued the merits" and "critiqued the quality" of the new spring tea (Lu and Cai 1995, 164–66). The tea contest was introduced to the Song court on a query from the emperor Renzong (r. 1022–1063), who wanted to know more about the Fujian style of examining tea. In response, the aforementioned connoisseur Cai Xiang, intendant of the imperial estates, wrote his *Record of Tea*. Only new, unscented tea from

1.10   Emperor Song Huizong (China, 1082–1135)
A Literary Gathering, Northern Song dynasty (960–1126)
Hanging scroll; ink and color on silk
184.4 x 123.9 cm
NATIONAL PALACE MUSEUM, TAIWAN, REPUBLIC OF CHINA

Emperor Huizong was not only a tea master and connoisseur of the highest order but a brilliant calligrapher and painter. In this large hanging scroll, he depicted a gathering of scholars seated at a large table in a park In the foreground, servants busily prepare tea for the party. Legend has it that Huizong created the scroll to commemorate a tea held in honor of a high official.

I.11   Tea bowl and cup stand, Jian ware, China, Song dynasty, twelfth century CE
Stoneware with glaze
Diam (mouth): 12.2 cm
©SEIKADO BUNKO ART MUSEUM, TOKYO

The marking known as "butterfly" is among the rarest glaze effects in Jian ware. Related to the small markings of "oil spot" glaze, which is known for its subtle sheen, "butterfly" glaze boasts a deep blue-black ground against which visually dynamic clusters of large luminescent spots appear to vibrate and flutter.

I.12   Attributed to Liu Songnian (China, ca. 1150–1225)
Tea Contest, Song–Yüan dynasties, 13th century CE
Hanging scroll; ink and color on silk
Present whereabouts unknown

This painting depicts a group of street peddlers engaged in a tea tasting contest. One contestant uses the "point" method of mixing powdered tea with a thin stream of water poured from the ewer into the tea bowl, while the others admire his technique and taste his wares.

Fujian was used for examining tea. As in the Tang, a very pale or "white" tea was preferred. The wafer was made of tea buds that produced a powder as white as fine paper. In one form of the game, the purity of the natural fragrance and the sweetness and smoothness of taste were criteria used to judge tea. Another game required full mastery of making tea, from breaking and pulverizing the cake to boiling water and wielding the whisk. A fine, thick froth was the goal, and the winner of the contest was judged by the way the foam clung, a feature known as "biting the bowl," and whether or not it betrayed unwanted traces of liquid, or "water scars." The close examination of the white froth required bowls of highly contrasting hues, the darker the color, the better.

Cai Xiang praised Jian ware bowls of "purple-black with hare's fur markings."[25] The thick, unctuous iron glaze on Jian wares was transmuted by fire into an extraordinary range of markings, inspiring names that referred to texture, pattern, and iridescence like "partridge feathers," "oil spots," and the "hare's fur" mentioned by Cai Xiang. Later, the emperor-aesthete Huizong (r. 1101–1125) wrote *Treatise of Tea in the Daguan Reign Period*, a discourse on the finer points of the tea contest. Huizong, a connoisseur and avid tea contestant, noted that bowls of "deep black" hue with minute markings of "jade gossamer" were best.[26] An extremely rare Jian ware glaze was known simply as "butterfly" (fig. 1.11), a blue-black color with clusters of luminous spots that appeared to vibrate and flutter (Marshall Wu 1998, 22–31, esp. 30; Rousmaniere 1996, 43–58). Like the rare tea they held, prized Jian ware bowls were sent in large quantities to the palace as imperial tribute from Fujian (Chang 1982, 10; see also Zhang Linsheng 1978, 79–90).

Deep within the walls of the palace in Kaifeng, tea was served to the emperor and his consorts in their private apartments by a personal staff supervised by the Court of Palace Attendants, a service agency comprised of eunuchs. At functions of state, high-ranking eunuchs worked closely with the Court of Entertainment and its Office of Fruit and Tea to arrange official receptions and banquets hosted by the throne. The emperor honored students of the National University and School for the Sons of the State in a ceremony punctuated by loud commands to "ascend the hall," "rise" after bowing, and "sit and take tea." Tea was one of the most important gifts presented to foreign rulers, ambassadors, and dignitaries. Visiting embassies returned to their native lands laden with return tribute, including gold and silver metalwork, ceramics, silk, and many varieties of fine tea disbursed from the great stores of the Court of Imperial Treasury. On imperial tours of inspection, the emperor presented tribute teas to monasteries and temples (Liang 1994, 190–99). Members of the prestigious Hanlin Academy, ministers and civil officials, military officers, and functionaries were given monthly allotments, as tea was considered one of seven necessities of daily life: fuel, rice, oil, salt, soy sauce, vinegar, and tea (Zhu 1985, 41–53; Liao 1996, 12).

In the pleasure districts of the Song capitals, Kaifeng in the north and Hangzhou in the south, teahouses abounded, packed cheek-by-jowl with restaurants serving gourmet banquets, brothels with beautiful and talented courtesans, and wine houses serving exotic drinks. Exquisite teas vied with fine wines, such as the costly Plum Blossom Steeped in Snow, in establishments with names like House of Pure Happiness and House of Eight Immortals.[27] One of many teahouse districts in Kaifeng was marked by grand architectural facades of crimson lacquer erected in the middle of the avenue (Meng [1174] 1982, ch. 2, 59). In the southern capital at Hangzhou, storied tea pavilions were covered with elaborate scaffolds decorated with fragrant flowers. Places like Mommy Wang's House of Tea attracted wealthy merchants, officials, and literati who gathered to taste the season's new tea. Paneled in fine wood and embroidered silk, the teahouse was scented with cut flowers and cedar trees grown stunted and gnarled as bonsai in small basins; scrolls of painting and calligraphy by famous

1.13   Gong Chun (China, active 1506–1521)
Teapot in the shape of a gingko burl, Ming dynasty
(1368–1644)
Modern lids by Huang Yulin (1842–1913) and Pei Shimin
(1892–1977)
Unglazed stoneware
H: 10 cm
NATIONAL MUSEUM OF CHINA, BEIJING

1.14   Teapot, Yixing ware, China, Ming dynasty, 16th century CE
(Tomb of Wu Jing, buried 1533 CE, Majiashan, Zhonghua
Gate, Nanjing)
Unglazed stoneware
H: 17.7 cm
NANJING MUNICIPAL MUSEUM
REPRODUCED FROM SHIH (1999)

1.15   Wang Wen (China, 1497–1576)
Brewing Tea, Ming dynasty, 1558 CE
Detail of handscroll; ink on paper
NATIONAL PALACE MUSEUM, TAIWAN, REPUBLIC OF CHINA

Yangxian tea was produced in Changzhou near the famous pottery town of Yixing near Lake Tai. Once lauded as Tang and Song imperial tribute, Yangxian tea was enjoyed as a rare tea in the repertoires of Ming tea masters such as Wu Lun and Wang Lai. Their discriminating taste and style were as sought after as the tea they served.

Wu Lun (1440–1522) was from Yixing, living among the surrounding "hills and streams" as a reclusive tea master known as Hermit of the Distant Heart (Central Library 1978, 253). He was friends with the renowned painters Shen Zhou (1427–1509) and Wen Zhengming (1470–1559) and crossed Lake Tai to visit the artists in Suzhou. As a tea master, Wu Lun was overtly partisan in his appreciation of the products of his hometown Yixing. He was not only partial to Yangxian tea but also promoted the teapots made at the local kilns by Gong Chun (active 1506–1521), a young servant in Wu Lun's own household who learned to make ceramics from an old monk at nearby Chinsha Temple (Wu Shan 1995, 1062). Gong Chun perfected the use of the local clays and their special properties, creating teapots supremely suited for steeping tea and thus starting the Yixing tradition of tea wares (see Bartholomew, this volume). His master Wu Lun, by serving Yangxian tea infused in a fine teapot made by Gong Chun, attained an extraordinary level of tea that was rarely surpassed by other tea masters in the Ming (fig. 1.13).

The connoisseurship of tea was an aesthetic realm removed from the mundane, a sphere of refinement and sophistication often shared among the literati at tea gatherings. On such occasions, a tea master was the center of a day devoted to artistic, literary, and culinary pursuits; his role was something akin to a master of ceremony. Wang Lai (1459–1528) was a favorite in Suzhou circles, traveling by boat, leisurely wandering here and there, "whistling and swaggering about in the mists and waves." Remembered as a witty and brilliant conversationalist,[39] Wang Lai often stayed as a guest in the garden studio of the famous painter Shen Chou, frequently presenting the elder gentleman with a gift of rare tea.

Once in the winter of 1497, Shen Chou was joined at his house by four other literati for an intimate gathering at which Wang Lai prepared and served tea with a Yixing pot (figs. 1.14, 1.15). The marvelously subtle art demonstrated by Wang Lai during the party so moved Shen Chou that he wrote an essay in praise of the tea master. The work no longer survives, but it was recorded that: "Shen Chou dedicated 'Gathering for Tea' to Wang Lai. Wang is fond of tea and his style of tea preparation is especially wonderful. He often brings Shen Chou beautiful tea, brewing and serving it to the old man, always in this fine manner. At this gathering, the old man sipped through seven cups and savored the full beauty of it all."[40]

In the sixteenth century, the taste for Yangxian tea gave way to Tiger Hill, a tea grown in the Suzhou area and the most famous tea of the Ming. Tiger Hill tea was known for its scent of "wintry beans" and a "pure and light taste" like "the scent of bean flowers." When brewed with spring water from Mount Hui in nearby Wuxi, the tea was clear "like the color of moon light" or "white like jade" (Owyoung 2000, 31–32).

Grown on the slopes of a small mountain by Buddhist monks, demand for the tea exceeded the limited annual yield. Covetous officials commandeered much of the production, and the monks routinely adulterated the tea.

As a rare tea, Tiger Hill was brewed with Yixing teapots made by the celebrated potter Shi Dabin (b. ca. 1567) who began his career by imitating the works of Gong Chun. Initially, he made "large" teapots (17.7 cm high), but under the influence of the literati, Shi Dabin created smaller pots (13.7 cm high; fig. 1.16) to better nurture the fragrance and flavor of tea. Highly prized for brewing tea, Shi Dabin's pots were also appreciated for their excellent workmanship and the fine, satiny patina they acquired through constant use. Although many tea drinkers preferred using Yixing wares, some thought that teapots of porcelain, pewter, silver, or gold made superior tea.

In the early seventeenth century, there were nearly fifty books devoted to the subject of tea. Wen Zhengheng (1585–1645), a great-grandson of the artist Wen Zhengming, wrote the *Record of Superlative Things*, a catalog of gentlemanly pursuits that included a section on the connoisseurship of tea. He recorded seven noteworthy teas, including Yangxian and Tiger Hill, and made recommendations on tea wares and equipage as well as boiling water, charcoal, and the tea room. Wen Zhengheng also noted a general change in harvesting and processing tea, from the selection of tea buds to the picking of slightly more mature leaves: "In harvesting tea, one need not pick too fine a leaf. Fine leaves are tea buds, these first teas are deficient, lacking in flavor." Yangxian tea with its small, pointed, oblate buds shaped like "birds' tongues" was the only exception to the rule (Owyoung 2000, 31–43).

At the end of the Ming, the tea tradition was nearly three thousand years old and had undergone centuries of development and appraisal, spurring innovation and changes in style. The one constant of tea was flavor. The paramount interest of the connoisseur was taste and the singular ability to summon experience and knowledge in the appreciation of tea. In the late Ming, there was no finer connoisseur than Zhang Dai (1597–1680?), a literatus with a most discriminating palate. On one occasion, Zhang Dai was served Yangxian tea, popularly known as Lo-chieh, by the region's foremost tea master Min Wenshui. In 1638, Zhang journeyed to the old capital of Nanjing to visit friends who had studied tea with Min Wenshui. They encouraged Zhang to visit Min at his studio. Zhang Dai arrived at sunset but had to wait for Min, a doddering old man of seventy, to return. When Zhang Dai began to speak, however, Min suddenly excused himself and only returned much later to ask what Zhang Dai wanted. Explaining that he had wished to meet the old tea master for a long time, Zhang said, "If I don't taste master Min's tea today, I just won't leave." Min Wenshui was pleased, invited Zhang into a well-appointed tearoom, and began preparing tea in a Yixing teapot, then serving the brew in an exquisite porcelain cup from the imperial kilns. As he looked dubiously at the undistinguished liquid in the cup, Zhang Dai was suddenly struck by its beautiful fragrance and shouted, "Excellent!" He

then asked, "What kind of tea is this?" Min Wenshui replied, "It's Langyüan, 'tea of the immortals,' a palace tea." Zhang Dai took a sip and said, "Don't fool me. It is made using the same method as Langyüan, but the flavor is not the same." Trying to cover up a smile, the tea master asked, "Does our guest know where it was produced?" Zhang Dai took another sip and queried, "Why is it so similar to Lo-chieh?" Min then stuck out his tongue and exclaimed, "Wonderful, wonderful!"[41]

Qing

The history of tea and the art it inspired continued to evolve through the Qing dynasty (1644–1912), invigorated by the keen interest and connoisseurship of the palace, court, and intelligentsia. The innovations and customs of the common people were also echoed in the marketplace, the forms of tea expanding from green teas to include white, black, red, yellow, and scented teas under myriad names. In the early Qing, Wuyi in Fujian produced a tea called Wulong. Commonly known as Black Dragon, or oolong, Wulong, like most teas, was made by heating leaves in a iron pan and drying them over a low fire. Brittle and green, freshly picked leaves were allowed to change chemically through the interaction of natural enzymes and oxygen, wilting in the process and turning color. Green tea underwent little oxidation of the leaves and retained a green color; Wulong was semi-oxidized, half russet and dark; and red and black teas were fully oxidized and dark in hue. In the case of Wulong tea, the heating by pan-firing arrested the oxidation, coloration, and deterioration of the leaves. Drinking fine Wulong produced a sensation known as *houyün*, or "harmony of the throat."

The Qing emperor Qianlong (r. 1735–1796) was a sinicized Manchu whose nomad ancestors had moved from Liaoning to conquer the Ming. As in the past, imperial tribute tea was sent northward to Beijing for palace use at court and state functions. The emperor followed the Manchu and Mongol custom of drinking milk-tea on a daily basis as well as serving it at official banquets and meetings. The Qianlong emperor drank milk-tea from a bowl carved from white jade and inscribed with his poetry (fig. 1.17). Tribute teas were also enjoyed by the Manchu, prepared and drunk in common fashion; the vast bulk of the tea, however, was distributed in the form of imperial gifts to officials, diplomats, and foreign princes. The dispersal of fine tea through foreign trade and diplomacy intro-

duced tea to a greater international audience, including Europe and America (Owyoung 2007).

The teahouse continued as an important feature of urban life. A morning at the teahouse was filled with the latest news and gossip, and business was often conducted over cups of hot tea. Ordinary and fine teas were prepared and served with small dishes of fruit, nuts, and seeds. Customers ordered tea and drank until their leaves steeped out and had no more flavor. The teahouse was also a place of entertainment. Storytellers were popular among the day crowd, their tales punctuated by the sharp rap of wooden clappers or the staccato of a beaten drum. In the evening, singers performed traditional songs accompanied by the lute or zither. Some houses were full-scale restaurants with several floors to accommodate customers coming to chat informally over tea or celebrate and feast.

The Qing literati greatly expanded the writings devoted to tea, compiling previous records into compendia and adding their own contributions to the literary tradition. Scholars wrote monographs on individual teas such as Tiger Hill and Dragon Well, detailing the origins and history of each, the peculiarities of processing, the pairing with specific spring waters, preparing tea with various utensils, serving, drinking, and critiquing. Like literature and alchemy, tea was an endeavor rich enough to engage fully the philosophical and intellectual mind. Historically associated with eremitic and spiritual life, tea offered a respite from worldly cares, yet it also provided the fortitude and clarity of thought to deal with them. The late Qing transmitted the scholarly tea tradition through modern, English-speaking literati like Lin Yutang (1895–1976). A native of Fujian, he drank Iron Goddess of Mercy tea infused in a small Yixing pot, made thick and strong, and served in small cups. Of the meaning of tea, Lin Yutang wrote "On Tea and Friendship" and the attitude of a tea drinker: "Thus chastened in spirit, quiet in mind, and surrounded by proper company, one is fit to enjoy tea." The "proper company" he recommended "must be small." He further explained: "To drink alone is called *secluded*; to drink between two is called *comfortable*…to drink with seven or eight is called [contemptuously] *philanthropic*" (Lin Yutang 1937, 331–31, esp. 224–27). An eminent man of traditional values, Lin Yutang wrote of tea as a cultural pursuit, a way of exploring the human condition and a means of bridging the spiritual gulf between East and West. ☙

1.16   Shi Dabin (China, b. ca. 1567 CE)
Teapot, Ming dynasty, inscribed 1597 CE
Yixing ware
H: 13.7 cm
HONG KONG MUSEUM OF ART COLLECTION, NO. C1981.0500

1.17   Jade bowl, Qing dynasty, 18th century CE
Nephrite jade
Diam: 16.6 cm
NATIONAL PALACE MUSEUM, TAIWAN, REPUBLIC OF CHINA

The Qianlong emperor favored this bowl as his personal drinking vessel for milk-tea. He was so fond of it that he composed a poem about it and had his verses carved on its sides.

Terese Tse Bartholomew

LEARNING POTTERY IN YIXING, CHINA

PRIOR TO THE MING DYNASTY (1368–1644), Chinese most often drank tea that was whisked in powdered form (ground from tea cakes) into hot water contained in bowls. During the Ming dynasty, however, tastes and practices changed (see Owyoung, this volume), and tea came most frequently to be prepared as an infusion of leaves steeped in hot water. This change necessitated a special vessel in which to steep the leaves and from which to dispense the brewed liquid: the teapot.

Located in Jiangsu Province to the west of Tai Hu (Lake Tai), Yixing, the pottery capital of China, had been a ceramic center since the Warring States period (480–222 BCE). Yixing potters began to make teapots early in the sixteenth century by modifying the existing design of wine pots. Their teapots, made from local clay (*zisha*, or "purple sand"), gained the approbation of Chinese connoisseurs and came to be considered the finest vessels for brewing tea. It is still believed that even in hot weather, tea left overnight in a Yixing pot will remain fresh. These teapots are never washed; the old tea leaves are simply removed and the pots rinsed in cold water. As a result, the interior of the pot soon develops a residual layer of tea. The exterior surface, due to constant use and handling by the collector, also achieves a rich patina. To this day Yixing teapots remain highly prized for their ability to retain the taste, color, and aroma of tea leaves, and some owners designate one Yixing teapot exclusively to one type of tea.

Yixing potters typically worked individually, selling greenware (unfired pieces) to local shops. After 1948, however, the government decided to seek out the best of the older generation of potters and have them train young men and women in traditional techniques. The Tangdu Pottery Cooperative was established in 1954, and this was the forerunner of Factory No. 1, the foremost "factory" producing Yixing ware for local consumption and export. It should be noted that "factory" is not used in the Western sense here and that all the tea wares produced in Yixing factories are made individually by hand and stamped with the name of the potter who made them (see fig. a.5b). The first batch of students who issued from the pottery cooperative are now some of the top potters of modern-day

A.1 Teapot in the shape of an ancient tile, Yixing, China, circa 1750
Stoneware
H: 12.1 cm
ASIAN ART MUSEUM, BEQUEST OF
MARJORIE WALTER BISSINGER, NO. 2003.60.A–B
PHOTOGRAPH BY KAZ TSURUTA

A popular method of decorating Yixing ware involves the use of wooden molds that are carved with a design in intaglio. The front panel of this teapot was pressed into such a mold incised with an inscription from an ancient tile. The resultant design reads: *changle*, or "joy forever."

A.2 Hexagonal teapot with molded decoration, Yixing, China, circa 1750
Stoneware
H: 8.9 cm
ASIAN ART MUSEUM, BEQUEST OF
MARJORIE WALTER BISSINGER, NO. 2003.59.A–B
PHOTOGRAPH BY KAZ TSURUTA

This teapot was made in Yixing for the European market. As with the teapot in figure a.1, it was decorated using wooden molds. The sides of the teapot depict two young, confronted dragons against a background of C-shaped clouds. The shoulder of the teapot is decorated with a pressed design of *ruyi* (head of the wish-granting wand). In Yixing today, such stamps are still available. Many teapots like this one can be found in European collections where silver replacements for the lid and spout are common.

A.3 Yang Pengnian (China, active early 19th century)
Hexagonal teapot, Yixing, circa 1800–1850
Stoneware, pewter, jade
H: 7 cm
ASIAN ART MUSEUM, BEQUEST OF
MARJORIE WALTER BISSINGER, NO. 2003.58.A–B
PHOTOGRAPH BY KAZ TSURUTA

Beginning in the nineteenth century, there was a trend toward decorating teapots for the Chinese market with beautiful calligraphy and poetry. In order to provide a suitable surface for such decorations, teapots had to be plain and simple. During this time some teapots were covered with pewter, which provided a softer surface for the carving knife. The knobs, handles, and spouts of pewter-covered teapots were often further embellished with jade.

A.4   Shao Shunchang (China, active early 19th century);
inscribed by Shao Erquan
Cylindrical teapot, Yixing, Qing dynasty, early 19th century
Purplish brown stoneware
H: 10.8 cm
QIN XUAN COLLECTION

This teapot bears a poetic inscription that reads: "A scholar reclines in the snow-covered mountain / A beauty arrives from the moonlit forest."

A.5a   Zheng Ninghou (China, active early 18th century)
Teapot with plum blossoms in relief, Yixing, circa 1700–1725
Stoneware
H: 8.3 cm
ASIAN ART MUSEUM, BEQUEST OF
MARJORIE WALTER BISSINGER, NO. 2003.57.A–B
PHOTOGRAPH BY KAZ TSURUTA

This teapot exemplifies a more refined form of the molded technique observable in figures A.1 and A.2. After being pressed into a wooden mold, the plum blossoms on this teapot are inset in panels so they appear as an openwork design. This highly decorative piece was made for the European market.

A.5b   Detail of figure A.5a showing the potter's name stamped on the bottom of the teapot.

A.6   Xu Yufang (China, active 1980s)
Segmented teapot in the shape of a chrysanthemum,
Yixing, 1980s
Red stoneware
H: 7 cm
QIN XUAN COLLECTION

A.7   Gu Meiqun stands in front of shelves of her Yixing ware. She holds a naturalistic teapot, the handle of which is a stem ending in a leaf. Two frogs perch upon the leaf.
PHOTOGRAPH BY BRUCE BARTHOLOMEW, YIXING, CHINA, 2008.

Yixing, and they in turn are training more students. Additional factories were established in the 1970s and 1980s, and at present there are potters who work in factories, while others work at home. Together they supply the hundreds of pottery shops in the Yixing area, and Yixing teapots are sold all over China as well as being exported to foreign countries.

I classify Yixing teapots by shape: geometric (based on spheres, cylinders, cubes, etc.; figs. A.1–A.5); naturalistic (modeled after tree trunks and plant and floral forms; see fig. A.7); ribbed (or segmented, based on stylized floral or plant shapes such as melon and chrysanthemum; fig. A.6); and miniature (small round teapots for drinking the strong brew preferred by the tea connoisseurs of Guangdong and Fujian provinces (Bartholomew 1981, 13). In the past, most potters specialized in one of the four shapes, but today, some talented potters work in a variety of styles.

Although in the course of my study of the history of teapots and their makers I have devoted more than thirty years to Yixing ware, the chance to actually try my hand at making it had, until recently, eluded me and with it the opportunity to gain a fuller understanding and appreciation of the pottery that I knew so well through observation and study. While in college I had taken ceramics courses, and I had been to Yixing a number of times. In 1996 I had in fact visited with every intention of learning how to make Yixing ware. I traveled with a group of Western potters, and we spent nine glorious days at Factory No. 5, the Taiwanese owner of which was kind enough to supply us with teachers (Bartholomew 1998, 24). While my friends all made wonderful teapots in collaboration with their Yixing teachers, however, I had to spend most of my time translating for them. It was a frustrating experience, and I swore that I would go back to Yixing and actually work with the wonderful purple sand clay as soon as I could.

My opportunity came in April of 2008, when having retired from my curatorial position, I once again traveled to Yixing, this time with my husband, Bruce, and our friend Dottie Low, a well-known San Francisco potter who also wanted to learn to make Yixing ware. We were fortunate to have as a teacher Gu Meiqun, an accomplished and versatile potter who makes teapots in various styles. I especially admire her pieces in the naturalistic tradition, which includes teapots in the shape of lotus leaves and blossoms (fig. A.7). Gu Meiqun had first learned to make pottery from her mother, and later she received instruction from some of the foremost potters trained in the 1950s.

I originally met Gu Meiqun in 1996 when she was working in Factory No. 5, as she was one of the teachers assigned to help our group. We kept in contact through the years, and she let me know that she had become a part-owner of Factory No. 5 in addition to continuing her own work as a potter. When she expressed a wish to hold workshops for foreign potters, I wrote to her immediately. As she was not yet set up for a workshop, she invited us to take lessons at her home.

Unlike many other well-to-do potters who have moved to urban areas, Gu Meiqun lives in the farming village of Yangzhu Qianman close to Lake Tai. The village lies east of the town of Dingshan, where most of the factories are located, and southeast of the city of Yixing. There, farmers make pots in winter after they have harvested their crops. Almost every household makes them, and trays of finished teapots and other tea wares drying in the sun outside the houses are as common as trays of dried turnips and other farm products (fig. A.8). Walking around at night, I saw entire families working away, supplying local shops with teapots and fancy containers for tea leaves and tea cakes (some of the *puer* tea from Yunnan Province is traditionally pressed into a flat cake).

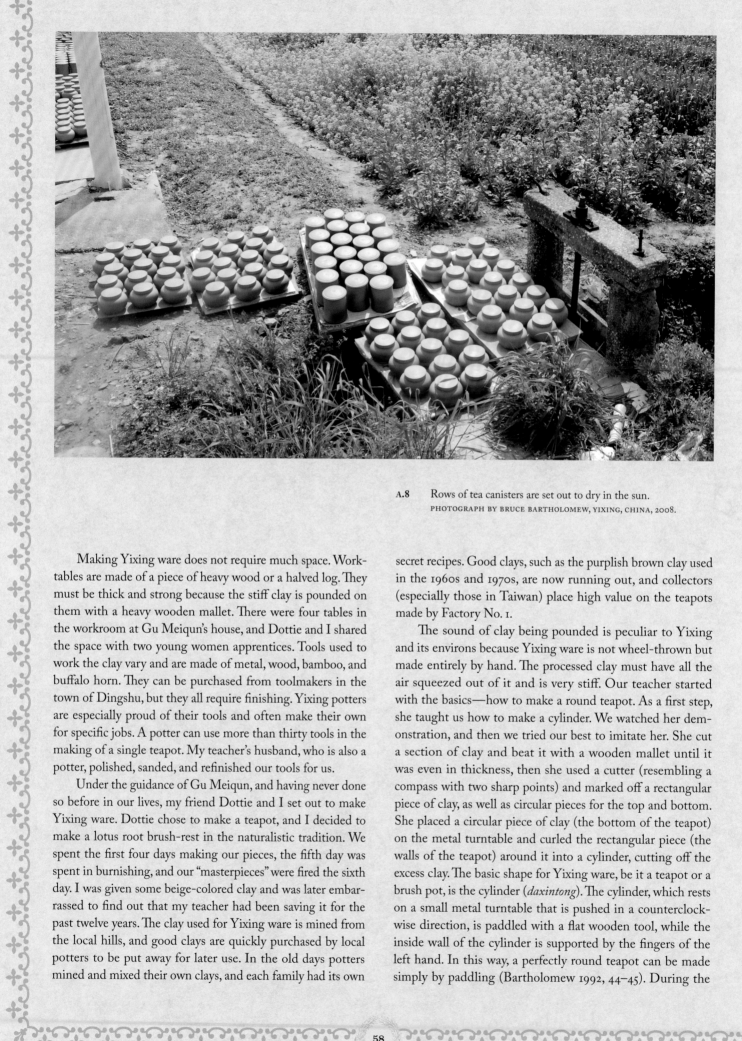

A.8   Rows of tea canisters are set out to dry in the sun.
PHOTOGRAPH BY BRUCE BARTHOLOMEW, YIXING, CHINA, 2008.

Making Yixing ware does not require much space. Work-tables are made of a piece of heavy wood or a halved log. They must be thick and strong because the stiff clay is pounded on them with a heavy wooden mallet. There were four tables in the workroom at Gu Meiqun's house, and Dottie and I shared the space with two young women apprentices. Tools used to work the clay vary and are made of metal, wood, bamboo, and buffalo horn. They can be purchased from toolmakers in the town of Dingshu, but they all require finishing. Yixing potters are especially proud of their tools and often make their own for specific jobs. A potter can use more than thirty tools in the making of a single teapot. My teacher's husband, who is also a potter, polished, sanded, and refinished our tools for us.

Under the guidance of Gu Meiqun, and having never done so before in our lives, my friend Dottie and I set out to make Yixing ware. Dottie chose to make a teapot, and I decided to make a lotus root brush-rest in the naturalistic tradition. We spent the first four days making our pieces, the fifth day was spent in burnishing, and our "masterpieces" were fired the sixth day. I was given some beige-colored clay and was later embar-rassed to find out that my teacher had been saving it for the past twelve years. The clay used for Yixing ware is mined from the local hills, and good clays are quickly purchased by local potters to be put away for later use. In the old days potters mined and mixed their own clays, and each family had its own secret recipes. Good clays, such as the purplish brown clay used in the 1960s and 1970s, are now running out, and collectors (especially those in Taiwan) place high value on the teapots made by Factory No. 1.

The sound of clay being pounded is peculiar to Yixing and its environs because Yixing ware is not wheel-thrown but made entirely by hand. The processed clay must have all the air squeezed out of it and is very stiff. Our teacher started with the basics—how to make a round teapot. As a first step, she taught us how to make a cylinder. We watched her dem-onstration, and then we tried our best to imitate her. She cut a section of clay and beat it with a wooden mallet until it was even in thickness, then she used a cutter (resembling a compass with two sharp points) and marked off a rectangular piece of clay, as well as circular pieces for the top and bottom. She placed a circular piece of clay (the bottom of the teapot) on the metal turntable and curled the rectangular piece (the walls of the teapot) around it into a cylinder, cutting off the excess clay. The basic shape for Yixing ware, be it a teapot or a brush pot, is the cylinder (*daxintong*). The cylinder, which rests on a small metal turntable that is pushed in a counterclock-wise direction, is paddled with a flat wooden tool, while the inside wall of the cylinder is supported by the fingers of the left hand. In this way, a perfectly round teapot can be made simply by paddling (Bartholomew 1992, 44–45). During the

A.9   San Francisco potter Dottie Low burnishes her teapot.
PHOTOGRAPH BY BRUCE BARTHOLOMEW, YIXING, CHINA, 2008.

A.10   Master potter Gu Meiqun stamps the teapot made by Dottie
Low with a seal bearing Dottie's Chinese name.
PHOTOGRAPH BY DOTTIE LOW, YIXING, 2008.

next few days, our teacher continued the process of making a teapot. Her technique was effortless with no wasted motion. She continued a tradition developed over five hundred years, whose techniques, passed from generation to generation, have reached perfection. The method was moderately difficult, and it definitely required a lot of practice. It was not something that could be mastered in the few days we spent there.

The various parts of the teapot, the handle and spout, for example, are attached with slurry. To make slurry, scraps of clay are mixed with water, using a special wooden tool. Yixing clay adheres very well with just a small amount of slurry. The smooth shiny surface of a Yixing teapot is achieved by burnishing when the piece is leather hard. One excellent tool for this task is thinly sliced buffalo horn, which is hard as well as flexible. After being soaked in water, the buffalo horn is held with the right hand and used to burnish the teapot until it is completely smooth (fig. A.9). Periodically, the buffalo horn is cleaned using a piece of towel to wipe off any excess bits of clay.

When Dottie finished her teapot, our teacher turned it upside down and supported the base with a wooden tool. Then she picked up a seal carved with Dottie's Chinese name and using a small wooden mallet, she made an impression in the finished piece with one stroke of the mallet (fig. A.10). This is an important part of the Yixing tradition; the potter proudly seals the finished work with his or her name (see fig. A.5B).

One of the joys of visiting Yixing is buying teapots, and examining them closely is another way of learning about this unique tea ware. Rows of shops selling nothing but Yixing ware can be found along the highway leading to Yixing, in the city of Yixing itself, the surrounding towns, and even in the villages. Depending on the maker, a teapot can range from US$1 to more than $30,000. Buying a good teapot can be a challenge. Some of the cheaper teapots are slip cast and have a rough finish. Ingenious potters buy a good teapot and make section molds from it. They press in the clay, attach the parts together, and take time on burnishing. From a distance, these teapots look very good. Closer inspection, however, will reveal the joints, and any self-respecting potter looks down on such practices. I look for a teapot having a body that is finely balanced by the spout and the handle and that demonstrates good workmanship and finishing. Most important of all, the spout must not drip, and I ask for water and test it on the spot. My policy is to go to well-known workshops run by famous potters and buy from young apprentices who do excellent work. Once they win a few prizes and become famous, their prices will skyrocket. The week that I spent working and learning in Yixing was an unforgettable experience, one I hope to repeat.

part 2

The Way of Tea in

JAPAN

Beatrice Hohenegger

TEA WAS PRAISED BY CHINESE DAOISTS as an elixir of immortality and has long been a revered beverage in spiritual practices. This is especially true in Japan where tea has had a central role in religious, cultural, and artistic pursuits, as well as in everyday life, for more than a thousand years. Tea first entered Japan, along with Buddhism, during the early Heian period (794–1185). It was introduced by monks who traveled to China to study Chan (Zen) Buddhism, a sect that had developed as a fusion of Mahayana Buddhism and Daoism (p. 33).

The patriarch of Zen Buddhism, Bodhidharma, or Daruma, as he is known in Japan (figs. 11.1–11.5), was born an Indian prince. He traveled to China in the sixth century to teach the wordless dharma, or the discipline of achieving enlightenment not through the study of sutras but through meditation—the Japanese word "*zen*" corresponds to the Chinese "*chan*," which is in turn derived from the Sanskrit "*dhyana*," meaning "eliminating distracting thoughts," or "meditation." Legend has it that while Daruma was in the course of a nine-year meditation, he fell asleep. When he woke up he was so angry at having broken his meditative state that he cut off his eyelids and threw them away. Where they touched the ground, a tea plant grew. Tea, thereafter, became the inseparable companion of monks and an invaluable aid in helping them to stay awake during meditation. Historically, of course, evidence exists that tea was used by Daoist monks long before Bodhidharma reached China.

11.1 Netsuke, Daruma, first patriarch of Zen, Japan, 19th century
Red coral
H: 3.9 cm

According to legend, Daruma's legs atrophied during the nine years he spent in meditation. This is why he is often portrayed as legless. Popular Japanese Daruma dolls, which are presented as tokens of good luck, are thus often egg shaped.

11.2 Chikanobu Shushin (Japan, 1660–1728),
Bodhidharma, early 18th century
Ink and colors on silk
41.5 x 17.5 cm

Daruma is usually portrayed without eyelids as, according to legend, he cut them off in rage for having fallen asleep during a nine-year meditation. The long-haired object below his face may be a fly whisk, an important symbol in Zen Buddhism (see fig. 11.4).

II.3 Signed Dosho I or II (Japan, dates unknown)
Netsuke, yawning Daruma, Japan, late 19th century
Wood, ivory, tortoise, green porcelain (?)
H: 4 cm
COLLECTION OF RICHARD R. SILVERMAN

In this netsuke, Daruma yawns as he emerges from his nine-year period of meditation. Many yawning Darumas are also shown stretching their arms after this prolonged period of immobility.

II.4 Signed Naomitsu (Japan, dates unknown)
Netsuke, Daruma with large *hossu* (fly whisk),
Japan, late 19th century
Ivory
H: 3 cm
COLLECTION OF RICHARD R. SILVERMAN

The fly whisk (*hossu*), an important symbol in Zen Buddhism, is often associated with Daruma. It is used to gently wave away insects without killing them. In Zen the *hossu* serves metaphorically to swish away the distracting thoughts that may surface during meditation.

II.5 Daruma, detail of illustration 39 from Engelbert Kaempfer,
De beschryving van Japan…Benevens eene beschryving van het koningryk Siam (*The History of Japan, Together with a description of the kingdom of Siam*), 's-Gravenhage, P. Gosse en J. Neaulme, 1729
Printed book
H (book): 33 cm
ROBERT E. GROSS COLLECTION OF RARE BOOKS IN ECONOMICS AND BUSINESS, ROSENFELD MANAGEMENT LIBRARY, UCLA

This illustration relates to a famous story in which Daruma met with the Chinese emperor Liang Wu, who as a devout Buddhist both studied scriptures and built temples. Despite his sincerity, the emperor could not grasp the principle of enlightenment through meditation. The meeting did not go well, and according to legend, Daruma left for the north, floating across the Yangzi River while standing on a reed.

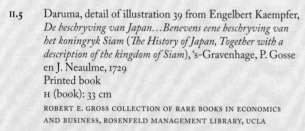

When it arrived in Japan, tea—most likely in the form of *dancha*, the compressed tea common in China at the time—was consumed in some aristocratic circles and at the imperial court. Records indicate that tea was served at the court of Emperor Saga (786–842). This initial contact was followed by a period of general indifference toward tea, during which its use was limited to Buddhist temples and religious ceremonies at court. It was not until the end of the twelfth century that interest in tea was renewed, when the Buddhist priest Eisai (1141–1215) brought back to Japan the powdered tea (known in Japan as *matcha*) then popular in Song China (960–1279). This has been called "the most important event in the history of tea drinking in Japan" (Varley and Isao 1989, 7). Eisai wrote a treatise, the *Kissa yōjōki*, extolling the medicinal benefits of tea according to Daoist principles, which contributed to the spread of tea consumption in Japan. During the thirteenth and fourteenth centuries tea drinking became more common as tea cultivation expanded—in Toganō northwest of Kyoto and later in the Uji district near Kyoto (fig. 11.6)—which, in turn, made it possible for the Japanese pastime of tea-tasting contests (*tōcha*) to emerge. These were different from the Chinese tasting contests where the frothiest tea was the best; in Japan the required skill was the ability to compare and distinguish teas on the basis of their provenance.

Tea drinking also spread among the military aristocracy, along with an increasing appreciation of Chinese art and craft objects (*karamono*), and especially tea utensils, which were considered valuable status symbols (see fig. 2.7, p. 82). At the same time, the warrior-aristocrats were attracted to the rigors of Zen discipline and often had Zen priests as advisers. These priests brought with them not only Buddhist precepts but also expertise in tea utensils and settings as well as specific rules (*sarei*)

11.6   Maruyama Ōzui (Japan, 1766–1829)
Tea Picking at Uji, 18th–19th century
Six-panel screen; ink, color, and gold flecks on paper
124.8 x 284 cm

During the Muromachi period (1392–1568) the Uji district south of Kyoto was considered the prime tea-producing region in Japan. Uji tea had the reputation of being the only real tea (*honcha*) and was clearly distinguished from all others, which were referred to as "non-tea" (*hicha*). In this rare scene, farmers gather tea during the summer for drying in covered sheds. Uji can be identified by the bridge in the distance at the left, a well-known landmark used both in painting and poetry to evoke the locale.

II.7   Tea caddy (*chaire*), Seto ware, Japan, 17th century
Stoneware
H: 12.2 cm
ROBERT W. MOORE

The *chaire*, or tea caddy, is most often tall and thin, made of ceramic or stoneware and fitted with an ivory lid. During a formal tea gathering both thick tea (*koicha*) and thin tea (*usucha*) are served. The *chaire* is used for the storing of tea for *koicha*. This caddy is an example of Seto ware, named after the Seto kilns—one of the Six Ancient Kilns of Japan.

II.8   Tea caddy (*natsume*), Japan, 19th century
Lacquerware
H: 7.3 cm
COLLECTION OF JOSE J. TERZ

The *natsume* is a tea caddy used to store the tea destined for the preparation of *usucha* (thin tea). Both thick and thin tea are made with *matcha*, a brilliant green powdered tea, but thin tea is usually prepared with only one-third the amount used for thick tea and is sometimes also of lower quality. This *natsume* is a particularly rare piece because of the raised lacquer decoration executed in Haritsu-style. Ogawa Haritsu (1663–1747) was a much-imitated lacquer artist, well known for creating lacquer works that resembled other materials, such as wood, tile, or bronze.

II.9   Tea caddy (*natsume*), Japan, 20th century
Lacquerware
H: 10 cm
ROBERT W. MOORE

Natsume are usually made of lacquered or untreated wood. They are wider and shorter than the *chaire* and have a flat lid and rounded bottom. They are called *natsume* because their shape resembles the jujube fruit (*natsume* in Japanese). This is a *hira natsume*, which is even flatter and wider than the usual versions. The red peaked shape on this example is a representation of Mount Fuji.

regarding tea drinking as it was practiced in their temples. Within the context of tea, the association between warrior elite and Zen priests produced one of the early forms of *chanoyu* (lit., "hot water for tea"), known in the West as the Japanese tea ceremony. In time, this type of *shoin* tea[2]—thus called in reference to the large, *shoin*-style reception rooms used for the gatherings—evolved into a lavish type of tea party in which aesthetic and decorative aspects, as well as connoisseurship of precious Chinese objects, became more important than the initial Daoist and Buddhist ideas underlying tea-drinking practice.

Toward the end of the fifteenth century, a reaction against this type of excess began to grow in the form of the "way of tea" (*chadō*), a path to enlightenment through the everyday gestures of preparing and serving tea in harmony with nature and fellow humans and in mindful awareness of the present moment. The focus moved away from the splendor and opulence of *shoin* rooms and *karamono* objects and toward the aesthetics of *wabi*—the appreciation of essence in the beauty of imperfection, impermanence, and austerity—which favored the small, simple *sōan* (hut) tea room as a retreat from the mundane, as well as rustic Korean (*koraimono*) and Japanese (*wamono*) tea objects (see fig. 2.8, p. 82; fig. 11.7) and wooden and bamboo utensils. The *wabi* tea room was generally small—four-and-a-half mats, or even two mats (the size of a standard mat is about 3 x 6 feet)—with the main space for serving the tea and an alcove (*tokonoma*) for the display of flowers or scrolls (figs. 11.10–11.12). The resulting form of *chanoyu* was *wabicha*, the tea of simplicity and sincerity of heart, which evolved during the sixteenth century through the contributions of three main figures: Murata Jukō (1421–1502), Takeno Jōō (1502–1555), and especially Sen no Rikyū (1522–1591), who is considered to have been Japan's foremost tea master (*sadō*) and who "most clearly defined the parameters and concerns of *chanoyu* as a way" (Hirota, 1995, 36). The essay by Dennis Hirota in this volume

11.10   Kanō Tanyū (Japan, 1602–1674);
        calligraphy by Gyokushū Sōban (1600–1668)
        Night Rain on the Xiao and Xiang Rivers, 1640
        Hanging scroll; ink on silk
        Calligraphic panel: 16 x 14.5 cm; image panel: 16.1 x 14.5 cm
        PRIVATE COLLECTION

The calligraphic inscription reads:

Gazing at the desolate shore, my spirits are broken
Sleet and drizzling rain mottle the evening sky
From a distant tent, a faint glow and sound of the flute
Facing the bamboo branches, my tears flow.

During the seventeenth century in Japan, a new style of tea emerged that was favored by daimyo, or Japanese feudal barons. It emphasized refined elegance over the rustic simplicity of Rikyū's *wabi* style. This scroll combining painting and poetry reflects the aristocratic taste of the daimyo tea master and connoisseur Kobori Enshu (1579–1647). It would have been appreciated along with other works of art in a tea room. The scroll pairs an intimate painting rendered in the *haboku*, or splashed-ink, style by Kanō Tanyū, a leading artist of the early Edo period, with a poem by Gyokushū Sōban, the 185th Chief Abbot of the great Zen monastery in Kyoto, Daitoku-ji.

LEFT

II.II   Furukawa Taiko (Japan 1872–1968)
         Pine Trees a Thousand Years of Green, circa 1950s
         Hanging scroll; ink on paper
         Image: 106.7 x 20.8
         PRIVATE COLLECTION

Calligraphy scrolls by Zen masters are displayed in the tea room to set the tone and mood of a gathering. The great tea master Sen no Rikyū considered scrolls produced by Zen masters to be the most important "utensil" used in the practice of the "way of tea."

Furukawa Taiko was one of the more prominent twentieth-century Zen masters and a longtime abbot of Myoshin-ji, the largest Rinzai branch of Zen Buddhism in Japan. The fourth character that appears on this scroll may be translated as "years." It is elongated and written with a continuous brushstroke to emphasize the sense of eternity

ABOVE

II.12   Kuga Kankei (Japan, 1817–1884)
         Tea bowl and verse on the theme of tea, mid-1800s
         Hanging scroll; ink on paper
         Image: 18.3 x 59.9 cm
         PRIVATE COLLECTION

The verse on this scroll may be translated as:

The pine breeze fills the tea bowl with moon and stars.
One sip awakens you from the long dream sleep.

Kuga Kankei was the 61st Head Abbot of the great Zen temple Eihei-ji and the spiritual leader of the Soto school of Buddhism during the turbulent end of the Tokugawa (Edo) period (1615–1868). Under his guidance Zen Buddhism entered the modern world.

offers a lucid and profound explanation of Buddhist thought as the foundation of the "way of tea" (see also Hirota 1995).

During the seventeenth century *chanoyu* as formalized by Sen no Rikyū reached the height of its popularity. Rikyū's heirs and successors founded the three main schools of tea that are still in existence today—Urasenke, Omotesenke, and Mushanokojisenke—and *chanoyu* became a national art form and a highly refined pastime practiced by courtiers, feudal lords, and wealthy merchants. This expansion, in turn, greatly fostered domestic ceramic production and the evolution of the unique Japanese pottery style and design. Yet, toward the end of the century, *chanoyu* itself came under increasing criticism, not only for its restrictive rules and etiquette and the exclusionary control exercised by the *iemoto* (grand masters) of the schools but also for the loss of underlying meaning and the corruption of the foundational values of *wabicha*. With regard to the latter point, the commentary by historian William McNeill is particularly incisive:

> Yet no matter how earnestly it has been renounced, the world has a way of creeping in by the back door. Innumerable saints and would-be saints of every religious persuasion have discovered that self-denial can turn into egotistical self-indulgence simply by exciting too much admiration from others. Similarly, monks who renounce all personal possessions in order to become collectively wealthy are recaptured by the world through the very excess of their virtue. The ambivalences surrounding *wabi* and other key concepts of the way of tea therefore keep company with comparable ambiguities pervading full-blown ascetic traditions. [Varley and Isao 1989, 255]

In part as a result of this state of things, a different "way of tea" began to take shape: *senchadō*, the "way of *sencha* tea." Grown not only as an alternative to *chanoyu* formalities but also as a rejection of the social strictures of a cultural environment controlled by military elites, *sencha* tea found its roots in the Chinese literati-style tea and made use of the steeped loose-leaf tea common in Ming China (1368–1644), as opposed to the powdered *matcha* (popular in Song China) used in *chanoyu*. *Sencha* tea drinking was done in a relaxed way while discussing poetry and the arts in the style of the gentleman-scholar and was often favored by artists and intellectuals as well as people who did not approve of the excessive worldly power of Zen masters. In the West the *sencha* tradition is not as well known as *chanoyu*, and Patricia Graham's essay in this volume represents a thoroughgoing and much-needed introduction to it.

The second half of the Edo period (1615–1868) saw the celebration of tea drinking expand beyond spiritual practice or privileged pastime, with tea utensils appearing as frequent

II.13   Ohara Mitsuhiro (Japan, 1810–1875)
         Netsuke, tea bowl and whisk, mid-19th century
         Wood, lacquer, ivory
         H: 3.8 cm
         LOS ANGELES COUNTY MUSEUM OF ART,
         RAYMOND AND FRANCES BUSHELL COLLECTION, NO. M.91.250.323
         PHOTOGRAPH ©2009 MUSEUM ASSOCIATES/LACMA

The tea whisk on this netsuke is carved with such extreme care that it seems to possess the lightness of bamboo. The artist left the whisk in plain ivory with a delicate *sumi* (charcoal) stain, but the material used for the bowl is fully concealed under stains and lacquer.

II.14   After Ohara Mitsuhiro (Japan, 1810–1875)
         Netsuke, teakettle, late 19th century
         Ebony, ivory inlays
         H: 2.8 cm
         LOS ANGELES COUNTY MUSEUM OF ART,
         RAYMOND AND FRANCES BUSHELL COLLECTION, NO. M.91.250.232
         PHOTOGRAPH ©2009 MUSEUM ASSOCIATES/LACMA

In this netsuke the texture of cast iron and the details of the tea kettle (*kama*) are painstakingly replicated. The ivory loops attached to lug handles on each side of the kettle would be used by a tea host to lower it onto the brazier.

II.15   Attributed to Kaigyokusai [Masatsugu] (Japan, 1813–1892)
Netsuke, charcoal and feather for use in tea, late 19th century
Ebony, ivory with staining, *sumi*
L (of log): 3.8 cm
LOS ANGELES COUNTY MUSEUM OF ART,
RAYMOND AND FRANCES BUSHELL COLLECTION, AC1998.249.185
PHOTOGRAPH ©2009 MUSEUM ASSOCIATES/LACMA

Specially prepared charcoal logs (*sumi*) are placed inside a brazier in the tea room, and a feather broom is used to dust the edges of the brazier. Kaigyokusai has focused upon the dramatic contrast of color, texture, weight, and relative delicacy in treating these two intimately connected objects.

II.16   *Kagamibuta* netsuke, Japan, circa 1850
Copper, ironwood, gold gilt
H: 4.5 cm
COLLECTION OF RICHARD R. SILVERMAN

Kagamibuta, or "mirror-lid," netsuke are nearly always round. This rare rectangular example depicts a brazier and kettle on a stand, a tea bowl and whisk, and a pair of *hibashi* (fire chopsticks), which are used to rearrange the coals in a brazier.

II.17   Signed Eiraku Hozen (Japan, 1795–1854)
Netsuke, tea brazier and kettle (*kama*)
Japan, circa 1850
Silver
H: 3.5 cm
COLLECTION OF RICHARD R. SILVERMAN

motifs on dress and household objects—as can be seen in the netsuke (figs. 11.13–11.21) and bed cover (fig. 11.22)—a widespread practice unique to Japan. The second, and significant, expansion of tea took place with the inclusion of women as students and practitioners of the tea ceremony, an almost exclusively male domain until the late Edo period. A major impact was given by the inclusion of *chanoyu* in women's school curricula, in an attempt to preserve Japanese cultural traditions against the massive Westernization of the Meiji period (1868–1912; Varley and Isao 1989, 188; figs 11.23–11.29). Reiko Tanimura's essay in this section traces this development from the almost nonexistent role of women in tea during the Muromachi period (1392–1568) to the overwhelming presence of women in tea today, analyzing the varying positions of women through the ages in the context of tea practice, from members of a privileged aristocratic class, to iconoclasts, to high-ranking courtesans and teahouse pleasure women, to social climbers in search of style and etiquette. This is a fascinating and vastly underresearched topic that certainly merits further attention; it is my hope that Tanimura as well as other scholars will use this essay as a stimulus to delve more deeply into the multilayered themes included in it. ❧

II.18 Signed Sesado Mitsuhiro (Japan, dates unknown)
Five *sencha* bowls in container, circa 1850
Bamboo, ivory
H (stacked bowls): 3.7 cm
COLLECTION OF RICHARD R. SILVERMAN

Five is the traditional number of bowls that make up a *sencha* set.

II.19 Signed Gyokuho (?)
Netsuke, *ochanoyu* (tea theme), Japan, early 19th century
Ivory, ebony
W: 5 cm
COLLECTION OF RICHARD R. SILVERMAN

This netsuke includes objects for *chanoyu* on the front: a lidded water jar (*mizusashi*), charcoal container (*sumitori*), and tea caddy (*natsume*). A feather broom is depicted on the back.

II.20 *Ryusa* netsuke
Japan, circa 1850
Ivory
W: 3 cm
COLLECTION OF RICHARD R. SILVERMAN

Ryusa netsuke are executed with a very delicate, lace-like carving, so that light shines through them. This example features all the principal tea utensils used for *chanoyu*.

II.21 Netsuke, tea master (*chajin*)
Japan, late 18th century
Ivory
H: 3 cm
COLLECTION OF RICHARD R. SILVERMAN

The tea master is either posed leaning forward or asleep.

II.22 *Yogi* (bed cover in the shape of a kimono)
with tea ceremony utensils and auspicious treasures,
Japan, Meiji period (1868–1912)
Paste-resist dyeing (*tsutsugaki*) on plain-weave cotton
L (center back): 171.5 cm

Coverlets in the shape of a kimono (*yogi*) became popular at the beginning of the Edo Period (1615–1868). Intended to be worn or wrapped loosely around the body for warmth in winter, *yogi* are much larger than a fashionable kimono. The decoration on this example was accomplished using the resist-dye technique known as *tsutsugaki*, which entails drawing a design freehand in rice paste on cloth; dyeing the cloth; and then washing the paste off. The areas covered by rice paste remain undyed. This particular design reflects the significance of the tea ceremony.

II.23   Portable set for outdoor tea ceremony, Japan, circa 1820
Lacquer, ceramic, bamboo, wood, cotton
h (tea box): 10.5 cm
PRIVATE COLLECTION

Portable tea sets reached their height of popularity during the mid-Edo period, as a consequence of improved roads and increased travel between Japan's two capitals, Kyoto and Edo (present-day Tokyo). This *chabako*, or tea box, contains the essential utensils required to enjoy tea outdoors: tea bowl, tea caddy containing the powdered tea, tea scoop, tea whisk in a special holder, and a linen wiping cloth and holder. All of the items have been miniaturized to fit compactly in the box.

By the mid-nineteenth century, interest in powdered tea among the general population had been supplanted by *sencha*, or steeped tea. Portable tea sets, however, continued to captivate wealthy collectors. This set demonstrates the shift from the functional to the precious with all its components intended to delight. The *chabako* has been lacquered with a complicated technique to simulate wood grain, then decorated with applied and inlaid gold. The ceramic tea caddy is delftware imported from Holland and fitted with an ivory lid, and the tea scoop has been fashioned from ivory with a carved rattle as its finial. This portable tea set is among the smallest functional sets known to exist.

II.24   Multifaceted tea caddy with various scenes, Satsuma ware
Japan, circa 1900
Stoneware with enamels and gold
H: 12.7 cm
LOS ANGELES COUNTY MUSEUM OF ART, GIVEN FOR MRS. EMMA
M. JESSUP BY HER DAUGHTER MARGARET, NO. M.86.221.3A-B
PHOTOGRAPH ©2009 MUSEUM ASSOCIATES/LACMA

Satsuma ware originated on the southern Japanese island of Kyushu during the late sixteenth century, after Japanese leader Toyotomi Hideyoshi invaded Korea (initially in 1592–1593) and brought skilled Korean potters back to Japan. This type of high-fired ceramic is characterized by rich and elaborate gold and polychrome decorations, and it became very popular in Europe during the late nineteenth century. This caddy was intended for *sencha* tea.

Gezigt op de haven van Nagasakie tijdens het verblijf van het fregatschip Cornelia en Korvette
Kapt. P. Breining augustus 1840

II.25 Kawahara Keiga (Japan, 1786–after 1860)
Aerial view of the Harbor of Nagasaki with the
Dutch frigate *Cornelia and Henriette*, circa 1840
Gouache on silk
Framed: 93 x 75 cm
PEABODY ESSEX MUSEUM, MUSEUM PURCHASE, NO. M20148

In 1639 Japan enacted a closed-door policy (*sakoku*), which prohibited all foreigners from entering the country. Even more extreme than the Chinese were at Canton, the Japanese built an artificial island called Deshima in the port of Nagasaki (the small half-moon of land that can be seen to the left of the Western ship in this painting). Among European traders, only the Dutch were allowed to operate, and they were restricted to using Deshima as a base. Limited trade was allowed with China, but no other nation was tolerated. This lasted until the Kanagawa Treaty of 1854 was concluded between Commodore Matthew Perry and the Empire of Japan, resulting in the opening of Japan to international trade.

II.26 Map of the Port of Nagasaki, detail of illustration 19
from Engelbert Kaempfer, *De beschryving van Japan…
Benevens eene beschryving van het koningryk Siam* (*The History
of Japan, Together with a description of the kingdom of Siam*),
's-Gravenhage, P. Gosse en J. Neaulme, 1729
Printed book
H (book): 33 cm
ROBERT E. GROSS COLLECTION OF RARE BOOKS IN ECONOMICS
AND BUSINESS, ROSENFELD MANAGEMENT LIBRARY, UCLA

The artificial island of Deshima, the roughly half-moon shape just left of the center of this map, was only six hundred feet long and two hundred feet wide. From this tiny speck of land Dutch merchants traded Japanese tea for two hundred years.

II.27 Tea set, Satsuma ware, Japan, Meiji period (1868–1912)
Earthenware, enamel paint
H (teapot): 19 cm
PACIFIC ASIA MUSEUM, GIFT OF MRS. WILHELMINA LOCKHART,
NO. 1984.55.47A-R

Satsuma ware was produced to a great extent for the Western market, but the decorations incorporated Japanese motifs. This magnificent Satsuma tea set includes enameled images of *rakan*, "one who has attained enlightenment," and dragons in a mythical setting.

II.28 Tea bowl, Oribe ware, Japan, 19th century
Ceramic, black glaze and white grass design
Diam: 14 cm
LOS ANGELES COUNTY MUSEUM OF ART,
GIFT OF HANS AND MARGOT RIES, NO. AC1997.182.7
PHOTOGRAPH ©2009 MUSEUM ASSOCIATES/LACMA

Oribe ware is named after the tea master Furuta Oribe (1544–1615). Oribe ware is a high-fired ceramic characterized by bold design and the use of dark-green copper glaze.

II.29 Tea bowl, Kyoto-Ninsei School, Japan, late 19th–20th century
Ceramic, glaze
H: 7.6 cm
ROBERT W. MOORE

This more recent tea bowl was created in the style of the later Ninsei school, using brightly colored enamels as well as silver and gold. Nonomura Ninsei is considered to have been one of the three great Kyoto potters of the seventeenth century, along with Ogata Kenzan and Aoki Mokubei (see fig. 3.14, p. 102).

Dennis Hirota

BUDDHIST THOUGHT AND THE WAY OF TEA

2

THE TRADITIONAL JAPANESE PRACTICE known in English as the "tea ceremony" or "way of tea" was referred to in early writings simply as *chanoyu*, or "tea in hot water." It evolved gradually out of a variety of tea-drinking practices, in part under the influence of Buddhist modes of thought and perception, and it reached the pinnacle of its development during the sixteenth century among the warrior elite and the affluent merchants who served them. *Chanoyu* has continued to be transmitted down to the present by the descendants of the early masters, adapting to immense changes in social conditions while at the same time preserving much of the manner, the ideals, and even the material culture of utensils, tea rooms, and gardens from earlier periods. Although a sizeable body of documents and writings on *chanoyu* has been preserved and transmitted over the centuries, practitioners have always preferred concrete instruction regarding the details of performance and knowledge of the manner and utensils of past masters to theoretical speculation about the significance of their art. Nevertheless, I will take up here aspects of Buddhist tradition that the early practitioners of *chanoyu* adopted as resources for understanding and developing their practices and for formulating the values and ideals that they sought to manifest.

Today in Japan and elsewhere, *chanoyu* is most often experienced in the form of demonstrations, large-scale tea events (*chakai*) in which tea is whisked and served to numbers of participants, and weekly group learning sessions where various segments of a tea gathering (*chaji*) are taught and practiced. In considering the Buddhist influences that contributed to the formation of *chanoyu* and the awareness of Buddhist principles embodied in tea practices, it may be helpful to keep in mind that the standard activity in *chanoyu* in its classical form is the tea gathering. A host and several guests come together in a small, carefully prepared tea room to share in a meticulously orchestrated sequence of events—laying of fresh charcoal in the brazier or hearth, a meal served in set stages, two services of powdered tea whisked in tea bowls (fig. 2.2). Ideally the gathering lasts about four hours. In their rusticity

2.1 Portrait sculpture of Gyōki, Japan, early 17th century
Wood, gesso, lacquer, pigment, gold
H: 92.71 cm
MINNEAPOLIS INSTITUTE OF ARTS,
THE ETHEL MORRISON VAN DERLIP FUND, NO. 95.85A–C

The Buddhist monk Gyōki (670/688–749) was considered a bodhisattva,
a practitioner who works with deep wisdom-compassion to help others
along the path to enlightenment. Many portraits of Gyōki exist, and it is
likely that images of him began to be made soon after his death. This portrait is remarkable for its realism, apparent in the deeply furrowed brow
and determined mien. The monk holds in his hand a *nyoi* jewel, a symbol
of the virtue of wisdom, said to hold the power to fulfill all wishes.

2.2 The intimate interior space of the Ennan tea room has been preserved and maintained in use by the Yabunouchi family of tea masters for four centuries. Shown at the back of the room is the mat where the host sits to prepare tea for the guests, who sit on the mats in the foreground. The necessary utensils have been set in place as if the service were in progress. The selection of utensils reveals the aesthetic of *wabi*. To the right of the host's mat is a container for freshwater modeled on a square well bucket. The pristine grain of the wood, together with that of the bentwood container for discarded water modeled on a monk's begging bowl, lend a sense of purity. At the center of the mat is a Japanese tea container (*chaire*); its silk brocade pouch is hung on the pillar. The tea bowl is rough Korean ware highly prized by the early tea masters, together with a bamboo tea scoop, whisk, and linen cloth to wipe the bowl. In their reticence and austere, natural beauty, these utensils contrast sharply with the fashion of earlier periods, which favored containers of bronze, tea scoops of ivory, and elegant Chinese ceramics. This tea room has been designated an Important Cultural Property by the Japanese government. COURTESY OF YABUNOUCHI-KE, KYOTO, JAPAN.

and austerity, the architectural features of the tea room and the small garden path of carefully laid stepping stones leading to its entrance typically suggest a rough dwelling secluded in the mountains. Within the muted light of the room, the guests enjoy together the faint trace of purifying incense, the sound of water boiling in the iron kettle, the hanging scroll inscribed, perhaps, by a Zen master, and of course the great variety of utensils—ceramics, lacquerware, brocades, bamboo, metalwork, ivory, and so on.

The actions performed in *chanoyu* are those most common and basic to everyday human life: serving and partaking of a meal in the company of others. But in the intimacy of the tea room, heightened attention is paid to every facet of the gathering, from the formal greetings exchanged between host and guests to the ash of the hearth, carefully laid and smoothed for each gathering but perhaps decades old, having been dyed with tea, cleaned, sifted, and reused many times. The participants are aware of every detail and engage all their senses, apprehending every movement in the close space of the room. Further, they share in the formal, overall rhythm of the gathering, widely familiar in traditional Japanese arts: *jo* (slow prelude), *ha* (development), and *kyū* (brisk conclusion).

The custom of whisking and drinking powdered tea was introduced into Japan in the late twelfth century by Zen Buddhist monks returning from training in Song dynasty China, and the ritualized tea drinking that was practiced in the medieval Japanese monasteries survives to the present. Our concern here, however, will not be to trace particular practices of *chanoyu* back to monastic roots but rather to consider the Buddhist modes of thought that the early *chanoyu* masters understood as informing their own aspirations and sensibilities as they practiced and perfected their art. For the sake of convenience, this essay will discuss strands of Buddhist tradition that influenced *chanoyu* under three central themes, taking them up in loose historical order: the life in a thatched-roof hut, the aesthetic of the "chill and withered," and the sense of astonishment at the everyday things of the world. Further, I will consider the first as related to Pure Land Buddhism, the second as reflecting general Mahayana Buddhist thought, and the last as connected with Zen Buddhism.

Pure Land Buddhism: The Attained Simplicity of the Thatched-Roof Hut

Buddhism was formally introduced into Japan in the sixth century in the form of statues and scriptures presented to the Japanese court by a Korean king. In the ensuing centuries, it became established as the official religion of Japan by the central government but was largely confined to the ruling classes. The state constructed temples in the various provinces and oversaw the training of monks and nuns, but the central activity of the clergy was the conducting of rituals such as chanting sutras for the protection of the country and offering prayers for the repose of members of the aristocratic clans in the next life. Contact between the clergy and the ordinary people was carefully restricted out of fear that preaching to the masses might foment social unrest. State authorization was necessary for any who would seek ordination and pursue monastic training.

Among the monks, however, there gradually emerged individuals who desired to pursue their religious disciplines apart from the ceremonial activities in the state- or clan-sponsored temples. For such monks, permission was sometimes granted for extended retreats to practice austerities in remote locations, but there were others who abandoned their positions in the monasteries and struck out on their own to perform religious practices in the mountains. Since ancient times, mountains had been viewed as sacred, the abode of deities and the spirits of the ancestors. While villages, fields, and urban life developed in the valleys and plains, the hills and mountains that rise in the background everywhere in the Japanese landscape were largely uninhabited. They were the sites of village shrines and the places where corpses were laid and the spirits gathered. As holy sites, the mountains were considered appropriate, as they continue to be today, for various kinds of religious praxis and the acquisition of spiritual power. There began to appear, therefore, men who departed from the official temple complexes in a kind of second renunciation, this time of the regulated ordained life, in order to go into the mountains. There they lived in caves or built simple huts and led austere lives devoted to solitary study and practice.

Various types of these practitioners emerged. Some alternated periods of solitary practice in mountain retreats with sojourns down among the villages, where they preached and performed rites for the villagers while traveling from place to place. Wandering monks begin to turn up widely in the popular tale literature from the latter part of the Heian period (794–1185). One early celebrated precursor is the Nara period monk Gyōki (670/688–749), who was called a bodhisattva for his activities to improve the lives of the common people, such as building roads and bridges (fig. 2.1). Another important early Heian period figure was Kyōshin (d. 866), venerated as a learned scholar-monk of the great Kōfukuji Temple in Nara. Eventually, however, he grew dissatisfied with the scholasticism of conventional doctrinal study and the ritualized praxis of the established temples and came to reject the accomplishments that had led to his lofty ecclesiastic rank and reputation for sanctity. Embarking on a meandering journey throughout Japan, he finally settled near a rural village. There he abandoned his monk's habit, built a thatched-roof hut, and took a wife. He lived in poverty and engaged in common labor, working in fields and carrying baggage for travelers, and he passed thirty years in utterance of the *nembutsu*, the name of Amida, "the Buddha of Compassion."

Kyōshin's life of religious devotion, which later inspired such major figures in Japanese Buddhist history as Shinran (1173–1263) and Ippen (1239–1289), was legendary: "Kyōshin, who settled in Kako, built no fence to the west: toward the Buddha-field of Amida, the gate lay open. Nor, befittingly, did he enshrine an image of worship; he kept no sacred books. In appearance not a monk nor yet worldly, he faced the west always, saying the nembutsu, and was like one to whom all

2.3 This garden path leads to a traditional tea hut. The massive, irregular stones, the moss and verdant foliage, and the weathered tree trunk all create an environment evocative of the timeless solitude of a mountain retreat. The stone lantern (*tōrō*) to the right of the path is lit with an oil lamp during night gatherings. COURTESY OF YABUNOUCHI-KE, KYOTO, JAPAN.

2.4 The *nijiriguchi*, or "crawling-in entrance," is visible on the exterior of the sixteenth-century Unkyaku tea hut of the Yabunouchi family. It is opened by sliding aside the small wood panel (directly above the straw sandals resting on the outside entryway). The *chanoyu* guests remove their footwear and enter the tea hut on their knees. In the upper right of the same wall, the two racks would have been used by samurai warriors to store their swords before entering the tea room; a stepping stone has been set in place for this purpose. COURTESY OF YABUNOUCHI-KE, KYOTO, JAPAN.

else was forgotten" (cited in Hirota 1989, 49).[1] We see here that the Buddhist path that Kyōshin adopted was the Pure Land tradition. This path is based on the vow of Amida Buddha, who brings all those who entrust themselves to him and say his name into the domain of his enlightenment, known as the Pure Land. There they attain Buddhahood and join in the compassionate work to liberate all beings caught in the pain of delusion. For Kyōshin, and for many who emulated him and other such *nembutsu* practitioners, receiving the Buddha's compassionate action was the direct way by which the bonds of craving and self-attachment in all its forms—including pride in religious attainments and personal merit—could be severed. It was a Buddhist path of simplicity, free of all the trappings of ostentatious religiosity, attained through profound self-reflection.

This model of the Buddhist life as neither monastic nor worldly—neither renunciative of secular life with others nor absorbed in the pursuits of ordinary society—reverberates through Japanese culture, and in the medieval period it was often expressed in terms of the semireclusive thatched-roof

hut of the Buddhist practitioner. One influential figure who sought to adopt the principles of the thatched-roof hut while continuing in his post at the imperial court was Yoshishige Yasutane (d. 1002), who built a small chapel with an image of Amida Buddha in the garden of his residence in Kyoto. After returning from duties at court each day, he would retire to the chapel to perform religious devotions, imagining himself dwelling in a hut deep in the mountains.

Yoshishige's garden chapel may be viewed as a prototype of the tea room of the later *chanoyu* masters, often a small, thatched-roof hut functioning similarly to suggest a mountain retreat secluded from ordinary secular life, even while standing on the grounds of an urban residence. Overt religious fixtures are absent from the tea room. In typical examples designed in the sixteenth century, the tea room is reached by a short path of stepping stones meant to evoke a mountain trail (fig. 2.3), and the low portal—the "crawling-in entrance" or *nijiriguchi*—is a minimal opening through which one must slide on hands and knees (fig. 2.4). Such features suggest a reenactment of a leave-taking from everyday life and help create the atmosphere of *chanoyu* as an environment detached from extraneous worldly concerns and focused on what is most essential. Within the austere tea room, one partakes of a meal and tea with a small number of companions, all of whom demonstrate complete attention and sincerity. Later tea masters, among them Sen no Rikyū (1522–1591) quoted below, used the image of the Pure Land to suggest the ideal ambiance of the tea gathering, evoking the scrupulous care given to the cleanliness and freshness of all aspects of the grounds and chambers, and the analogous purity of spirit of each participant.

> Since the fundamental intent of [the ideal of] *wabi* lies in manifesting the pure, undefiled Buddha-world, once host and guest have entered the garden path and thatched hut, they sweep away the dust and rubbish [of worldly concerns] and engage in an encounter with mind open and entire. ["Record of the Words of Rikyū," *Nampōroku*, cited in Hirota 1995, 236]

> Chanoyu of the small room is above all a matter of performing practice and attaining realization in accord with the Buddhist path. To delight in the refined splendor of a dwelling or the taste of delicacies belongs to worldly life. There is shelter enough when the roof does not leak, food enough when it staves off hunger. This is the Buddhist teaching and the fundamental meaning of chanoyu. We draw water, gather firewood, boil the water, and make tea. We then offer it to the Buddha, serve it to others, and drink ourselves. We arrange flowers and burn incense. In all this, we model ourselves after the acts of the Buddha and the past masters. ["Record of the Words of Rikyū," *Nampōroku*, cited in Hirota 1995, 217]

2.5 The thatched-roof Ennan tea hut belonging to the Yabunouchi family conveys a rusticity that lends the performance of *chanoyu* an air of tranquility. The roof is equipped with a skylight that allows for modulations of light within the tea room. See figure 2.2 for the interior of this teahouse. COURTESY OF YABUNOUCHI-KE, KYOTO, JAPAN.

2.6 The interior of the Unkyaku tearoom (see fig. 2.4 for the exterior) is remarkable for its daring use of space. At the rear is the host's entrance and the mat for preparing tea. Guests sit on the two mats visible in the foreground. This room was a gift to Yabunouchi Kenchū, the founder of the Yabunouchi tradition, from his companion in *chanoyu*, Sen no Rikyū. They had both studied under Takeno Jōō. The gourd-shaped plaque at the upper right was inscribed by Rikyū and is dated 1581. COURTESY OF YABUNOUCHI-KE, KYOTO, JAPAN.

These allusions to Pure Land Buddhist teachings refer not merely to details of the environment of *chanoyu* but more importantly to fundamental attitudes that inevitably manifest themselves in the comportment of host and guest. In other words, the poverty represented by the thatched-roof hut of the *nembutsu* practitioner was above all a poverty in spirit, free of attachment to worldly fame and advantage (figs. 2.5. 2.6). Hōnen (1133–1212), who established the *nembutsu* path in Japan, stated on his deathbed: "If you would entrust yourself to the nembutsu,… become the same as the unlettered women and men who enter the Buddhist path while remaining at home, and without assuming the manner of a sage, simply say the nembutsu with wholeness of heart" ("The One-Page Testament of Hōnen" [*Ichimai kishōmon*], cited in Hirota 1995, 244). It is this sincerity of life in the thatched-roof hut, stripped of all pretense to religious accomplishment, that the tea masters sought to emulate. One *chanoyu* document from the period of its mature development at the close of the sixteenth century, when expertise as a master required broad learning, full-time training, and artistic discernment, models itself on Hōnen's famous statement to express the essential spirit of Pure Land Buddhism as adopted in *chanoyu*:

Though you may have acquired fine utensils, both native and Chinese, if you entrust yourself to this way of tea, then you should—becoming an impoverished person ignorant of even a single written character, or the same as the women and men who enter the Buddhist path while remaining at home—without assuming the manner of a "person [well versed in chanoyu]," simply heat the water with wholeness of heart. ["The One-Page Testament of Rikyū," cited in Hirota 1995, 245]

Mahayana Buddhist Thought in the Formation of *Chanoyu*

Chanoyu is one among a number of traditional practices or arts that developed during the medieval period and were influenced in their aesthetics and performance by Buddhist modes of thought. Other examples that precede *chanoyu* historically include classical poetry (*waka*), incense appreciation, flower arrangement, Noh theater, and linked verse (*renga*). The connection with linked verse is particularly illuminating when considering the nature of the Buddhist influence on *chanoyu*. Both arts evolved in part, over the course of several centuries, out of popular entertainments such as parties for linking verses beneath blossoming cherry trees and tea-tasting contests offering prizes.

Among the warrior elite, tea drinking was a feature of gatherings that sometimes included bathing or the lavish display of exotic goods and treasured artworks from the Asian continent, and formal Chinese-style ceremonial and ritualized serving of tea was also adopted from Zen monastic life. Eventually, however, less-public and more-restrained practices appeared. It was during the Muromachi period (1392–1568) that many of the features now considered typical of traditional Japanese architecture were incorporated into the drawing rooms and inner chambers of warrior residences, including tatami-mat flooring, square pillars with sliding papered partitions, and the alcove, split-leveled shelving, and low writing-shelf adopted from Zen temple design. Such chambers afforded atmospheres of privacy and intimacy and became sites for social interaction among small gatherings of associates. Keenly conscious of the court nobility with their centuries of refined cultural traditions and elaborate norms of comportment, the feudal lords sought their own sense of decorum and social accomplishment. Linked verse and *chanoyu*, with their conventionalized modes of social interaction in part served this purpose when practiced within the recently developed architectural spaces. At the same time, as arts, they both developed far beyond the merely social.

The Buddhist influence on these arts may be considered in terms of two broad topics: (1) the notion of the discipline of learning and practicing an art as a "way" of personal spiritual development; and (2) the nature and requirements of artistic mastery, including the self-restraint necessary to foster the communal enactment of the gathering by all the participants and to achieve the elevated aesthetic ideals governing the art and its performance. The close intertwinement of these two themes—personal training and the religiously defined aesthetic sensibility—informed both linked verse and *chanoyu* at the high point of their development and imparted to them their most distinctive qualities. Moreover, it was linked verse that in the late fifteenth and early sixteenth centuries, directly provided the nascent practice of *chanoyu* with both a highly developed practical model of group performance and various conceptual structures for articulating its ideals and aesthetic principles.

In a session of linked verse, a small party of participants creates a sequence of verses, usually of one hundred links of alternating 5-7-5 and 7-7 syllables. Each link, together with the one preceding and, independently, the one following, produces a semantic unit and approximates the classical Japanese poetic form: 5-7-5-7-7. The entire sequence is composed according to detailed rules designed to generate a dynamic balance between cohesiveness and novelty, with carefully modulated transitions in seasonal themes, most conspicuously between cherry blossoms and the autumn moon, several times in the session. The poets sought shifts in mood, setting, persona, theme, and season, while at the same time achieving an overall rhythm, a kind of lyric journey.[2]

During the medieval period, linked verse superseded the earlier traditions of court poetry (*waka*) as the most vibrant and popular form of poetic composition, reaching its height with the work of the Buddhist monks Shinkei (1406–1475) and Sōgi (1421–1502). The early masters who are credited with first formulating the practices of *chanoyu*, Murata Jukō (1421–1502) and Takeno Jōō (1502–1555), were both well-acquainted with linked verse and its practitioners, and they may be said to have been the genuine inheritors of crucial elements of the legacy of linked verse. Thus, in order to consider the traces of Buddhist thinking in relation to *chanoyu*, I will look in particular at its debt to practitioners of linked verse.

Art as a Way

The term "the way of tea" (*sadō* or, more recently, *chadō*) to indicate *chanoyu* does not come into use until the mid-seventeenth century. The notion was widespread from the medieval period on, however, that learning and performance of any of a variety of arts and disciplines embody the "way" and that mastery of such an art or skill both depends on and leads to knowledge of the "way."[3] Clear expression of the various aspects of this idea is found in widely read works of the period such as Kenkō's *Essays in Idleness* (ca. 1330), but in relation to *chanoyu*, perhaps the most significant figure is Shinkei. In addition to articulating a highly developed conception of the way of the arts based on his extensive learning as a Buddhist monk, Shinkei appears to have exerted direct influence on the early founders of *chanoyu*. We will consider first, therefore, several of the aspects of the concept of art as a way in the writings of Shinkei and then turn to their presence in *chanoyu*.

Perhaps the most striking feature of the notion of the way of the arts is the breadth of its application. Figures such as Kenkō and Shinkei recognized the presence of the way in a broad spectrum of human activities. Shinkei mentions scholarship, Buddhist training, calligraphy, poetry; games such as *go*, Japanese chess (*shōgi*), backgammon; wind and string instruments, dance, and singing; kickball, *sumō*, and martial arts. Kenkō enumerates a similar range and includes in his essays anecdotes about, for example, the forester's training in tree climbing as exhibiting the principles of the way. It appears that in the eyes of these poet-monks, the acquisition and genuinely skillful performance of almost any form of human endeavor is characterized by common features termed "the way." Thus, the master of an art or discipline is one who apprehends the way. Further, this dimension of a deepening awareness of human experience acquired through training in one art gives rise to knowledge of principles of conduct applicable to all arts and to human life in general. Masters, therefore, speak of the principles of the way as common to all the arts.

Underlying this view is the experience of the mastery of a skill or activity as necessarily involving a transcendence of the ordinary self, a relinquishment of attachment to one's attainments and the distractions of concern over self-worth. Thus, the process of training requires single-minded dedication and unstinting effort extending over one's entire lifetime, and at the same time, in order to advance to authentic mastery, one must cultivate a profound reflection on the nature of one's own existence and the limitations of one's abilities. Shinkei recorded the following advice concerning the need for continuous practice underpinned by self-reflection:

> Question: After a person has received training in this way [of linked verse] for a number of years, is it possible to discontinue it for even a short time without altogether losing one's bearings?
>
> Answer: Although you may have accumulated years of diligent study, if you are negligent even briefly in your practice, you will fall back with nothing to show for your previous efforts. It is written [in the Confucian Analects]: "Reflect on yourself three times each day."
>
> The finest *shakuhachi* player of recent times, Ton'a, said: "If I were to leave off practicing for three days, I would lose the ability to play." These words hold true for all the ways. [Shinkei, *Sasamegoto*, cited in Hirota 1995, 147]

Further, for the medieval mind, a significant element of training was the guidance of a genuine master who grasped the way. Mastery might be apparent, but the path of acquisition was not necessarily direct. Thus Shinkei admonished, "in all the ways it is impossible for one to know what lies beyond one's own level of accomplishment" (Shinkei, *Sasamegoto*, cited in Hirota 1995, 146). Further, he cautioned that "not to seek out and come to an understanding of the master's heart and mind, so that teacher and disciple reveal to each other their inmost concerns, is like a poor man from morning to night counting the treasures that belong to another" (Shinkei, *Sasamegoto*, cited in Hirota 1995, 147). The failure to recognize one's shortcomings or the attempt to conceal them from others is a major impediment to personal actualization of the way.

Shinkei's conception of art as a way passed directly into *chanoyu*. We find his advice on practice echoed in a letter by Jukō:

> Nothing will hinder one more in the practice of this way [of *chanoyu*] than feelings of self-satisfaction and self-attachment. It is altogether reprehensible to envy skilled practitioners or to scorn beginners. One must approach the accomplished, beseech their least word of instruction, and never fail to guide the inexperienced.... Moreover, however cultivated one's manner, a painful self-awareness of one's shortcomings is crucial. [Jukō, "Letter on Heart's Mastery," cited in Hirota 1995, 198)

Here, in relation to *chanoyu*, we find the same admonitions concerning self-attachment and the need for reflection that govern the way in all the arts.

What is most pronounced in Shinkei and what highlights the particular relevance of this thought for *chanoyu* is his assumption that the way of the arts and the Buddhist path are essentially convergent. Thus, he not only repeatedly asserts that training in the arts and Buddhist praxis manifest the same basic principles, but he also freely adopts Buddhist concepts and analogies in discussing issues of linked verse. In this, he differs from earlier literary figures like Kamo no Chōmei and Kenkō for whom art is a way but may itself become the object of worldly attachment and thus an obstacle to final religious attainment. Although the various arts as the way are a means of refining one's existence and attaining knowledge of profound truths about the proper conduct of human life, in the end Kenkō viewed them as potential entanglements that could block the Buddhist path. In Shinkei, however, we find a different message, "If you dedicate yourself totally to this art [of linked verse], so that you even come to embrace the conviction that it is the single matter of grave concern, you will advance. Do not imagine it is easily and ordinarily accomplished" ("Master Shinkei's Instruction," cited in Hirota 1995, 174). The phrase "single matter of grave concern" usually indicates the Buddhist goal of liberation from samsara, the endless cycle of death and rebirth. Thus, in this passage, Shinkei suggests that total devotion to the practice of linked verse can serve the same end as Buddhist praxis, and we find no hint of Kenkō's concern.

In employing Mahayana Buddhist ideas of emptiness and nonduality, Shinkei was able to achieve a fuller convergence or superposition of art and Buddhist practice. This was accomplished by forging a more complex conception of the path of practice than the linear model envisaged by Kenkō:

> If you do not set your mind on [genuine] enlightenment, how can you gain liberation from the samsaric bondage operating within the practice of poetry? In the dharma, even the mind of great awakening to the teaching of emptiness may yet be pulled down to the condition of discriminative grasping. But in the Tendai teaching of emptiness that is itself nondual with form, the ten realms, including the six realms of unenlightened beings and the four realms of awakened sages, are all said to embody the one form of formless reality.... In the *Lotus Sutra*, it is taught that all things are poised upon emptiness.... The beginner enters from the shallow into the deep, and once having attained the depths, emerges again into the shallow: this is the essential rule of all ways. [Shinkei, *Sasamegoto*, cited in Hirota 1995, 160–61]

While recognizing the danger posed by attachment to one's achievements in an art ("samsaric bondage operating within the practice of poetry"), Shinkei overcomes the lingering dualism of sacred and profane that ultimately demands a rejection of art in order to achieve enlightenment. The Buddhist teachings themselves, as cast in human concepts, belong to

2.7   Tea bowl, Temmoku ware, China, Song dynasty (960–1279)
Ceramic, glaze
H: 12.8 cm
ROBERT W. MOORE

The collection of Chinese art objects (*karamono*) was popular among the military aristocracy in feudal Japan. Many such objects were brought back to Japan by Zen priests visiting China. The term "Temmoku" is the Japanese rendering of Tianmu Shan (Eye of Heaven), the name of a Chinese mountain range where, according to legend, Japanese visitors to a monastery originally acquired tea bowls with the characteristic black or dark brown Temmoku glaze, which is extremely high in iron content.

2.8   Tea bowl, Ido style, Korea, 16th century
Ceramic, glaze
H: 6.8 cm
ROBERT W. MOORE

At the time Korean bowls first arrived in Japan, they were frequently just rice bowls adapted to tea drinking. The rustic simplicity of Korean craftsmanship was, however, completely in tune with the spirit of *wabi* and was therefore embraced by tea master Sen no Rikyū. The appreciation of Korean objects was referred to as *koraimono*.

the realm of forms and may become the objects of discriminative attachment. What is critical in the way is apprehending, through practice, the formless reality or emptiness prior to conceptual grasp that pervades the world of forms. Thus, practitioners of linked verse or other arts traverse a path of training that leads from the detailed poetic forms and conventions and gestures and bodily movements, acquired by study and imitative drill, to a gradual maturation in which they come to enter the profound mastery that transcends all forms and all worldly attachments. The path, however, does not end in the depths of self-transcendence but leads back to the elemental forms of the art, so that the master inhabits once again the realm of convention, this time manifesting an ineffable freedom and spontaneity of spirit.

Tea masters have traditionally eschewed talk on a theoretical level, preferring to treat the myriad particulars of concrete situations: the proper rhythm and sound of water cast in the garden path when the host, using a wooden bucket and ladle, freshens it before the departure of guests, or the balance of texture, color, and glaze of the utensils. Nevertheless, Shinkei's delineation of the way as leading "from the shallow into the deep," then emerging "again into the shallow," was introduced directly into the traditions of *chanoyu* at its roots and has provided an enduring paradigm by which practitioners have integrated the material and spiritual dimensions of their praxis.

The Aesthetic of the Chill and Withered

Another dimension of Shinkei's work that had a significant influence on the formation of *chanoyu* was the concrete delineation of aesthetic principles as rooted in Buddhist perceptions and praxis. In the medieval period, the center of cultural creativity shifted from the imperial court to the newly ascendant warrior aristocracy and the activity of Buddhist practitioners. As depicted in the literature of the Heian period, the court nobles took pleasure in lives of exquisite refinement and romantic intrigue, and they were forlorn (*wabi*) with the desolate (*sabi*) existence if ever—for political reasons—they were exiled from the capital. During the medieval period, however, the tranquil life of the secluded thatched-roof hut came to take on new aesthetic value. Playing the lute or composing poetry alone while watching the moonrise deep in the mountains offered the possibility for the expression of an austere awareness that pierced the variegated surface of life in society to touch the reality of human existence.

Shinkei's work provides one of the most explicit articulations of the spiritualized medieval aesthetic of the inconspicuous and subdued: "Nothing is more exquisite than ice. The stubbled fields of early morning, with needles of ice formed where sleet has glazed the cypress bark of the roof, or the dew and hoarfrost frozen upon the withered grasses and trees of the meadow—what is there to match this loveliness, this beauty? (Shinkei, *Hitorigoto*, cited in Hirota 1995, 43). Using such terms as "chill," "slender," and "withered," Shinkei states that mastery of the way naturally manifests an aesthetic of the unobtrusive and unadorned, of spareness and solitude in contrast to an exuberant grasping after life or clamorous multiplicity. Further, he underpins this aesthetic sensibility by referring to Buddhist thought. Here, I will cite two examples.

The personal realization of the Buddhist truth of the impermanence of all things permeates the medieval mind, and in relation to the way of art, becomes an impetus to wholehearted endeavor. Shinkei states:

> Masters have said that it is the same whether you seek to enter the path of dharma and realize the wellspring of mind, or whether to study this way and awaken to what is most deeply moving. There are those who take it for granted that they will be alive in the morning; absorbed with the multifarious hues of things they cling to their treasures, and content with their own brilliance they give not a moment to self-reflection. There is hardly a chance that such people will attain mastery.... We come and go amid the illusions of this world, and whether prominent or humble, wise or foolish, the stream of our breath is more tenuous than a strand of hair, scarcely lasting to day's end. It is utter folly to rely on things of the self in spite of this, confident that life will last a hundred or a thousand years; or to be intent upon pleasures and flattered by fame, distracted and deluded in every direction. When the body turns to dust and ashes, what will become of this strand of breath? Nor is this only of myself; I wish to realize fully the way in which all things arise, and whither they vanish. [Shinkei, *Sasamegoto*, cited in Hirota 1995, 143]

In genuine practice, the "multifarious hues of things" and the "illusions of this world" dissipate, and with one's own desires grown meager, one becomes able to apprehend and give voice to "what is most deeply moving," that is, "the way in which all things arise, and whither they vanish." Shinkei's aesthetic of the "chill and withered" manifests the experience of standing on this tenuous borderline of existence, pervaded by one's own emptiness or nonexistence. Here there arises a selfless appreciation of the existence of things and a genuine compassion for others.

Shinkei developed the apprehension of impermanence beyond the temporal dimension into an insight into the present. This may be seen in the following passages of instruction to a disciple:

> The attitude of heart and mind is central. In looking upon the scattering blossoms or falling leaves, in contemplating the dew on the grasses and trees, be ever wakeful in your heart to [the true nature of] the dream of this world and your mind of illusions, conduct yourself with gentleness, and let your mind be drawn to *yūgen* (the profound and subtle). ["Master Shinkei's Instruction," cited in Hirota 1995, 173]

2.9   Rokubei (Japan, dates unknown)
Kyoto tea bowl, circa 1720–1750
Ceramic, glaze
H: 12 cm
ROBERT W. MOORE

This bowl, decorated with cherry blossoms and maple leaves, is signed "Rokubei," probably the second-generation potter in a long line of famous master potters who came from the Rokubei family.

> Turn your attention to the faint and undistinguished (*kasukanaru*). It is the link like white plum blossoming within the bamboo grove, like seeing the moon through rifts in clouds, that is engaging. There is no pleasure in verses that are like branches of multipetaled cherry or crimson plum lopped off when the blossoms have opened and are scattering, or like the full moon of autumn. ["Master Shinkei's Instruction," cited in Hirota 1995, 174]

It is that which is hidden and only faintly perceptible that holds aesthetic interest, for it stands on the verge of our awareness and reminds us of the dimension of the ungraspable or inconceivable that permeates all things. Where our "mind of illusions"—our everyday, discriminative grasp of the objects of the world from the stance of the self—is drawn into the faint and undistinguishable, an astonishment at the beauty of the ordinary arises.

Shinkei's aesthetic entered into *chanoyu*. The early tea master Jōō recorded: "An old master [probably Jukō] said, 'After you have become a renowned master of chanoyu…you should devote yourself wholly to tea in the mode of *wabi*. The priest Shinkei states that linked verse should be withered and reduced by cold. Chanoyu should ultimately become like this'" (Jōō, "Record of Yamanoue Sōji," cited in Hirota 1995, 68–69). In *chanoyu* practice, the ways in which this aesthetic manifested itself concretely are various, but in general it may be seen

2.10   Tea bowl, Karatsu ware, Japan, 18th century
Ceramic, glaze, iron pigment
H: 7.2 cm
ROBERT W. MOORE

2.11   Tea bowl, Karatsu ware, Japan, 18th century
Ceramic, glaze
H: 7.3 cm
ROBERT W. MOORE

Most Japanese pottery is named after the location of its kilns. This bowl is from Karatsu, a ceramic center that flourished at the end of the sixteenth century. The local clay is sandy with a high percentage of iron.

in a growing inclination away from elegant Chinese ceramics—Temmoku tea bowls and celadon vessels—toward rough Korean and Japanese wares for daily use (figs. 2.7–2.11); away from elaborate displays of various kinds of utensils; toward smaller, plainer chambers; and away from large-scale entertainments in favor of small, highly focused gatherings.

Creating a Cohesive Gathering

Linked verse and *chanoyu* share a fundamental dimension as arts of the *za*: the gathering of participants in a carefully prepared space to enact as a group the temporal creation that is their art, the composition of a sequence of verse links or the conduct of a tea gathering (fig. 2.12). In both arts, painstaking attention is given by all the participants to fulfilling their particular roles in bringing about a successful gathering. This sense of joint artistic creation in which success in performance arises from the interaction of the group and not individual talent stands in strong contrast with modern Western conceptions of individual artistic genius. Within the traditions of linked verse, Shinkei stands upon more than a century of detailed manuals that spell out not only the rules governing the sequence of verse links but also the preparation of the setting for the session, but he adds a characteristic perspective:

In general, we do not have our own way in this world, so we cannot determine who our friends will be or what kind of people we will associate with. Nevertheless, encountering good friends is of crucial importance in every discipline. However concentrated or composed the group may be, if there are even one or two participants whose hearts are not transfixed [by awareness of the nature of human existence], that session will inevitably leave a sense of disappointment. [Shinkei, *Sasamegoto*, cited in Hirota 1995, 140]

The attention to nurturing the fragile spirit of the gathering expressed by Shinkei is also found in early records of instruction in *chanoyu*: "Concerning the manner of the guest: attention should be given to building a unified gathering.... From the moment you enter the garden pathway until the time you depart, hold the host in most respectful esteem, in the spirit that that encounter will occur but once in your life. Worldly gossip has no place here" (Jōō, "Record of Yamanoue Sōji," cited in Hirota 1995, 205). In both Shinkei and the words of Rikyū quoted here, we find recourse not only to the Buddhist apprehension of impermanence but also to the insight of interconnectedness with others, so that one's own existence is not perceived as autonomous and individual but as necessarily communal and interdependent. The enactment of this truth is an ideal of the arts.

2.12 *Saru no sōshi emaki* (*Tale of the Monkeys*), detail, Japan, Muromachi/Momoyama period, 1560–1570
Hand scroll; ink and colors on paper
L (entire scroll): 13.29 m
©TRUSTEES OF THE BRITISH MUSEUM;
BEQUEATHED BY SIR A. W. FRANKS, NO. 1902.6-6.01

Zen Buddhism and *Chanoyu*: Spontaneous Action and the Apprehension of Things

The contact with Buddhism among the feudal military governors and wealthy merchants who supported and developed the practices of *chanoyu* was most significantly with Zen priests and temples, where powdered tea was first introduced. Further, Zen monks familiar with Chinese language and customs served to facilitate diplomatic and trade relations with the Asian continent. Thus, when the early masters of *chanoyu* looked to Buddhist tradition for guidance or support, they turned most readily to Zen, while also inheriting the traditions of the thatched-roof hut from Pure Land Buddhism and the aesthetic of the chill and withered from Mahayana. Direct reference to Buddhist ideas, however, is extremely rare, and the records of tea masters are filled chiefly with the concrete details of their practices. This avoidance of the abstract is itself, perhaps, one point of commonality shared with practitioners of Zen.

The influence of Zen Buddhist tradition on *chanoyu* is clearest in two interrelated characteristics of the way of tea: the sense that the things and events of everyday life can become the locus for the manifestation of what is real and the notion of the "working" or spontaneous activity and acuity of the accomplished tea master. For illustration, I will turn to several anecdotes from the records of *chanoyu*. The first relates a well-known legend regarding the origins of the practice:

While employing personified monkeys to illustrate a narrative about the domestic lives of persons of high rank, this remarkable hand scroll provides a valuable picture of the preparation of tea as well as the earliest known depiction of a *renga* gathering. In the detail shown here, the *renga* master sits in the back row center, wearing a black robe. He holds a tea bowl in his hand with its stand set in front of him. He would make the final judgment as to the best verse links and would be respected for his knowledge of the rules of *renga*. Seated to the right is a scribe at a low desk who would record the verses. Other figures are participants. At the extreme left, out of the way, tea is prepared and carried to the guests. The tea bowls are probably Japanese wares made in imitation of Chinese Temmoku. Such bowls were conventionally placed on lacquered stands.

It was with Zen master Ikkyū of Daitokuji Temple that drinking tea first came to be perceived as possessing the way of Zen as its essence. Jukō of Shōmyōji Temple in Nara, a disciple of Master Ikkyū, had an appreciation for the preparing and serving of tea and performed it daily. Ikkyū noticed this and, seeing that tea might accord with the wondrous realm of Buddhist attainment, recreated the spirit of Zen in the whisking of tea. Thus was established the way of tea. [*The Zen Tea Record*, cited in Hirota 1995, 263]

Although no clear evidence exists for a relationship between Jukō, named in later records as the founder of *chanoyu* as an independent performance art, and Ikkyū, famed for his eccentricity as well as his calligraphy and poetry, the latter did have connections to various figures in the arts, and the idea that he provided encouragement for treating the serving of tea as a medium of Buddhist awareness is not necessarily far-fetched. The legend of Zen Buddhist inspiration at the origins of *chanoyu* was widely accepted among later tea practitioners, and we see in this account the notion that Buddhist attainment inhabits and makes numinous the world of the ordinary.

According to the following passage from a seventeenth-century record of Rikyū's *chanoyu* practice and instruction (fig. 2.13), the tea master Jōō used the following well-known poem by Fujiwara Teika to convey the spirit of *chanoyu*:

> As I gaze far about—
> there's neither blossom
>   nor crimson leaf.
> At sea's edge: a rush hut
>   in autumn dusk.

This poem may be understood as expressing an aesthetic close to that of Shinkei: the negativity suggestive of contemplative practice by which delusive perceptions have been eradicated, so that one has arrived at an awareness pervaded by an aesthetic appreciation of the plain and unadorned (fig. 2.14–2.16). The passage continues, however, noting that

Rikyū, having discovered another poem [expressing *chanoyu* in the spirit of *wabi*], often wrote it out with the one above, adopting them as articles of faith. The second poem is by Ietaka:

> To one who awaits
> only the cherry's blossoming
> I would show:
> spring in the mountain village,
> with new herbs amid snow.

…People in the world of society spend their time wondering when blossoms will open on this hillside or in that grove, day and night turning all their attention outside themselves and never realizing that those blossoms and leaves lie within their own hearts and minds. They delight merely in colors and forms visible to the eye…. As for all the previous year's blossoms and leaves, the snow has buried them utterly, so that the mountain village has become a place where there is nothing; in its thoroughgoing solitariness it has the same significance as the rush hut.

From that realm of "not a single thing," acts possessed of the power to move us spontaneously arise here and there quite naturally. That is, without any outside exertion of will or effort, that which is true and authentic manifests itself, just as, when spring has come, the snow that has covered all greets an awakening vigor in things, and in scattered patches where it has melted, herbs wholly fresh in their greenness gradually put forth two or three leaves. ["Record of the Words of Rikyū," *Nampōroku*, cited in Hirota 1995, 234]

In this interpretation of Rikyū's intent, we see depicted a phase of mastery that perhaps parallels Shinkei's returning movement from the deep to the shallow. Here, however, there is an emphasis on the spontaneous immediacy of the authentic, perhaps reflecting the spirit of Zen Buddhism. In terms of

2.13   Hasegawa Tōhaku (Japan, 1539–1610)
Portrait of Sen no Rikyū, 16th century
Hanging scroll

Sen no Rikyū is often identified as the master who, through his innovations in tea room design, utensils, and tea manner, brought the development of *chanoyu* in the mode of *wabi* to its most austere and radical level. Born into a wealthy merchant family, he had the economic means to devote himself to *chanoyu* practice from his youth, and he eventually became the trusted tea advisor and associate of the most powerful warlords of the day, Toyotomi Hideyoshi. At nearly seventy, he was commanded to commit ritual suicide. Today, Rikyū's descendants carry on the Sen family tradition in the most widespread schools of *chanoyu*.

2.14   Tea bowl, Akaraku ware, Japan, circa 1790–1800
Ceramic, glaze
Diam: 8 cm
COLLECTION OF S. BABA AND J. KECK

Raku ware employs sandy clays that are hand molded and firing techniques in which the tea bowls are abruptly removed from the kiln and
quickly cooled. Originally, these techniques were developed, under the
guidance of Sen no Rikyū, from those used for roof tiles. Previously,
utensils adopted for *chanoyu* were "discovered" items originally intended
for other purposes, such as the well bucket used as a freshwater container,
Korean bowls, or rough ceramic jars for seed or other farming-realted
uses. Rikyū carefully instructed the early Raku potters regarding the
shape, color, size, and features he desired, creating tea bowls of great
austerity and richness. "Akaraku" may be translated as "Red Raku."

2.15   Tea bowl, Raku ware, Japan, 19th century
Ceramic, glaze
H: 7.1 cm
COLLECTION OF S. BABA AND J. KECK

Raku tea bowls are considered by many the ideal vessel for *chanoyu*. A
long line of Raku-family potters has continued to produce tea bowls
since the time of Sen no Rikyū (1522–1591); the current master, Raku
Kichizaemon XV, was born in 1949.

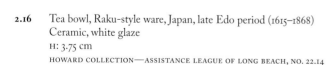

2.16   Tea bowl, Raku-style ware, Japan, late Edo period (1615–1868)
Ceramic, white glaze
H: 3.75 cm
HOWARD COLLECTION—ASSISTANCE LEAGUE OF LONG BEACH, NO. 22.14

performance, one has become able, through practice, to act with aptness in one's situation "without any…exertion of…effort," and in terms of one's surroundings, things emerge to a fresh appreciation as they are genuinely free of any imposition of will.

In a more practical vein, one more typical of the stories circulated among practitioners, the following anecdote about Rikyū conveys the same elements of practice:

> [During the tenth month] Rikyū and [his son] attended a morning gathering hosted by a certain person. In a morning storm, the leaves of an oak had fallen and scattered [onto the stepping stones], and the surface of the garden path gave precisely the feeling of a mountain forest. Rikyū, looking back [on the garden], said, "All of this is engaging. But the host, being unaccomplished, will probably sweep up the leaves."

> Just as he thought, after the intermission not a single leaf remained. At that time, Rikyū commented, "As a general rule concerning the cleaning of the garden path, if guests are to come in the morning, one should sweep the previous evening; if at noon, one should sweep in the morning. After that, even if fallen leaves should collect, the accomplished practitioner will allow them to lie as they are." ("Pointing to the Moon: Sōtan's Anecdotes of Rikyū's Tea," cited in Hirota 1995, 250–51).

2.17 Sen no Rikyū, Japan, Edo period, 19th century
Gofun (pulverized shell and glue), silk, paper, pottery, wood, paint
H: 24.1 cm
AYERVAIS COLLECTION
PHOTOGRAPH BY MICHAEL AYERVAIS

Figures like this one, known as *ningyo*, have an ancient history in Japanese culture, and during the Edo period (1615–1868), examples depicting Noh characters were popular among merchants. This figure probably belongs to this genre, as both *chanoyu* and Noh continue to be appreciated in Japanese culture.

Patricia J. Graham

DISSENSION IN THE WORLD OF TEA

The Fashion for Sencha and Chinese Culture in Early Modern Japan

3

TODAY JAPAN'S MANY TEA MANUFACTURERS produce mainly three types of green leaf tea, *bancha*, *sencha*, and *gyokuro*. The brownish colored *bancha* (common tea) is made from mature leaves picked late in the season. It is the most inexpensive, widely consumed leaf tea in Japan. Citizens from the lower classes may have begun drinking a boiled, coarse-leaf tea that was the precursor of *bancha* as early as the fifteenth century, at first using leaves and small twigs left over from production of powdered tea for *chanoyu*, popularly known as the "tea ceremony" in the West (see Hirota, this volume). By the nineteenth century, *bancha* had become so prevalent and so inexpensive that it was the standard tea sold to travelers at humble stalls in cities and along well-traveled routes (fig. 3.2).

Sencha and *gyokuro* teas are finer in quality and taste than *bancha* because they are made from young and tender leaves harvested in spring. *Sencha* (lit., "boiled tea") is an old term with multiple meanings. Although the word usually refers to green tea made from young tea leaves, it can also indicate a brewing method in which green leaf tea is thrown into a kettle of boiling or just-boiled water, or a formal tea ceremony using

3.1   Sesson Shūkei (Japan, ca. 1504–ca. 1589)
       Chikurin shichiken zu (*The Seven Sages of the Bamboo Grove*),
       mid-16th century
       Hanging scroll; ink and light color on paper
       102.6 x 51.8 cm
       PROPERTY OF MARY GRIGGS BURKE, NEW YORK
       PHOTOGRAPH BY BRUCE SCHWARZ

One of the most popular of the Daoist- and Confucian-themed paintings created for sixteenth-century Japanese warriors was *The Seven Sages of the Bamboo Grove*. The image had been known in Japan since the ninth century (Murase 2000, 177). This version was created by the Japanese Zen monk-painter Sesson Shūkei and depicts the legendary group of aged, Confucian-trained civil servants who escape from their stressful jobs to drink massive quantities of wine, dance about, and compose poetry in the seclusion of a bamboo forest. In this unusual Japanese interpretation, women and children also appear. Although images such as this seemingly contradicted the obligatory requirements of service to one's warrior overlord in Japan, their popularity increased in the late sixteenth century as artists and patrons reinterpreted the underlying Chinese message of protest against a stultifying political order as one that simply celebrated an aesthetic pastime.

3.2   Andō Hiroshige (Japan, 1797–1858)
        Fukuroi, Tōkaidō gojusan tsugi (Outdoor Tea Stall at Fukuroi,
        from the series The Fifty-Three Stations of the Tōkaidō),
        Hōeidō version, station no. 28, 1832–1833
        Full-color woodblock print
        Image: 22.5 x 35.7 cm
        COLLECTION UCLA GRUNWALD CENTER FOR THE GRAPHIC ARTS,
        HAMMER MUSEUM. PURCHASED FROM THE FRANK LLOYD WRIGHT
        COLLECTION, NO. 1965.30.53

This print by Andō Hiroshige depicts laborers resting at a tea stall at the
Fukuroi station along the great Tōkaidō Road.

leaf tea. The most refined and costly green leaf tea processed in
Japan, *gyokuro* (jade dew), derives its flavor from shading the
leaves for a time during the early spring growing season. Like
bancha, *sencha* is served informally, but the finest grades of both
sencha and *gyokuro* are usually reserved for special occasions or
for serving at formal tea ceremonies.

Few in the West know of the existence of a formal Japanese tea ritual for green leaf tea (*senchadō*, the "way of *sencha*")
or that in the first half of the nineteenth century this ritual
surpassed the older *chanoyu* tea ceremony in popularity. Westerners are also largely unaware that *senchadō* remains a living
tradition practiced by many thousands today in Japan. In *sencha* tea ceremonies, hosts steep tea in tiny teapots and serve it
to guests in delicate cups (fig. 3.3).

The *sencha* ceremony developed and quickly gained a following in the second half of the eighteenth century among
intellectuals who admired Chinese culture. By the early nineteenth century, emulating Chinese intellectual pastimes was
wildly popular among the general population, and the popularity of *sencha* soared. Its relegation to comparative obscurity by
the early twentieth century reflected a momentous shift in the
Japanese consciousness, with the center of the nation's intellectual universe swinging away from China and toward the West
in the late nineteenth century. The lack of familiarity with the
sencha tea ceremony outside of Japan today stems largely from
the perceived primacy of *chanoyu* as exemplar of pure Japanese
aesthetic and cultural values, an idea that developed during the

late nineteenth century, when the nation sought to distance itself from its centuries-long adulation of China. Since that time, prominent politicians, scholars, and collectors, in collaboration with Japan's tea school headmasters, have been engaged in promoting *chanoyu* and perpetuating carefully constructed myths designed to maintain its elite status.

Until quite recently, most scholarship on the tea ceremony in Japan's cultural history has overemphasized the role of *chanoyu* in the early modern period (coinciding with the Tokugawa or Edo period, 1615–1868). In actuality, *sencha*, as well as the Chinese or Chinese-style arts created and appreciated within its orbit, played an important part in shaping early modern culture.[1] In 1998, reflecting this new-found appreciation, Yamada Jōzan III (1924–2005) became the first potter specializing in *sencha* wares to be designated a Living National Treasure.[2]

Discussion of *sencha* serves as a point of departure for observing broader sociocultural issues including the mechanisms by which Japan adopts a foreign custom; Japan's changing relationship with China and how it has affected the popularity of this Chinese-influenced custom; the practical ramifications of cultural absorption of a pursuit like tea drinking—how this simple act stimulated the production of new and varied types of material culture; and how art and the related issue of aesthetic taste become integrally tied to larger social issues, especially the formation of personal and collective cultural identity.

3.3   Women of the Ogawa School in Kyoto perform a *sencha* ceremony. PHOTOGRAPH COURTESY OF THE JAPAN SECTION OF THE KANSAS ASIA SCHOLARS PROGRAM, 2003.

Chinese Literati Culture in Premodern Japan

The *sencha* tea ceremony is the result of many centuries of admiration for Chinese learning in Japan. Premodern Japan was essentially bilingual (Smits 2007, 105). Beginning in the seventh century, literate Japanese—aristocrats, elite samurai, and Buddhist priests—learned to read and write in Chinese as well as Japanese and were taught to appreciate Chinese artifacts. Imported Chinese documents included legal codes, Buddhist texts, treatises on philosophy, and literary writings. Much of the imported literature expressed the ideals of the Chinese literati, whose tenets encompassed the complementary spiritual and ethical traditions of Daoism and Confucianism, both introduced in the seventh century.[3]

Chinese literati typically upheld a Confucian-derived moral obligation to help better society through government service or teaching but paradoxically yearned for a Daoist reclusive life apart from worldly affairs. Since ancient times, literati had vowed to serve only fair and compassionate monarchs. When they disagreed with authorities, they often retreated into lives of reclusion. In their poetry, prose, and paintings, the Chinese literati extolled the spiritual and medicinal benefits of tea, which they consumed as an adjunct to their erudite lifestyles.

In the Muromachi period (1392–1568), Chinese literati philosophy had an especially strong impact on the elite warriors who controlled Japan because of the warriors' close relationship with Chinese Chan (Zen in Japanese) monks and traders. The writing of Chinese literati imported to Japan

during this time—together with Chan Buddhism and writings by Japanese admirers of Chinese culture—frequently mentioned tea using the term *sencha* (Joichi 2007). Paintings created for the warriors of sixteenth-century Japan abound with images of Confucian sages and Daoist recluses (fig. 3.1; Brown 1997; Watsky 2006).

In the seventeenth century, after decades of internal strife among regional warrior clans, warlords of the Tokugawa clan established themselves as the supreme military commanders, or shoguns, and unified the country. To secure their hegemony, they created a strict social hierarchy that classified citizens into status groups according to their birth, ranking their own group, samurai warriors, above others that included farmers and urban merchants. By the late seventeenth century they had begun encouraging all citizens to study Confucianism because that creed specified each person's function in society and thereby helped instill in their subjects a moral rationale for submission to authority. Ironically however, this encouragement of Confucianism stimulated curiosity about other, nonsanctioned interpretations of Chinese intellectual thought, including that associated with heterodox literati. Soon, Japanese scholars and writers who disagreed with the Confucian policies promulgated by the shoguns championed the penchant of the literati for reclusion as a symbol of their marginalization.[4]

Because political instability in China and legal restrictions by Japanese authorities made it impossible for Japanese

3·4   *Tōkan shobō no zu* (*A Chinese Scholar's Study in Nagasaki*),
Japan, early 19th century
Single-sheet woodblock print; ink and colors on paper
37 × 25 cm
KOBE CITY MUSEUM

This print features *sencha* accoutrements, including a brazier, teacup, and small teapot, which are visible in the cabinet behind the figures, on the right.

3·5   The main room at Shisendō (Abode of the Poetry Immortals), the former residence of Ishikawa Jōzan (1583–1672), is exemplary of the open spaces favored by Japanese devotees of the Chinese literati. The design of the Shisendō served as a model for later *sencha* tea rooms.
PHOTOGRAPH BY PATRICIA GRAHAM, KYOTO, 1997.

to visit China throughout most of the Tokugawa period, they had to glean knowledge of Chinese philosophy and customs from imported books and contact with Chinese citizens, including amateur and professional artists who emigrated to Japan or established temporary residence there as merchants (Jansen 1992; Addiss 1986). Nagasaki, Japan's sole legally sanctioned international port between 1635 and 1859, became the initial conduit for most of this knowledge (Graham 1998, 24–38; Itabashi Kuritsu Kyōdō Shiryōkan 1996). Circulation of illustrated woodblock-printed books and larger, single-sheet prints by Japanese artists beginning in the eighteenth century helped familiarize Japanese citizens who could not visit Nagasaki with the large Chinese community there, which included scholars. Many of these prints, including an early nineteenth-century example by a Japanese artist (fig. 3.4), included images of *sencha* accoutrements. The shoguns allowed only a small number of Nagasaki's Chinese residents to reside elsewhere in Japan, including a group of emigrant Chinese Chan monks who founded a new sect of Zen called Ōbaku.

These Ōbaku monks came to Japan to flee the turmoil that arose in China around the time the Qing dynasty Manchus vanquished the Ming Empire in 1644. The shoguns took the unprecedented measure of permitting them to establish a new temple, Manpukuji in Uji, near Kyoto, in 1663. Soon thereafter they founded branch temples throughout the country. Ōbaku's charismatic monks bolstered the sect's broad appeal and succeeded in converting large numbers of followers. Beyond the persuasiveness of their religious doctrine, the Ōbaku monks attracted attention because of their education in Chinese literati traditions, about which eager students in Japan desired to learn. Because they drank *sencha* during religious rituals and more informally throughout the day, the tea became so closely identified with the monks that it became popularly known as "Ingen *cha*" (Ingen tea) after the sect's patriarch Ingen (Yinyuan in Chinese, 1592–1673), who became regarded as the founder of the *sencha* ceremony in Japan.[5] It was not until around 1735, however, that Japanese tea manufacturers near Manpukuji in Uji began to widely produce *sencha*.

As part of their efforts to legitimize their Zen lineage and gain converts from other Japanese Buddhist sects, the Ōbaku monks asserted the spiritual supremacy of the leaf tea they drank over the more familiar powdered tea of *chanoyu*, closely associated with older Japanese Zen sects. The Japanese-born Ōbaku monk Gettan Dōchō (1636–1713), a direct disciple of Ingen, first articulated the Ōbaku position on tea in a lengthy prose-poem, *Sencha uta* (*Ode to Sencha*) of circa 1694, which was included in his book of 1703, *Gankyokō* (*Manuscript of the Rock Dweller*).

Tea from Jiangnan is excellent,
Better than other teas, it has a wonderful flavor.
Not only can it drive away the devil of sleep
But because it also dispels heat and thirst it is the
    elixir of immortals.
Ever since Lu Yu loved tea,

It was planted everywhere throughout the Tang
　　dynasty.
Mengding and Jiangxi are two of the best varieties
　　of tea;
Wuyi and Guzhu are also famous.
I only regret that it is not grown in Jugan,
And not a single word has been written about it
　　there.
In Sangyu and Zhenggu people appreciate tea.
A festival of processing tea has taken place there
　　since the time of emperor Noudi.
Eisai brought the famous tea seeds and shared them
　　with the monk Kōben [Myōe] at Umeoka
　　[Takao].
There, the valleys are deep, the dew is pure and the
　　tea leaves grow in profusion.
They are both bitter and sweet and make the tongue
　　feel cool.

Akamatsu Enshin liked the taste, the great monk
　　[and painter; see fig. 3.1] Sesson composed
　　lengthy poems praising tea.
When mountain tea was measured out as a treat to
　　official lay guests,
Visitors on horseback stirred the dust up to the white
　　clouds.
Then the shogun living at Rokuonji [Kinkakuji]
　　appeared
And ordered his official Yoshihiro to plant Uji tea.
The fertile land stretches up to my home.
Field after field of tea creates broad green spaces.
The locals trade it to make a living and care for the
　　tea plants as if they are precious jade.
They cultivate them and trim them diligently, and
　　fear the possibility of frost coming at night.
When the time of the Qingming festival approaches
　　[early March], the weather is warm.
Spring thunder awakens the insects and the tea
　　shoots emerge.
Crowds gather, picking tea to the beating of drums.
The tender leaves fill the baskets and are selected,
　　roasted, and prepared with great care.
The first cup is offered to the Shogun.
Who can resist the famous teas, "Sparrow's Tongue"
　　and "Dragon's Body?"
The teas "Falling Mortar" and "Jade Dust" appear
　　light gold.

The fire roars in the brazier signaling that springtime
　　is filling the room.
In the iron kettle, the water boils into bubbles shaped
　　like duck eyes.
The green tea fills up the Korean tea cup.
Guests drink in turn and exclaim that the taste is
　　like nectar.

The calligraphy and painting on the walls are pre-
　　cious works by the monks Xigeng and Muxi.
They have been studied and imitated for eons.
Notable among the followers of *wabi* are Jōō and
　　Shukō.
Samurai in fine clothing crowd into the tea room.
Yet rural recluses also appreciate tea.
These humble men do not approve of attending
　　expensive tea gatherings;
They prefer simplicity and dwell in mountain huts.
By Lake Biwa, someone is brewing *sencha*.
The aroma of the brewing leaves seeps out of the pot.
Neither tea scoops nor whisks are needed.
Tea is brewed strong and drunk to moisten the bowels.
After three cups his spirits are elevated,
And he leans on the windowsill to listen to the reed
　　flute.
Zen monk friends pass by and inquire about what is
　　taking place there.

They are shown tea cups as an answer.
Zhaozhou liked to test his visitors.
They understood his bluntness and accepted the con-
　　sequences.
Other people can compete for entry into the immor-
　　tal land of Lu Tong,
I am content to brag about my own fine home.
　　[translation mine; cited in Graham 1998, 55–56]

The poem portrays *sencha* as better than *chanoyu* because
as followers of the latter formalized their ceremony, they came
to disregard the importance that early Japanese Zen monks
had placed on the spiritual benefits derived from tea. Instead
the practice had become an avocation celebrating an ostentatious display of material possessions. Gettan noted that only
humble recluses who drank *sencha* (by implication the Ōbaku
monks themselves) understood the spiritual value of drinking
tea as transmitted from the ancients.

The defiant position of the Ōbaku monks, who left their
homeland in protest for a life of reclusion in Japan, resonated
with admirers of the Chinese literati, who emerged in the
mid-seventeenth century, around the time the monks arrived
in Nagasaki. One of the earliest of these admirers Ishikawa
Jōzan (1583–1672) came from a family of samurai loyal to the
Tokugawa clan. When he was in his early fifties, after heroic
service in the civil wars that led to the Tokugawa victory, dis-
satisfaction with the life of a warrior compelled Jōzan to retire
to Kyoto, where he settled in a rural retreat to write Chinese
poetry and study the writings of the Chinese literati (Rimer et
al. 1991). His elegant but rustic residence, the Shisendō (Abode
of the Poetry Immortals), a reference to Chinese rather than
Japanese poets, serves as a model for later *sencha* tea rooms
(fig. 3.5). Its informal and open plan centered around a raked
gravel garden contrasts sharply with the characteristic small,
closed spaces of *chanoyu* tea rooms. Jōzan was revered as the

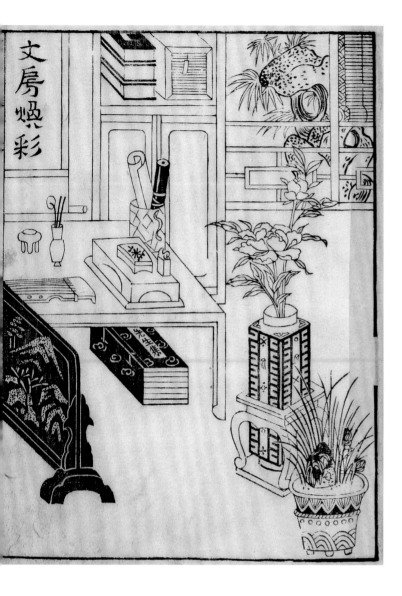

3.6   Ōeda Ryūhō (Japan, ?–ca. 1756)
Illustration from *Gayū manroku* (*Miscellaneous Records of Elegant Pastimes*), 1762
Woodblock-printed book; ink on paper
21 x 16 cm
PRIVATE COLLECTION, JAPAN

Ōeda Ryūhō's posthumously published seven-volume guide to the life-style and environment appropriate to devotees of the Chinese literati spawned a raft of similar publications. This illustration includes features typical of a Chinese scholar's room, including a writing desk with writing implements, rolled-up scrolls, a *qin* (zither), and incense set; a potted plant and vase of flowers in the right foreground; a bound set of books under the table; a free-standing, single-panel screen with landscape design; and a large gnarled rock visible outside the window.

founder of the literati tradition in Japan, but *sencha* follow-ers came to consider him as their spiritual progenitor as well (Anjōshi Rekishi Hakubutsukan 2007). This latter develop-ment is somewhat ironic, however, for although he aspired to the life of a Chinese literatus and knew of the Ōbaku monks and their tea-drinking traditions, scholars have not uncovered evidence that Jōzan himself actually drank *sencha* (Graham 1998, 57–63; Ōtsuki 2004, 247–59).

Jōzan's descriptions of his life of seclusion are permeated by the spirit of *fūryū* (lit., "floating with the wind"), a word derived from the Chinese term *fengliu*, which had entered the Japanese vocabulary by the eighth century and originally car-ried associations of courtly elegance and refinement. As the *wabi* aesthetic of *chanoyu* gained ascendance, especially from the time of Sen no Rikyū (1522–1591), however, the meaning of *fūryū* shifted to conform with *wabi* ideals (for a discussion of *wabi*, see Hirota, this volume). The famed Kyoto poet Matsuo Bashō (1644–1694) also emphasized this concept. *Fūryū*, as interpreted by both Jōzan and Bashō, derived from their familiarity with Chinese writings. To them, *fūryū* implied a deep understanding of Chinese literati culture, preferences for wanderlust and an eremitic withdrawal from the world, and devotion to simple pleasures, as epitomized by literati models such as the *Seven Sages of the Bamboo Grove* (see fig. 3.1). Jōzan's and Bashō's usage of the term became the guiding principle and dominating aesthetic in the *sencha* tea ceremony.

Bashō had developed his ideas about *fūryū* from his close study of Daoism (Qiu 2005). Others of his time also began exploring this philosophy. The influential Kyoto Confucian philosopher Ogyū Sorai (1666–1728), incorporated Daoist con-cepts of *ki* ("marvelousness," "strangeness," or "eccentricity") and *ga* (elegance) into his ideas about Confucianism. He pro-moted *ki* in his stress on personal spiritual cultivation, noting that each person should develop his innate talents and incli-nations as a way to reach his moral center. He qualified this emphasis on individualism, however, with the assertion that personal activities should be elegant (*ga*), a term used inter-changeably with *fūryū*. Following his dictum, individuals with similar interests banded together in coteries often centering on a pivotal figure. Their avocations, inspired by those of the Chinese literati, included participatory group events featuring painting Chinese-style pictures, composing impromptu poems, playing the *qin* (a zither-like instrument), and admiring antiq-uities. *Sencha* drinking flourished in this environment.

As literacy increased during the Tokugawa period, appre-ciation for Chinese learning deeply permeated Japanese culture. Numerous writers grew famous for their Chinese-language poetry inspired by the literati (Watson 1976; 1990), while oth-ers published woodblock-printed books that provided practi-cal information for aspiring Japanese followers of the Chinese literati. Ōeda Ryūhō (?–ca. 1756), the son of a wealthy Osaka merchant, wrote the first of many such guides, *Gayū manroku* (*Miscellaneous Records of Elegant Pastimes*), posthumously pub-lished in 1762. It instructed readers in the creation of a proper literati environment. The preface described how Ryūhō had

pursued the reclusive life of Chinese Daoist sages in his youth and clarified that although he eventually returned to the city, he continued to devote himself to scholarly pursuits. Within his book's seven volumes, he lovingly described and illustrated assorted literati objects in a Japanese vernacular text liberally sprinkled with quotations in Chinese (fig. 3.6).

Soon after Ryūhō's work was published, Chinese literati themes became familiar in paintings by artists of diverse ateliers throughout Japan's major urban centers (Graham 2001). Typical of such works is a scroll by Nakabayashi Chikkei (1816–1867), an artist who specialized in paintings in Chinese literati styles (fig. 3.7). He learned about literati ways from one of his painting teachers, Yamamoto Baiitsu (1783–1856), a specialist in Japanese literati-style painting, a famous connoisseur of Chinese paintings and antiquities, and a central figure in the promotion of *sencha* (Graham 1983; 1986). Beginning in the 1830s, Baiitsu and his friends frequently gathered to examine each other's Chinese art collections, all the while drinking *sencha*. Baiitsu initiated a Japanese literati tradition, which lasted until the early twentieth century, of recording for posterity descriptions of the Chinese arts displayed at these gatherings and the appearance of the rooms in which they were featured

3.7 Nakabayashi Chikkei (Japan, 1816–1867)
Scholars Enjoying Tea, 19th century
Hanging scroll; color on silk
149.69 x 85.41 cm
LOS ANGELES COUNTY MUSEUM OF ART,
FAR EASTERN ART COUNCIL FUND, NO. AC1994.146.1
PHOTOGRAPH ©2009 MUSEUM ASSOCIATES/LACMA

Typical of Chinese literati, these scholars are enjoying the drinking of tea, prepared and served by youthful attendants, in an outdoor setting.

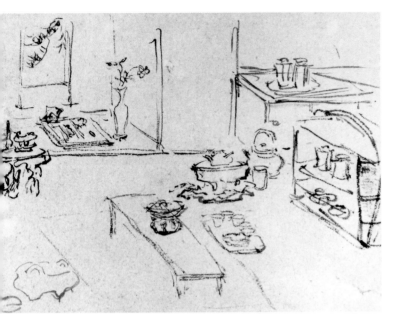

3.8a,b Yamamoto Baiitsu (Japan, 1783–1856)
Sketches of Chinese-Style Rooms for Serving *Sencha*
Mounted on a folding screen; ink on paper
Top: 13.7 x 17.7 cm; Bottom: 12.8 x 17.8 cm
NAGOYA CITY MUSEUM

In the upper sketch, a famous spare-looking Chinese landscape painting that was owned by Baiitsu hangs in the alcove, which is adorned with a simple Chinese-style flower arrangement in a bottle vase and a display of literati-style writing implements. The room depicted in the sketch below looks like a transplanted Chinese interior with its tile floor (instead of the usual Japanese tatami mats) and seemingly authentic Chinese furnishings: a table in the center of the room surrounded by stools for guests, a chair for the host set beside a smaller table with a rootwood base—atop which sits *sencha*-making equipment—and on the right, a tall rootwood display stand for an ancient Chinese bronze vessel used as a flower vase.

BELOW

3.9 Tsubaki Chinzan (Japan, 1801–1854)
Sencha shoshū (*Small Sencha Gathering*), 1838
Detail of an accordion-folded, woodblock-printed book;
ink and colors on paper
H: 12.4 cm
PRIVATE COLLECTION, JAPAN.

The literati painter Tsubaki Chinzan was one of the attendees at the small *sencha* gathering he illustrated to commemorate a friend's birthday. He modestly portrayed himself at the top right with his head cut off (we know this is a self-portrait as inscriptions near the figures identify them).

(Miyazaki 1996). These rooms, unlike those used for *chanoyu*, functioned mainly as painting or writing studios for their owners, or as elegant reception rooms for guests (much like the expansive room in Ishikawa Jōzan's residence, see fig. 3.5). As portrayed in two sketches that Baiitsu brushed of his own studio, these rooms would be decorated with Chinese furniture, paintings, and decorative objects with *sencha* accoutrements prominently displayed (figs. 3.8a,b).

Sometimes, more formal or larger group gatherings of literati aficionados took place at restaurants or teahouses in urban entertainment districts. For one party held in Edo (present-day Tokyo) in 1838, an illustrated woodblock-printed book was produced as a memento for partygoers and friends unable to attend (fig. 3.9). It captures the informal atmosphere in which guests mingled admiring each others' treasures, primarily *sencha* implements.[6]

Such gatherings served as the first exhibitions of Chinese literati-style arts in Japan revealing that interest in Chinese literati philosophy and pastimes went hand-in-hand with appreciation of *sencha*. *Sencha* played such a prominent role in the assimilation of Chinese literati culture in Japan largely due to one individual, Baisaō (lit., "the old tea seller," [1675–1763]; formally known as Kō Yūgai), an eccentric, enigmatic, Japanese-born follower of Ōbaku Zen, who ceaselessly championed tea's spiritual and medicinal benefits (Baisaō and Waddell 2008).

Formation of the *Sencha* Tea Ceremony

The shoguns mandated the participation of samurai in formal rituals, including *chanoyu*, in order to differentiate them from other status groups. Japanese citizens reacted to the close association of *chanoyu* with the shoguns in two ways. Some better-educated urban commoners, following the lead of wealthy sixteenth-century merchants, created their own *chanoyu* ceremonies to signify their cultural sophistication even though they were effectively blocked from any upward mobility. Others, principally intellectuals of various status groups who admired the Chinese literati—for example, samurai scholars, well-educated merchants, and bohemian artists—considered the shoguns' regime repressive and responded by decrying *chanoyu* as pretentious (Graham 1998, 56, 75–76; Varley and Kumakura 1989, 174–76). Many in this group began to drink *sencha*, which had no mandated rules of etiquette. *Sencha* was attractive because of its association with their Chinese literati heroes and its potential as a symbol of resistance to the shoguns. Many of these early *sencha* drinkers coalesced around the person of Baisaō.

Later followers of *sencha* embraced Baisaō with as much fervor as aficionados of *chanoyu* demonstrated for Sen no Rikyū. Unlike Rikyū, however, Baisaō did not consider himself a tea master, just a purveyor of *sencha*. He also became well known for his Chinese poetry based on literati themes and *sencha*. The son of a physician from western Japan near Nagasaki, he joined a branch temple of the Ōbaku sect near his home at age twelve, soon after the death of his father. After visiting

3.10 Itō Jakuchū (Japan, 1733–1800)
Portrait of Baisaō
Ink on paper
113 x 44.5 cm
PRIVATE COLLECTION, JAPAN

All extant portraits of Baisaō portray him, as Jakuchū has here, with a scraggly beard and jutting chin, sporting the wild look of the eccentric Chinese sages he so admired.

Manpukuji and other Ōbaku temples in search of spiritual guidance and serving for a time as steward at his home temple, he moved to the Kyoto area in 1724 and resided for a time at Manpukuji. After he left Manpukuji in 1730 and until the time of his death, he lived in Kyoto, earning his living not as a Zen priest but as an itinerant seller of *sencha*, which he offered from a portable bamboo stall that he carried on his back and set up at Kyoto's famous scenic spots. The attraction of his stall for passersby was not only the flavor ot the tea but also the beguiling messages of its purveyor. He called his tea stall Tsutentei (Pavilion along the Pathway to the Immortals) and his tea utensil basket Senka (Den of the Sages), both allusions to the Chinese literati. Alongside his tea stall, Baisaō hung a banner inscribed with the characters "*seifū*," an abbreviation of the term *sei-fūryū* (pure elegance), to express the literati values that he felt *sencha* embodied.

One of his poems persuasively describes the reasons he thought prospective customers should drink his *sencha*:

> This place of mine, so poor,
> I'm often even out of water;
> But I offer you an elixir,
> To change your very marrow.
> You'll find me in the pines,
> By the Hall of a Thousand Buddhas,
> Come take a drink—who knows?
> You may reach Sagehood yourself.
> [translation by Norman Waddell;
> cited in Graham (1998, 70)]

Not surprisingly, Baisaō attracted a devoted coterie of admirers among the many followers of Chinese learning in Kyoto and neighboring Osaka (Kano 2005). Prominent among them was Kimura Kenkadō (1736–1802), a former Osaka sake brewer who, after having his fortune confiscated by the authorities,[7] opened a stationery shop that became a gathering place for the prominent writers and artists of his day. Kenkadō was famous for his vast collection of Chinese books and botanicals, and he was also a talented amateur painter in the literati mode. Another of Baisaō's admirers, the celebrated painter Itō Jakuchū (1733–1800), brushed several portraits of his mentor, including one that shows the old tea seller gazing into the distance, wearing the robe of a Daoist priest and carrying the tools of his trade on his back (fig. 3.10).

During his lifetime and shortly after his death, Baisaō's disciples began the process of transforming the drinking of *sencha* from an informal pastime into a ritualized custom. Ōeda Ryūhō, in addition to penning the first guide to literati culture in Japan (see fig. 3.6), authored the first manual on *sencha* appreciation, *Seiwan chawa* (*Chats on Tea by the Azure Harbor*), published in 1756. Very quickly, many other guides to *sencha* appeared, some authored by Baisaō's immediate followers, others by less-intimate admirers, and still others by disciples of his close followers.[8] By the early nineteenth century, some authors of these guides began using terminology borrowed from *cha-*

noyu. Although this may seem incongruous given the earlier antagonism between these two tea ceremonies, *chanoyu* was by far the more widely known and practiced. It was logical therefore that the promoters of *sencha* would appropriate familiar terminology to describe their own tea ritual.

Baisaō's closest friends, meanwhile, took the lead in defining appropriate utensil types. As a frugal monk, Baisaō lived simply with few possessions, and though he stressed the flavor of his tea, he deeply revered the small assortment of Chinese tea-making paraphernalia that he owned. He directed that some pieces should be burned after his death but bequeathed others to his closest friends, who likewise treasured them. This begat the preference of his admirers for preparing *sencha* using only tea utensils that resembled those of Baisaō, either imports from China or wares made to their specifications by Japanese artists.

The published *sencha* manuals and the avowed preferences for certain utensil types began the process of transforming *sencha* into a distinctly Japanese tea ritual. They helped increase market demands for *sencha* utensils and arts reflecting literati taste, resulting in the creation of opportunities for artists to specialize in the production of *sencha* serving utensils and to produce paintings and other decorative arts—such as bamboo flower baskets in Chinese literati styles—appropriate for display at *sencha* gatherings (Graham 1999, 2002).

The *Sencha* Boom in Nineteenth-Century Japan

The aforementioned Kimura Kenkadō played a large role in Baisaō's apotheosis and the formalization of the *sencha* tradition by commissioning copies of Baisaō's tea wares from Japanese artists and by creating an illustrated record of Baisaō's utensils. First produced as a handwritten sketchbook, it survives today in an expanded woodblock-printed album of 1823 with illustrations (most copied from Kenkadō's sketches) by Aoki Shukuya (ca. 1737–1802), a disciple of another of Baisaō's friends (fig. 3.11). Inscriptions alongside each picture record the identity of the object's owner.[9] As noted in the album, many of Baisaō's possessions had gradually come into the possession of an aficionado of the Chinese literati known as the Master of Kagetsuan (Hermitage of Flowers and Meadows), the artist name of Tanaka Kakuō (1782-1848). Kakuō, an Osaka sake brewer, founded the first formal *sencha* tea ceremony school.

The most famous object illustrated in this album is a seventeenth-century Chinese stoneware teapot (second from right in fig. 3.11, with two cups), which Baisaō presented just before his death in 1763 to his friend Ike Taiga (1723–1776), Shukuya's teacher.[10] Baisaō's followers identified it erroneously as a product of the famous Yixing kilns of China. This mistake reflects the fact that although imported books on Ming material culture lauded Yixing wares, *sencha* fans had few opportunities to see actual examples, as these were not imported in great numbers until several decades later (Itabashi Kuritsu Kyōdō Shiryōkan 1996). Baisaō's teapot was actually a more common, unglazed, side-handled stoneware vessel, known as a "*kyūsu*" in Japanese and utilized in China for brewing medicinal herbs.

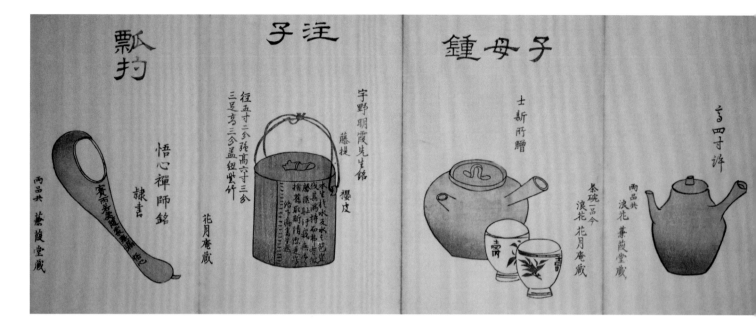

Because of Baisaō, unglazed side-handled teapots became a popular import to Japan, and Japanese potters frequently copied them.

Baisaō also owned some Chinese porcelain tea cups (see fig. 3.11, adjacent to the famous teapot), decorated with simple designs of tea plants in underglaze blue. Although these porcelains were more refined and elegant in appearance than the teapot, they also represented commonly produced types of ceramics. Baisaō must have liked them for their simple monochromatic designs—a *fūryū* aesthetic—that resembled literati ink paintings. Baisaō's preference for this underglaze blue ware resulted in its popularity for *sencha* tea utensils (fig. 3.12).

Because Baisaō and many members of his coterie resided in Kyoto, that city became the first locus of production for *sencha* utensils. The Kyoto potter Aoki Mokubei (1767–1833) was the first to specialize in wares for *sencha*. He copied Baisao's *kyūsu* illustrated in Shukuya's album (Graham 1998, fig. 38) and produced many porcelain wares with underglaze blue designs. He was also responsible for augmenting Baisaō's meager repertoire of utensils with new types based on his study of various Chinese ceramic vessel glazes and designs. By chance he learned how to re-create these from Chinese pottery manuals that he encountered in the library of his acquaintance Kimura Kenkadō. One of the most popular new types of *sencha* wares he devised was *kinrande* (gold brocade) with overglaze red enamel and gold leaf decoration (fig. 3.13). Examples of Chinese wares with this glaze were already admired in Japan, having first gained popularity in seventeenth-century *chanoyu* circles, but Mokubei was the first to apply the glaze to ceramics used for *sencha*.

Mokubei, a connoisseur of Chinese antiquities and an amateur literati painter, was an avid fan of *sencha* himself.[11] He often made tea wares for use at *sencha* gatherings he hosted. His last, ill-fated, project was for a large group of teapots and cups that he intended to distribute to one hundred guests of a *sencha* gathering he planned for the early spring of 1833 in

3.11 Aoki Shukuya (Japan, ca. 1737–1802)
Baisaō chaki zufu (Pictorial Record of Baisao's Tea Utensils), 1823
Detail of an accordion-folded woodblock-printed album;
ink and color on paper
H: 20.6 cm
PRIVATE COLLECTION, JAPAN

3.12 Nin'ami Dohachi (Japan, 1783–1855)
Teapot, Edo period, mid-19th century
Porcelain with underglaze blue designs of phoenixes and cranes
H: 8.5 cm
SAINT LOUIS ART MUSEUM, FRIENDS FUND, NO. 96:1992A,B

3.13   Eiraku Hozen (Japan, 1795–1854)
        Set of five teacups, Edo period, mid-19th century
        Porcelain with *kinrande* (overglaze red enamel and gold leaf)
        and underglaze blue designs
        Each cup: 3.8 x 5.7 cm
        SAINT LOUIS ART MUSEUM, MUSEUM SHOP FUND, 355:1991.1–.5

The potter Eiraku Hozen was born slightly after Aoki Mokubei (1767–1833) who was the first Kyoto potter to specialize in *sencha* ware (see fig. 3.14). Mokubei is credited with re-creating the Chinese-style *kinrade* glaze that Hozen used on these cups.

3.14   Aoki Mokubei (Japan, 1767–1833)
        Kyūsu (side-handled teapot), 1832
        Stoneware
        H: 10 cm
        SAINT LOUIS ART MUSEUM, WILLIAM K. BIXBY TRUST FOR ASIAN ART,
        NO. 126:1985A,B

Kyoto. Unfortunately, he had trouble with the firing process, fell ill from the effort, and passed away before completing the pieces. His daughter distributed finished pieces to friends at his funeral instead. Some of these unglazed mold-made teapots still survive (fig. 3.14). They feature a four-character inscription in raised relief, *Minun shiseki* (Sleeping among Clouds, Crawling in the Rocks), an oblique reference to Chinese literati who sought refuge from the difficulties of the world by dwelling in seclusion in mist-drenched mountains.

In 1835, shortly after Mokubei died, *sencha* popularity surged following the invention of a new growing and processing technique for green tea. This resulted in the creation of a new and even more flavorful variety of tea, *gyokuro*. It was following the introduction of *gyokuro* that the previously mentioned Tanaka Kakuō came to play a pivotal role in the establishment of a formal *sencha* tea ceremony. A devotee of Ōbaku Zen, Kakuō became famous for the fine flavor of his *sencha*, as seen in a small woodblock book on the meaning of *fūryū* to various Osaka luminaries (fig. 3.15). Kakuō considered *sencha* his path to spiritual communion with the ideals of the Chinese literati, and his tea owed its delicate taste to his recognition that the flavor of *gyokuro* could be further enhanced by systematic preparation and using only the purest water.

Kakuō outlined tea preparation methods according to differences in settings, social situations, levels of formality, varieties of utensils, and how each of these points related to two distinct tea brewing methods. One of these, *encha*, entailed first placing tea leaves in a teapot and then filing the pot with hot water. The other method (which Baisaō had used) was essentially the reverse: tea leaves were thrown into a teapot already filled with hot water. Kakuō's success at tea brewing stemmed from knowledge gained in the management of his family's sake business. By 1838, Kakuō began calling himself *iemoto* (headmaster) of Kagetsuan (now the name of the *sencha* tea school he founded), and he began teaching people his tea preparation method, which he refined and adapted to accord with the wide variety of *sencha* serving utensils that had come to be used in different social circumstances. He recorded his instructions for preparing *sencha* in a secret manuscript that survives in handwritten copies produced by disciples in the late nineteenth century. His was the first of many such guides to *sencha* that borrowed *chanoyu* terminology for distinguishing variations in serving procedures and utensils depending on the level of formality of the occasion. From this time on, interest in *sencha* surged among diverse social groups, including commoners, courtiers, and elite samurai who had formerly only participated in *chanoyu*. Soon, in response to growing interest in *sencha* and associated literati aesthetics, other knowledgeable literati began to teach *sencha* etiquette as professional *sencha* tea masters. Following the literati emphasis on individuality, they desired to create their own unique preparation methods, setting the stage for the establishment of numerous schools of *sencha*.

The *Sencha* Tea Ceremony in Modern Japan

After the demise of the Tokugawa government in 1868, literati-style *sencha* gatherings continued, sometimes in conjunction with new government-sponsored public exhibitions of Chinese arts. Principal participants and organizers of the public events included prominent art dealers, businessmen, and politicians who had themselves studied the values of *sencha* and literati arts in their youths (Guth 2006; Graham 2003; Seikadō Bunkō Bijutsukan 1998). The most prominent among the new generation of *sencha* enthusiasts attended the *Seiwan chakai* (*Azure Sea Tea Gathering*), a multiday extravaganza held in Osaka in 1874, which featured suites of rooms both as sites of tea ceremonies and as model environments for display of Chinese antiquities. Tanomura Chokunyū (1814–1907), the leading literati painter and scholar at the time, illustrated a woodblock-printed book depicting this event (fig. 3.16).

Chokunyū's younger friend, Tomioka Tessai (1836–1924), the most important literati painter of the modern era, was one of many who continued to promote Chinese learning in the late Meiji era (1868–1912), when Japan had turned its attention to the West. Admiration for China had waned in the mid-nineteenth century, when the Japanese observed China's economic collapse as a result of humiliating defeats at the hands of British, French, Russian, and American forces, as well as the increasing inability of the Qing emperors to quell peasant rebellions. After American warships under the direction of Commodore Perry sailed into Yokohama Bay in 1858 and forced Japan to allow more international trade, the Japanese government—particularly after the Meiji Restoration of 1868—sought rapidly to industrialize following Western models in order to avoid the fate of China and to be able to successfully compete in global markets. Nevertheless, the Chinese literati values of *sencha* had become so assimilated that they contributed to the shaping of Japan's modern national identity as self-proclaimed preserver of East Asian wisdom in the early twentieth century. This change in attitude is evident in Tessai's scroll of *Blind Men Critiquing Beauty*, completed

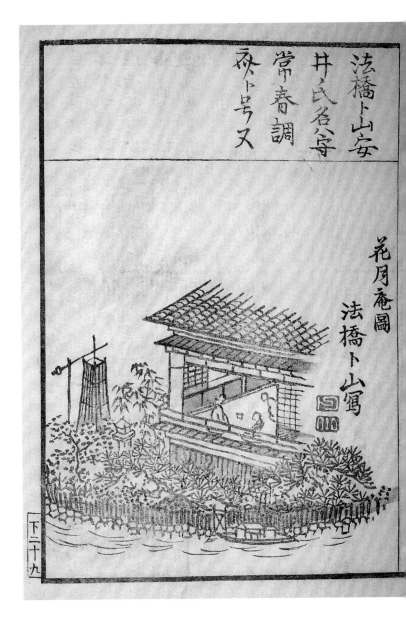

3.15 Yasui Bokuzan, illustrator
(Japan, active early nineteenth century)
Kagetsuan zu (*Picture of Kagetsuan* [*Hermitage of Flowers and Moonlight*]), from the book *Naniwa fūryū hanjōki* (*Records of the Elegant Pleasures of Life in Osaka*), 1830–1844
Woodblock-printed book; ink and light colors on paper
24 x 16 cm
KANSAI UNIVERSITY LIBRARY

Tanaka Kakuō is shown in this print brewing *sencha* by moonlight at his Kagetsuan (Hermitage of Flowers and Moonlight). Kakuō himself was also called Kagetsuan.

3.16 Tanomura Chokunyū (Japan, 1814–1907)
Pictorial Record of Famous Utensils Used at the Azure Sea
Tea Gathering (*Seiwan meien zushi*), 1875
Woodblock-printed book
H: 17 cm
PRIVATE COLLECTION, UNITED STATES

around 1920, a humorous and nostalgic painting that gently mocks the Chinese antiquarian spirit that he and others continued to admire (fig. 3.17). Tessai was one of a small group of purists who preserved the spirit of literati tea well into the twentieth century. During his lifetime others began transforming *sencha* into an etiquette system for women, in an effort to maintain its vitality at a time when *chanoyu* was rapidly superseding *sencha* in popularity.

Although the *sencha* tea ceremony ultimately absorbed many structural elements from *chanoyu*, its underlying aesthetic stems from a very different source, that of the introspective Chinese literati, who sought spiritual fulfillment through communing with nature and strove to express their individuality and spark their intellectual curiosity in morally uplifting pastimes. *Sencha* played an important role in bringing the world of the Chinese literati to life in Japan. In the process of so doing, however, its followers invariably altered its nature as they incorporated Japanese inclinations for ritual and order. Still, elements of the original Chinese literati spirit remain in the appearance of the accoutrements and room furnishings of *sencha*, and even in the institutional structure of its tea schools. More than fifty autonomous schools of *sencha* flourish throughout the country today. Many are led by women, a situation unheard of within the *chanoyu* establishment, and many retain association with Ōbaku Zen through their membership in a *sencha* association at the Ōbaku head temple of Manpukuji.

3.17 Tomioka Tessai (Japan, 1836–1924)
Bihyō mōgun (*Blind Men Critiquing Beauty*),
early 20th century
Hanging scroll; ink and color on silk
22.9 x 29.4 cm
NELSON-ATKINS MUSEUM OF ART, KANSAS CITY, MISSOURI.
GIFT OF I. GROUPP AND JULIEANN WHITE GROUPP, 73-48/2
PHOTOGRAPH BY JOHN LAMBERTON

Reiko Tanimura

THE SACRED AND THE PROFANE

The Role of Women in Edo Period Tea Culture

4

WHEN THE ART CRITIC AND PHILOSOPHER Okakura Kakuzo (1862–1913) chose *wabicha*, the form of *chanoyu* perfected by Sen no Rikyū in the sixteenth century, as a typical example of Japanese arts and the mentality that guided them, he referred to it as "a religion of the art of life" (Okakura 1906). The choice of the term "religion" was apt both metaphorically and historically. *Chanoyu* is replete with rituals, as are many religions, and Buddhism had directly influenced its development in Japan (see Hirota, this volume).

Chanoyu (lit., "tea in hot water"), or the "tea ceremony," as it is popularly referred to in the West, may be defined as a performing art that is created through (1) the drinking of special tea by a host and guest following strict procedures; (2) the employing of specific types of tea utensils; and (3) the use of a defined space, a tea room or tea hut. The host and guest exist at the intersection of these three elements, and the cup of powdered green tea is the symbol of the relationship between the two parties. The roles of host and guest are clearly distinguished, but both participate as equal partners and cooperate in order to create a unique, respectful relationship. Merely drinking tea to satisfy thirst is in no way the same thing as *chanoyu*. *Chanoyu* is defined by its ritual and transforms the drinking of tea into something numinous.

In view of the unique intimacy fostered by the "tea ceremony," it is perhaps not surprising that very few formal records of women's involvement are to be found in the texts on the subject of tea and the voluminous records of tea gatherings that exist dating back to the Edo, or Tokugawa, period (1615–1868). While such sources are useful and deserve examination, it must be recognized that they tell only one story. As a cursory glance through the illustrations in this essay will reveal, other sources tell a different tale.

4.1 *Teinai yuraku zu (Pleasure within the Residence),*
detail, Kyoto, Japan, 17th century
Six-fold standing screen; color on paper
82 x 274.7 cm
SUNTORY MUSEUM OF ART, TOKYO

While a group plays cards in the demimonde, a *kamuro*, or young maid, of about age ten prepares tea. *Kamuro* often served high-ranking courtesans and were in training to become courtesans themselves. Although this is not an instance of *chanoyu*, the girl demonstrates that even at a young age she has already learned the correct procedures for serving tea to guests.

The influence of Confucianism during the Edo period is often adduced as a reason for the lack of female participation in *chanoyu* (as I will discuss in greater detail below). Yet while this paternalistic philosophy certainly impacted female involvement, it also, rather paradoxically, required that women—in addition to producing heirs—meet high cultural standards including some knowledge of *chanoyu*. Meanwhile, away from the world of wives and mothers where Confucian thought had most impact, standing screens portray the pleasures of the demimonde, and Ukiyo-e prints depict high-ranking and cultured courtesans serving tea to their guests in special tea rooms (fig. 4.1). While the existence of such ostensibly "profane" *chanoyu* cannot be ignored, there is very little documentation of it. The records of the sophisticated salons have never been made public, and the activities of prostitutes and common entertainers were rarely, if ever, recorded.

In addition to considering the portrayals of women's tea in works of art, an examination of general texts, literary works, and surviving tea rooms from the period yields a fuller and more accurate picture of the nature and extent of women's participation in *chanoyu*. In this essay I will consider a variety of sources, some of which have only recently come to light, in an attempt to reconstruct women's *chanoyu*. It is also my intention to correct superficial understandings of the role of women in Edo period Japan and by extension in Japanese society, where, ironically, today it is estimated that 90 percent of *chanoyu* practitioners are women.

Women and Tea before
the Development of *Chanoyu*

By the fourteenth century, spectacular tea gatherings restricted to the Japanese political and military elite were held in special rooms decorated with Chinese art and craft objects. These gatherings continued into the fifteenth century. Tea consumption was not yet ritualized at this point, however, and drinking tea remained an entertainment for the upper classes. On the whole, these lavish events were intended only for men, but there is evidence of some involvement by women.

Hino Tomiko (1440–1496), for example, the wife of the eighth Muromachi shogun, Ashikaga Yoshimasa, seems to have enjoyed the tea culture of this period. She is recorded as having donated substantial amounts of tea to the court in 1479 and 1481 (*Oyudono no ue no nikki 1* 1957, 98, 208), and two valuable Chinese tea bowls were among her possessions at the time of her death (*Oyudono no ue no nikki 2* 1958, 497).

Kyōzuin, a member of a major Buddhist Pure Land temple, left records of tea gatherings that she had enjoyed with her family during the Tenmon era (1532–1555; Kagotani 1995, 259–68). She decorated all the rooms in her residence at the temple with valuable Chinese imports following the strict standards set forth by specialists working for the Muromachi shogunate. It is unlikely, however, that either Kyōzuin or Hino Tomiko made tea themselves. Making tea in front of guests was not a job for a noble host or hostess at this time. There-

fore, although these ladies enjoyed tea gatherings, they cannot be said to have participated in *chanoyu*.

The Refinement of *Chanoyu*:
Sen no Rikyū and *Wabicha*

In the sixteenth century, Sen no Rikyū (1522–1591) perfected *wabicha*, a style of *chanoyu* marked by its simplicity and peaceful silence and influenced by Zen thought (See Hirota, this volume). The *wabicha* style of tea is one of the most famous of Japanese performing arts, and it remains the contemporary standard for *chanoyu*.

The descendants of Sen no Rikyū established the three most famous schools of *chanoyu*, known as the Sen schools (see below). These schools still dominate *chanoyu* today as they have for nearly four hundred years. They continue to be run as rigid hierarchies based on the *iemoto* system in which the *iemoto*, or the head of the particular branch of the family, holds the top position and has absolute authority to grant the right to teach the school's methods. Various ranks are achieved by the practitioners, or followers, belonging to the school. The Sen schools are not, however, the only schools of *chanoyu*, as will be seen.

The *wabicha* of Sen no Rikyū especially appealed to the warrior lords engaged in the closing stages of a century of civil wars, and it quickly became popular. Although Sen no Rikyū himself was not a warrior, warriors often looked up to him as a tea master. Many records of tea gatherings held by these warriors survive, and two of them mention women. As far as I have been able to determine, the first of these was held by Kobayaka Takakage (1533–1597) on the twenty-fifth of the ninth month in the fourth year of the Bunroku era, or 1595 (Kamiya 1977, 311–12). Takakage, a retired lord, invited his son Hidetoshi, who was also his successor, and Hidetoshi's wife of ten months to a gathering. The wife and her maids took seats in the main tea room, and Hidetoshi and all the other male guests took tea in another room. The women were entertained for a whole day with tea, sake, and music performed by professional musicians. This gathering demonstrates the unusual consideration that Takakage displayed to his daughter-in-law.

The second tea gathering where a woman was present was held by Hosokawa Sansai (1563–1645) on the fourteenth day of the fifth month in the ninth year of the Kan'ei era, or 1642 (Matsuyama 1974, 239–40). Sansai, a warrior lord, invited a nobleman to a tea gathering at his mansion in Kyoto. There were eight more people present including Sansai's brother, his son, five male guests, and a granddaughter, about whom nothing else is known. Sansai was a famous follower of Rikyū, and it is therefore possible that this gathering might have observed *wabicha* style. Apart from these two instances, I know of no others including women held during this period. These two records indicate that a few women attended *chanoyu* tea gatherings, but only when a family member acted as a host or other family members attended with them.

The Women of the Sen Family

As Sen no Rikyū's fame as a tea master grew, he served as tea ceremony officer for the military leader Oda Nobunaga and for Toyotomi Hideyoshi, who unified Japan following the period of civil wars. From Hideyoshi, Rikyū received extensive landholdings. In 1591, however, for reasons that still remain unclear, Rikyū suddenly fell afoul of his patron and was forced to commit suicide.

Rikyū had two sons, the first of whom did not have male offspring. His second son, Shōan, was a child from the first marriage of Rikyū's second wife, Sō'on. Shōan was adopted by Rikyū, and it is alleged that he married Rikyū's illegitimate daughter and that they in turn had a son named Sōtan (1578–1658). Sōtan succeeded Shōan to the Sen school leadership, and his three sons established three separate lines of Sen families. They were the founders of the Omotesenke, Urasenke, and Mushanokōjisenke schools that still exist today. Even though the marriage of Rikyū's daughter and his stepson, Shōan, was not openly acknowledged, the lineage of the Sen family can be said to have been transmitted through the female line.

We know little of Rikyū's first marriage, but his second wife, Sō'on, is said to have understood her husband well and to have frequently given him beneficial advice. Although no record of tea gatherings performed by Sō'on has been found, anecdotal evidence connects her to *chanoyu*. Her great-grandson Kōshin wrote that she permanently revised the size of the silk cloth used at the tea ceremony (Kōshin 1975, 84), and according to the *Chawa shigetsu shū* (Kusumi [1701] 1975, 212), when Rikyū and Sō'on talked about the height of the incense burner used in the tea room, they immediately recognized that the same idea had occurred to them simultaneously. These traditions portray Sō'on as certainly familiar with *wabicha* and as an important supporting figure to her husband.

In 1591, when Rikyū committed suicide, Sōtan, his grandson, was only thirteen years old and a student at a Zen temple. When permission was granted for restoration of the Sen family following Rikyū's death, Sōtan returned home and with his father, Shōan, worked toward the revival of Rikyū's style of *chanoyu*. Sōtan took over leadership of the family from his father in 1600. That same year the Toyotomi clan was defeated by Tokugawa Ieyasu, who was designated shogun by the emperor and transferred the seat of government from Kyoto to Edo (present-day Tokyo). In addition he established a rigid Confucian-based social hierarchy with the samurai class at the top and no possible upward mobility for merchants, artisans, or farmers (see Graham, this volume). Even wealthy merchants and townsmen had no way to improve their class standing. One outlet for achieving greater status within one's own class, however, was to gain rank within a tea school. *Chanoyu*, as noted earlier, was greatly appreciated by the warrior class, and now it was coveted by those who wished to emulate them. Thus *chanoyu* can be said to have acquired a "profane" aspect even as practiced by men, for it came to serve as a means of personal, as well as commercial, advancement in addition to presenting the opportunity for establishing a unique relationship between host and guest.

While Sōtan is a central figure in the Sen family history, until recently not so much as the name of his wife was known. Documents recently discovered in the Omotesenke archives, however, have shed light on this (Omotesenke 2008). Sōtan married his second wife, Sōken, before 1612. While he himself avoided direct involvement with the shogun or powerful lords—possibly in view of his grandfather's fate—he encouraged his sons to build such relationships after he retired.

Some interesting differences in perspective between Sōtan and his wife Sōken are recorded. For example, when one of his sons finished constructing a teahouse for a member of the shogun's family, the Tokugawa, Sōtan expressed the hope that the son would be successful as a tea specialist. Sōken, however, sent a letter to the same son hoping that the lord would be fond of the teahouse and give him an additional reward (Omotesenke 2008, 348). Sōken also requested that her son send money to her quickly because she had to prepare for New Year's Day (Omotesenke 2008, 354).

Surviving letters from Sōtan show signs that he was often depressed, and he sometimes complained to his sons that Sōken was loud and sarcastic (Omotesenke 2008, 238, 240). These letters counter the notion that Edo-period Japanese women were universally submissive and oppressed by men. Sōken, by contrast, seems not only to have felt free to express herself but also to have controlled the household finances. In addition she took care of her daughter's son, who was adopted to become the head of the Sen family. Her letters show that she encouraged her grandson to practice *chanoyu* and observed him carefully and lovingly (Omotesenke 2008, 356, 359). After her sons started serving the domain lords as tea specialists, necessitating absences from home, she seems to have become even more involved in the family business, and she herself described the process of selling a tea bowl for one hundred *ryō* to one of her sons (Omotesenke 2008, 363–64).

Although Sōtan lived as a commoner, he did have a special relationship with Empress Tōfukumon'in (1607–1678). Handicrafts that the empress made and gave to Sōtan have been preserved at the Sen house, and Sōtan presented a tea stand to her. It is unclear what prompted such a special relationship between the empress and a commoner, and although it cannot be verified, it is now thought that Sōken may have been one of Tōfukumon'in's ladies-in-waiting. A letter written by Sōken in 1650 (Omotesenke 2008, 350) records that Tōfukumon'in told Sōtan to select various tea utensils for her. This recently published letter has, for the first time, revealed that the commoner Sōtan procured tea utensils for the empress. Considering all the surviving evidence, it seems clear that Sōken also had a special connection with Tōfukumon'in.

Over the centuries each Sen house accumulated innumerable documents, records of tea gatherings, and tea utensils. Even by the end of the Edo period—the middle of the nineteenth century—however, only a few names of women can be found in the lists of followers of the Sen schools (Geinōshi Kenkyū Kai 1976, 715–30). Hundreds of tea gatherings for men were recorded by the Sen families, but only a few that

women attended. It is nonetheless clear from the examples of Sō'on and Sōken that at least some women of the Sen families actively supported the heads of the houses and their heirs in the family business. The Sen families have not to date been especially keen to open their archives to the public, but as more scholars gain access, the history and roles played by the Sen women will become clearer.

Court Ladies and Tea

Both Empress Tōfukumon'in and her husband, the 108th emperor Go-mizuno'o, were known to enjoy *chanoyu* with their family, and as noted above, the empress had a personal connection with Rikyū's grandson, Sōtan, and his wife. One of the daughters of Tōfukumon'in, Princess Shina no miya (1642–1702), also possessed a good knowledge of tea (Tanihata 2005, 281–87). She married the noble Konoe Motohiro (1648–1722), and the couple held tea gatherings together. Most of the tea gatherings in which she participated were held in aristocratic villas and attended only by relatives of the emperor. They harked back to fifteenth-century tea gatherings held before the development of *chanoyu* (Seigle 2002, 4–13). Tōfukumon'in and Shina no miya seem to have been leaders of women's tea culture in the court at this time.

Members of the closed society of the court had intermarried since the seventh century, and they lived within a confined area of Kyoto. Court ladies often attended tea gatherings held by court nobles, and they enjoyed companionship with other guests, including males. It seems, however, that they were interested neither in the philosophy of *chanoyu* nor in creating fresh relationships through tea gatherings. Tea culture was simply a fashionable amusement for them, and it was thought to lack the classical roots of such pastimes as composing poems, playing the *yakobue* (a Japanese flute), or calligraphy. As a consequence, these aristocrats soon lost interest in tea culture, and its leadership passed to the Sen houses and samurai (Tanihata 2005).

Tea and *Tayū*

In the Edo period, *chanoyu* was performed by *tayū*, who were highly regarded entertainers of the demimonde and worked in areas such as Shimabara in Kyoto, where various kinds of sophisticated arts were developed. From the early Edo period on, the term *tayū* had been used to refer to an elite group of women who trained in many disciplines beginning at an early age and were far from being merely prostitutes. By the late Edo period, starting around 1760, *tayū* had in fact become so proud of their rank that they stopped dancing and playing musical

4.2   Yoshiiku Ochiai (Japan, 1833–1904),
       Gokakoku…Gankirō ni oite sakamori no zu
       (*Five Nations…Merrymaking at the Gankirō Teahouse*), 1860
       Woodblock print (triptych); ink on paper
       Each block: 36.5 x 24.5 cm
       CHADBOURNE COLLECTION OF JAPANESE PRINTS, LIBRARY OF CONGRESS,
       WASHINGTON, D.C., NO. FP 2–CHADBOURNE, NO. 101A,B,C

Following the Kanagawa Treaty of 1854, which opened Japan to international trade, foreigners became increasingly present in Japan. This print depicts Gankirō, one of the most famous and luxurious entertainment establishments in Yokohama, which was one of the first ports opened to foreigners. The atmosphere at Gankirō was very different from that of the seventeenth-century Shimabara discussed later in this essay.

instruments, such as the samisen, for their guests. Music and dance were instead performed by geisha, who were specialists in these arts.

In addition to their personal beauty and exquisite attire, *tayū* had to achieve a high level of skill at calligraphy, flower arrangement, performing the tea ceremony, dancing, singing, composing poems, playing musical instruments, and so forth. While maintaining a certain dignity, they were also expected to open their hearts to each of their guests. The *tayū* had to appear to be the ideal woman, highly sophisticated and completely conversant with the social graces. They fascinated court nobles and wealthy merchants in Kyoto, particularly during the seventeenth century.

One *tayū*, Yoshino (1606–1643), acheived fame as the favorite of the top-ranked noble Konoe Nobuhiro (1599–1649), although she eventually married Haiya Shōeki, a wealthy and cultured merchant. A textile, *Yoshino kandō*, was named after her, and the novelist Ihara Saikaku drew inspiration from her for *Kōshoku ichi-dai otoko* (*The Life of an Amorous Man*), his fictional masterpiece. With respect to *chanoyu*, it is said that Yoshino preferred to use a two-mat tea room with a large round window. It is in fact suspected that the two-mat tea room of Kōdai-ji Temple in Kyoto was once hers, although this cannot be verified.

Tea in the *Ageya*

Tea was served in a variety of establishments during the Edo period. The *chaya* (teahouse), a term now obsolete in Japan, indicated a place for entertaining people, usually an establishment where tea and meals were served to customers. A sumo *chaya*, for example, would serve those who came to watch a sumo match. Instead of the expensive powdered green tea of *chanoyu*, cheaper and inferior boiled tea was served at a *chaya* (fig. 4.3). Over the course of the Edo period, however, the word *chaya* gradually shifted in meaning to suggest a place where sexual favors were provided (fig. 4.2). The *chaya* has often been mistakenly conflated with the *ageya* from which it differs markedly.

The *ageya* was a completely different environment, one that catered to a much more refined clientele. *Ageya* were elegant restaurants or salons where banquets and dinner parties were held accompanied by the entertainments of geisha and *tayū*. Some extant Ukiyo-e prints depict a *tayū* performing a tea ceremony for her guest in a special tea room within an *ageya* (fig. 4.4).

The novel *Tōkaidō meishō ki* (*The Reports of the Tōkaidō Road*)—the title of which refers to the road running from Kyoto to Tokyo—was published in 1660/1661 and includes a description of a tea ceremony performed at an *ageya* by a *tayū*

4.3   Suzuki Harunobu (Japan, 1725–1770)
Kasamori Osen, 18th century
Woodblock print
19 x 29.3 cm
TOKYO NATIONAL MUSEUM, A-10569-143

There were various types of *chaya* in the Edo period, and some of them were depicted in works of art, particularly if popular girls worked there. This establishment, where a famous beauty named Osen (shown at the center of the print) worked, was a large *chaya* near Kasamori shrine in Yanaka. The red columns in the background are the entrance to the shrine. The two clients at the right are samurai and clearly interested in Osen.

named Yachiyo (Asai [1682] 2002, 200–201). Within the novel, the narrator reports that Yachiyo used a tea room and tea utensils the like of which he had never seen and that she made tea so excellently and with such elegance that it seemed as if a goddess had descended from the heavens to do so. Although this is clearly a work of fiction, the author intended that his account appear credible to his readers, even if they could never hope to experience such a memorable event.

The character Yachiyo was, in fact, modeled upon a real seventeenth-century *tayū*. The historical Yachiyo produced some masterpieces of calligraphy, reproducing classic poems composed in the Japanese medieval period (fig. 4.5). Her portrait has resided for several centuries at Sumiya (fig. 4.6), a surviving example of an *ageya* located in Shimabara in Kyoto (figs. 4.7–4.14). In order to get a better sense of Yachiyo's *chanoyu*, it is helpful to examine four extant tea rooms at Sumiya: two Kakoi-no-ma (one on the first and one on the second floor in the main building) and Kyokuboku-tei and Seiinsai Chaseki (two tea huts in the garden).

The Kakoi-no-ma (The Enclosed Space) on the first floor of Sumiya is thought to have been remodeled, based upon the tea room of a Zen temple, in 1787 (fig. 4.9). Architecturally, it follows some of the norms of a formal tea room, for

4.4   Isoda Koryu-sai (Japan, active 1764–1789)
       Chashitsu (room for tea ceremony), late 18th century
       Woodblock print
       29.3 x 19 cm
       TOKYO NATIONAL MUSEUM, A-10569-3990

A *tayū* prepares to perform *chanoyu* in a tea room as a guest enters through
the *nijiriguchi*, or "crawling-in entrance." The decor of this tea room clearly
departs from the austere *wabicha* aesthetics advocated by Sen no Rikyū.

4.5   Yachiyo (Japan, b. 1635; retired 1658) and the tayū Kofuji
       (Japan, b. 1622; retired 1644) and Kaoru (Japan, active 1655–1660)
       Calligraphy, Kyoto, seventeenth century
       Ink on paper
       31.7 x 622 cm
       SUMIYA HOZON KAI

This is an excellent example of the elegant calligraphy produced by *tayū*.

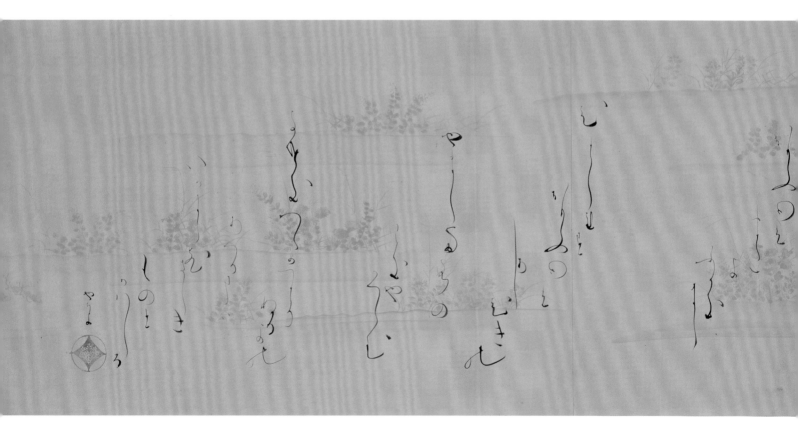

instance having *tsukubai*, a water basin for ritual cleansing, at the entrance; a *nijiriguchi*, a small door referred to as the "crawling-in" entrance; and a *tokonoma*, or an alcove.

By contrast, the red wall of the Kakoi-no-ma on the second floor (fig. 4.10) might initially appear strikingly original. In the first half of the Edo period, however, some locales, usually those having a public function, were decorated in this manner. Examples of such red walls exist in the villas of the emperor (among them the Villa of Katsura) and temples (Hiun-kaku in Nishi Honganji Temple). Even though it is not without precedent, the color choice does create a rather remarkable impression in the context of a tea room.

Kyokuboku-tei (The Hut of Bent Logs) has a more complicated and unique appearance due to the fact that, apart from the floor and a small section of the wall, it is made completely of bent wood and curved beams fitted together (fig. 4.11). It therefore tends to put the viewer somewhat off balance. Although this tea hut is very different from ordinary tea rooms, it is clear that the sixth head of the Omotesenke endorsed its construction. Traditionally the Japanese hung wooden boards showing the name of the room or house at an entrance. A board reading "Kyokuboku-tei" that was written by the sixth head of Omotesenke still hangs at the entrance of the hut (fig. 4.12). Based on the year of his death, Kyokuboku-tei is thought to have been built before 1730.

Seiinsai Chaseki (The Tea Room of Silence and Loneliness; fig.4.13) is thought to have been designed by the famous tea master Yasutomi Tsunemichi Seiin-sai (1715–1788), who married a daughter of the head of the Yabunouchi tea school, which possessed a high reputation and was founded at the same time as the Sen schools. The facade of this tea hut has a rustic appearance, but the inside is unique. Ordinarily the floors of Japanese tea rooms are square or rectangular and covered with tatami mats, but the floor of this room is irregular and one of the segments is actually triangular (fig. 4.14).

There is a unique quality to all four of these *chanoyu* environments at Sumiya. The two tea huts in fact differ markedly from conventional tea rooms. The other rooms of Sumiya are also highly original and beautifully executed to the extent that the building's style as a whole might be deemed excessive. It is interesting, however, that famous tea masters, the sixth head of the Omotesenke and a member of the Yabunouchi, whose styles of *chanoyu* were considered orthodox, apparently endorsed the construction of the tea rooms and huts at Sumiya. These two tea masters definitely accepted the tea performed by *tayū*, and their attitude toward it seems more positive than might have been expected. It is also known that the owners of Sumiya used these rooms for *chanoyu* and for gatherings where haiku were composed (Nakagawa 2002, 29–31). This would seem to indicate that the gap between the *chanoyu* of *tayū* and "ordinary" *chanoyu* was not unbridgeable. Considering the valuable tea utensils and unique tea rooms preserved at Sumiya, we can see that even though the tea performed by *tayū* was different from *wabicha*, it was not merely the drinking of tea, but *chanoyu*.

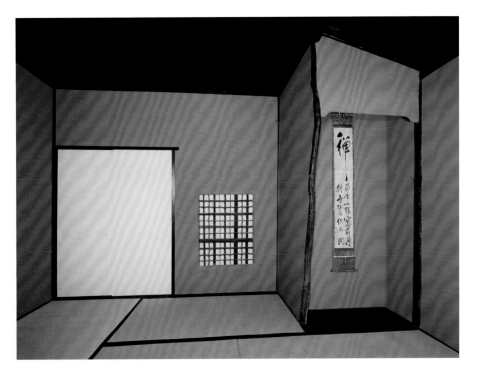

CLOCKWISE FROM UPPER LEFT

4.7 This view of the facade of Sumiya, a famous *ageya* in the Shimabara district of Kyoto, gives a sense of the size of the establishment (see fig. 4.8). SUMIYA HOZON KAI.

4.8 This side door of Sumiya (see fig. 4.7) is hung with long red *noren* (curtains) and leads to a kitchen. The gold design featuring three ivy leaves on the *noren* is the family crest of Sumiya. SUMIYA HOZON KAI.

4.9 The Kakoi-no-ma tea room on the first floor at Sumiya was next to the owner's private room. Successive owners are known to have held haiku-composing gatherings in it. It seems to have served a more private function than the three remaining tea rooms in the Sumiya. SUMIYA HOZON KAI.

4.10 The red wall of the Kakoi-no-ma on the second floor of Sumiya is striking, but it would not have been unprecedented in the first half of the Edo period. The pole supporting the alcove is slender and bent and contributes to the novel impression conveyed by the room. SUMIYA HOZON KAI.

OPPOSITE

4.6 Portrait of Yachiyo, Kyoto, Japan, 17th century
Hanging scroll; ink and color on paper
81.7 x 33.2 cm
SUMIYA HOZON KAI

The *tayū* Yachiyo was known for her calligraphy (see fig. 4.5). She also appeared as a character in the fictional *Reports of the Tōkaidō Road* (1660/1661), where her performance of *chanoyu* was described in the most glowing of terms.

CLOCKWISE FROM UPPER LEFT

4.11 The Kyokuboku-tei tea hut on the grounds of Sumiya efficiently combines pieces of bent wood. The wooden board bearing its name (see fig. 4.12) was written by the sixth head of the Omotesenke, Kaku kaku sai (1678–1730). SUMIYA HOZON KAI.

4.12 A close-up view of the entrance to Kyokuboku-tei (see fig. 4.11) reveals the inscribed wooden board in greater detail. SUMIYA HOZON KAI.

4.13 The Sumiya tea hut known as Seiinsai Chaseki is thought to have been designed by the tea master Yasutomi Tsunemichi Seiin'sai (1715–1788), who had a close relationship with the Yabunouchi family. SUMIYA HOZON KAI.

4.14 The interior of the Seiinsai Chaseki tea hut (see fig. 4.13) reveals an irregular floor pattern with a triangular segment directly under the window. SUMIYA HOZON KAI.

In volume seven of the previously mentioned *Life of an Amorous Man* by Ihara Saikaku, the narrator describes a tea ceremony performed by Takahashi, a *tayū*, at an *ageya* called Hachimonjiya. This establishment no longer survives, but it was formerly, like Sumiya, one of the leading *ageya* in Shimabara. In Saikaku's day *ageya* were relatively small-scale institutions, so it is not clear how closely his account was based on reality. It does, however, reveal what Saikaku, and by extension his readers, thought was appropriate, or ideal, tea for a *tayū*:

> On the morning of the first snow, Takahashi suddenly came up with the idea of holding a tea ceremony. The hanging scroll in the tea room always suggests the issue of the day's ceremony, but a blank scroll was hung that day. Some tea utensils were new, but they would be thrown away after the ceremony. These utensils were only for the guests of that day. Takahashi sent a servant to a famous riverside in order to draw fresh water and the guests appreciated this gesture very much. When all the guests had settled in the room, she started the ceremony by asking each of them to compose haiku, a short poem, and to write it down on the blank scroll. During the intermission, while the guests were relaxing outside the room, she announced the latter half of the ceremony by playing a samisen cheerfully. This style of announcement was so fresh and unique that the guests enjoyed it very much. When they returned to the room they found a vase without any flowers. The guests supposed that the *tayū* were the best flowers for the day. Takahashi made tea so delicately that the guests said it was as if they had seen Rikyū himself making tea. After the tea ceremony, the guests became more relaxed and started drinking sake. [Ihara (1682) 1996, 198–99][1]

Although tea ceremonies held at *ageya* are apt to be thought of as a simple commercial means to entertain guests, it is clear that the tea performed by *tayū* was not merely a prelude to other intimacies. Rather, it was full of deliberate and ingenious devices invented by the *tayū* to create a sophisticated personal relationship with each guest. The *tayū* followed the strict procedures for making tea and used special tea utensils and rooms. Clearly, both the *chanoyu* practiced by the tea schools and that practiced by the *tayū* had important personal and commercial ramifications, and both inspired artists, poets, and novelists through their use of ritual. Given the approbation that extant literature and artworks of the period seem to give to the practice of *chanoyu* by *tayū*, one is led to wonder what prevented ordinary women from performing it more frequently and openly.

Confucian Thought and Edo Period Women

As noted at the beginning of this essay, the relatively small number of Edo period women who are documented as performing *chanoyu* is often attributed to the pervasiveness of

Confucian thought. The Confucian perspective on *chanoyu* was, however, ambiguous, as a brief survey of literature intended for the education of women and girls will demonstrate. *Onna daigaku* (*Instruction for Girls*) was first published between 1716 and 1736, and it is representative of texts aimed at Edo period women and girls. The following passages are especially relevant to the practice of *chanoyu*:

> From her earliest youth a girl should observe the line of demarcation separating women from men, and never, even for an instant, should she be allowed to see or hear the least impropriety. The customs of antiquity did not allow men and women to sit in the same chamber, to keep their wearing apparel in the same place, to bathe in the same place, or to pass anything to each other directly from hand to hand.... Of tea and wine she must not drink over much.... She should strictly adhere to the rule of separation between the sexes. [*Onna daigaku* 1980, 202–5]

Women in the Edo period followed these rules so that their behavior would not be misunderstood by others. Some literary works deal with such "misunderstandings" resulting specifically from *chanoyu*. Perhaps the most noteworthy of these is a *bunraku* puppet play written by Chikamatsu Monzaemon (1653–1724) and titled *Yari no Gonza kasane katabira* (*The Double Suicide of Archer Gonza*)—first performed in 1717. Osai, the heroine of the play, is the wife of a samurai tea master whose family has passed down a secret *temae* (the advanced procedures of *chanoyu*). The hero, Gonza, is a young samurai who has been asked to serve the guests at a formal tea gathering to celebrate the wedding of his lord's son. In order to make a good impression on his lord, Gonza asks Osai to show him the documents describing the *temae*. She finally agrees, on the condition that Gonza marry her daughter and join her family, and she asks him to meet her in the tea room late at night. When someone spreads insinuating rumors about their meeting, however, the couple is driven to a double suicide even though there was nothing illicit in their behavior (Chikamatsu 1998, 585–687).

From the play we learn that Osai knew where her husband kept the record of the secret *temae*, although she seems not to have learned the procedures herself. This is in keeping with what we know of the women of the Sen family, who appear to have supported the male tea practitioners in their family but were not expected to perform *chanoyu* themselves.

Onna chōhōki (*The Record of Women's Great Treasures*) is a unique text read by women at all levels of society from about 1700 to 1850 (Arima et al. [1692] 1989). It treats the everyday lifestyle of women in considerable practical detail. Volume 4 specifically encourages women to learn some arts: "Calligraphy. Composing poems.... Playing board games. Practicing the art of incense. Practicing *chanoyu*. Composing linked verses and haiku.... Studying hairdressing. Studying the proper way to discipline maids." While it is clear that this influential book

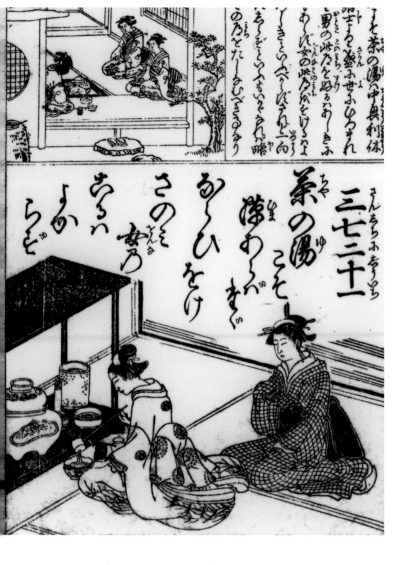

4.15 Instruction in *chanoyu*, from *Onna kuku no koe*
(*First Instructive Songs for Women*), Japan, 1787
Woodblock-printed book
14 x 21 cm
WASAN-KENKYU JYO (WASAN INSTITUTE), NO. 132

encouraged women to learn *chanoyu*, it contains no descrip-tion of tea other than that provided under the heading "How to Drink Tea": "You should take a cup from the teacup stand with your right hand. After drinking, transfer it to your left hand and then put it on the tatami mat. The waitress takes it and places it back on the teacup stand. When the tea is hot, you should sip the tea moderately, and not wave the cup around" (Arima et al. [1692] 1989, 51). *Onna chōhōki* describes how to drink tea in a social setting, but it clearly has no detailed infor-mation on the specific features of *chanoyu*. In contrast *Otoko chōhōki* (*The Record of Men's Great Treasures*), written by the same author, described the detailed procedures for *chanoyu* and illustrated how to place tea utensils (Nihon Shigaku Kyōiku Kenkyūjo 1985, 142–46).

In another text for women published in 1787 (fig. 4.15), *Onna kuku no koe* (*First Instructive Songs for Women*), the author remarks that

> Generally speaking, *chanoyu* has spread over Japan since Rikyū perfected its style. It is not bad for men to enjoy it, but it cannot be good for women to do so. However, it may also not be good for women to know nothing about it. This is why women should know a little *chanoyu* and it may be good for women who have much free time to learn it. However, it is not good for women to be addicted to it. [2]

Men with a particular interest in *chanoyu* belonged to a tea school and increased in rank there, but women were not expected to gain either advanced skills or school rank. Women seem to have learned the basics of *chanoyu* just in order to learn proper manners, to appear cultivated, and to gratify their family, or, in the case of servants, to serve their masters. Thus, it seems that Confucian views of proper behavior for women at least prevented them from performing *chanoyu* among people outside the family and from using tea rooms and tea utensils freely.

The End of the Edo Period
By the end of the Edo period, in the mid-nineteenth century, the number of women who learned *chanoyu* seems to have increased (figs. 4.16, 4.17). In 1825 some women's names appear in the list of followers of the Horinouchi school, which was part of the Omotesenke (Geinōshi Kenkyū Kai 1976, 715–30). Nineteenth-century textbooks for women give more details of *chanoyu* (e.g., *Onna shōrei ayanishiki* 1841 and other texts; see also Ōmori 1993, 290–95), and nuns and wives of Bud-dhist priests had *chanoyu* lessons in the countryside (Takai 1991, 37–41).

4.16   Keisai Eisen (Japan, 1791–1848)
        Ro-biraki (*Opening of the Fireplace in October*),
        from Jūnikagetsu nishikie (Twelve Months of Ladies),
        second half of 18th century
        Woodblock-printed book
        25.4 x 18 cm
        NATIONAL DIET LIBRARY, NO. 2-8-2-1

The hairstyle of this woman does not suggest that she belonged to the samurai class, and her rank remains unclear. She is not a *tayū*, but she could be either a geisha or a commoner.

4.17   Utagawa Toyokuni (Japan, 1769–1825)
        Nijū-yon konomi imayō bijin (*One of the Twenty-four Women*),
        late Edo period, 19th century
        Woodblock-printed book
        37.4 x 23.5 cm
        NATIONAL DIET LIBRARY, KIBETSU, NO. 2-7-2-2

This appears to be a high-ranking woman from the samurai class. While she is clearly engaged in the preparation of tea, it is not possible to determine the tea school to which she adheres.

On an individual level, some remarkable women—often members of the families of wealthy merchants and farmers—learned *chanoyu* as a sophisticated accomplishment (fig. 4.18). Their teachers were most commonly the wives of Buddhist priests or nuns who ran temples themselves. Among these talented and exceptional women was the poet Ōtagaki Rengetsu (1791–1875). She was adopted by the Ōtagaki, a samurai family serving at Chion-in Temple in Kyoto. From ages eight to sixteen, she served the Matsudaira family as a lady-in-waiting at Kameoka castle in Tanba. Surrounded by other cultivated women, she developed talent in the areas of poetry and calligraphy. It is probable as well that she had the opportunity to learn *chanoyu* in this environment and would have had access to more refined tea utensils than many other women.

As her adoptive family did not have an heir, Rengetsu eventually returned to her home. There she married twice, her second husband dying when she was only thirty-two. It was at this time that she became a Buddhist nun, adopting the name Rengetsu (Lotus Moon) and establishing a reputation as a poet. She is known to have taught poetry to *tayū* in Shimabara, and she wrote at least one poem inspired by the area. Rengetsu later began to make tea ware for use in the Chinese-inspired *sencha* tea ceremony (see Graham, this volume, for an in-depth discussion of *sencha*). Some of the tea utensils she made for herself still survive (Fister 1988, 144–55). The reclusive life that Rengetsu led as a nun allowed her the freedom to develop her natural talents.

Although the Sen schools were very influential in the Edo period, they were not considered proper for the samurai class to attend as samurai could not be subordinate to the commoners who ran the schools. The school considered appropriate for

samurai was the Sekishū school, founded by the daimyo, or domain lord, Katagiri Sekishū (1605–1673). Sekishū did not follow the *iemoto* system and establish a house and hierarchy like the Sen; rather, when a student was sufficiently talented, he was recognized as a master and allowed to establish his own school. One such Sekishū master, Ōguchi Shō'ō (1689–1764), was the author of *Tōji-no-tamoto* (*Senior Lady's Sleeves*), a text on tea for women dated 1721 (Nomura 1985, 188–223). Using Rikyū's wife Sō'on as an example to demonstrate that women had the necessary character for *chanoyu*, he proceeded to describe tea utensils, procedures, and manners for both the hostess and guest. Although he emphasized that women should observe strict manners with men in order to avoid misunderstandings, he did describe the way in which a woman should share a cup of tea with a man: she should put the cup on the floor and pass it to the man instead of handing the cup to him directly. Thus, Ōguchi clearly imagined women not only hosting tea gatherings, but also entertaining men at them.

In the records of a prominent later follower of the Sekishū school, we can see that this actually happened. Ii Naosuke (1815–1860), a member of a powerful domain family and a major political figure, recorded more than 170 tea gatherings in his life, including 34 tea gatherings with women present (Tanihata 1996). As noted earlier, there are very few such records, so these are very valuable.

There were normally five participants, including Naosuke, and on average two were women. There are thirty different female names, most of them occurring several times. Some of these women were members of Naosuke's family, including his two concubines, and many of the rest were ladies-in-waiting. The other male and female guests may have been friends.

OPPOSITE

4.18   Masayuki Shinsai (Japan, 1760–1848)
        Two women at a ceremony; one teaching another
        the serving of tea, undated
        Woodblock print; ink on paper
        13.97 x 18.73 cm
        SCRIPPS COLLEGE, PURCHASED BY THE AOKI ENDOWMENT
        FOR JAPANESE ARTS AND CULTURES, NO. 2000.1.15

Toward the end of the Edo period, the number of women who practiced *chanoyu* seems to have increased. On an individual level, some women—often members of the families of wealthy merchants and farmers—began to learn the art of tea as a sophisticated form of entertainment.

ABOVE

4.19   Yōshū Chikanobu (Japan, ca. 1838–1912)
        Womens Activities of the Tokugawa Era: Tea Ceremony,
        circa 1896–1897
        Woodblock print (triptych); ink on paper
        35.56 x 72.07 cm
        SCRIPPS COLLEGE, PURCHASED BY THE AOKI ENDOWMENT
        FOR JAPANESE ARTS AND CULTURES, NO. 2006.1.7

This woodblock print was created during the Meiji period, about twenty years following the collapse of the Edo government. It reflects a sense of nostalgia for the sophisticated culture that existed among the families of high-ranked Edo period samurai. The woman seated at the left, a member of the samurai class, prepares tea for her guests.

Eight of the thirty-four gatherings were conducted by hostesses, and Naosuke's daughter hosted two of the eight. The hostesses seem to have chosen the tea utensils themselves, and while these were neither time-honored nor valuable, they revealed a seasonal sensibility and refined tastes. Women also preferred to use personally significant utensils, for instance gifts from or pieces made by Naosuke.

While we know that Naosuke sometimes taught his style of tea to ladies-in-waiting himself (Nakamura [1914] 1978, 40) and that he personally followed the guidelines in *Toji-no-tamoto*, women of Naosuke's school seem not to have been given either rank or title. They were, however, treated as followers of the school, their attendance was recorded, and records of tea gatherings run by women were maintained just as for men's gatherings.

Naosuke was a consistent advocate for samurai culture as practiced in *chanoyu* and attempted to restore the spirit of the Japanese warrior (Tanimura 2004, 137–50). Through his promotion of women's tea, he portrayed an ideal, spiritual mentality for samurai women (fig. 4.19), and he encouraged women to develop a sensitivity to their surroundings (Tanimura 2001, 202–3). With the beginning of the Meiji period in 1868, however, samurai culture was effectively destroyed, and the Sekishū school lost its influence. Despite this, respectable women continued to learn *chanoyu* as a proper accomplishment (fig. 4.20). The stance toward it, however, gradually came to approximate that of Western families in the Victorian era toward piano lessons (fig. 4.21). In other words, *chanoyu* gradually became a social nicety devoid of much of its original content and purpose.

4.20   Toyohara Kunichika (Japan, 1835–1900)
Tea Ceremony, 1883
Woodblock print; color on paper
36.8 x 24.4 cm
LOS ANGELES COUNTY MUSEUM OF ART,
GIFT OF S. SHIMIZU, NO. M.74.104.2
PHOTOGRAPH ©2009 MUSEUM ASSOCIATES/LACMA

4.21   Ogata Gekko (Japan, 1859–1920)
The tea ceremony from the series Fujin Fuzoku Zukushi
(Women's Customs and Manners), 1897
Woodblock print: ink on paper
32.5 x 22 cm
SCRIPPS COLLEGE, PURCHASED BY THE AOKI ENDOWMENT
FOR JAPANESE ARTS AND CULTURES, NO. 2001.2.89

Although at first the woman in this print might appear to be from the
late Edo period, her Western-style wedding ring reveals that the print
was created later, during the Meiji era (1868–1912) when the custom of
wearing a ring of this sort first appeared in Japan. She is enjoying the
practice of *chanoyu*, which would have been considered a sophisticated
accomplishment at the time Kunichika created this print.

CLOCKWISE FROM UPPER LEFT

4.22   The chapel of the convent of the Congregatio Sororum Missionariarum Cordis Jesu (The Congregation of the Missionary Sisters of the Heart of Jesus) is located in Kamakura. PHOTOGRAPH BY REIKO TANIMURA, JAPAN, 2008.

4.23   The facade of the main tea room with a wooden board bearing the name of the mission's founder Joseph Reiner. The Japanese characters were written by a woman tea master of the Sekishū order. PHOTOGRAPH BY REIKO TANIMURA, KAMAKURA, JAPAN, 2008.

4.24   In the interior of the main tea room, the transom bears the signature and exhortation of the missions's founder Joseph Reiner: "Seid edel, trau und gut" (Be dignified, faithful, and good). PHOTOGRAPH BY REIKO TANIMURA, KAMAKURA, JAPAN, 2008.

4.25   The interior of the main tea room contains a hanging scroll and a statue of the Virgin Mary atop a built-in desk. The scroll reads: "*Banri ichijyō no testsu*" (A line of iron through the ten-thousand-mile road). This saying—employed by Zen priests—refers to the act of concentrating singlemindedly without giving in to distraction. The founder of the Sekishū tea school, Katagiri Sekishū, is said to have gained inspiration from these words. PHOTOGRAPH BY REIKO TANIMURA, KAMAKURA, JAPAN, 2008.

This trend toward trivializing the performance of *chanoyu* by women was maintained until the years following World War II. The defeat provoked revolutionary social changes in Japan, and instead of just enjoying themselves through the performance of *chanoyu*, women became eager to gain rank and title in a specific tea school. Discussing the population of the *chanoyu* community in 1998, sociologist Etsuko Katō has noted that "a high ranking *chanoyu* teacher of the Urasenke school in Tokyo teaches 300 pupils, about 15 of whom are men while about 285 are women practitioners" (Katō 2004, 98–99). Most female tea practitioners today are housewives who are not particularly wealthy. They turn to *chanoyu* as a field where they can achieve and be formally recognized by an authority, the head of the tea school. One has to wonder, again, however, how far the true meaning of *chanoyu,* of creating a relationship over a cup of tea, has been preserved. At present, the popularity of *chanoyu* among younger women seems to be eroding, as further social changes offer them an ever-expanding array of careers and pastimes.

The Sacred in Women's Tea

There is at least one instance in which women may have led *chanoyu*, via a rather unexpected route, back to its numinous beginnings and away from the pursuit of rank and status. In a Catholic convent located in Kamakura, near Tokyo (fig. 4.22), there are several tea rooms. These range from a room of fifty-four tatami mats to one of only two tatami mats. They are not open to the public. The main tea room is called the Reiners Room, after the priest who founded the mission. Above the entrance door of the tea room, there is a wooden board written by a female tea master of the Sekishū school (fig. 4.23). The transom bears a copy of the founder's signature and exhortation (fig. 4.24), and a scroll written by a Zen monk hangs in the alcove. On the built-in desk beside the alcove stands an abstract sculpture of the Virgin Mary in prayer. It is a simple room with a peaceful atmosphere (fig. 4.25).

The tea rooms are special places for nuns to pray and meditate, particularly during retreats. They learn the procedures of the Sekishū school, but when they can make tea following the procedure without thinking, they stop taking lessons. They do not seek rank in the school, and the school respects them so much that it would never require this of them. The tea rooms are places for nuns to pray for peace in the world and to communicate with God.

The encounter between the nun and God has in this case replaced the interaction between host and guest central to *chanoyu*. Ii Naosuke said that the final aim of his tea was to grasp the absolute reality that makes up the phenomenal world. He called this *dokuza kan'nen* (seated alone in meditation). The nuns seem to have independently rediscovered his concept and to have restored the "sacred" to the experience of *chanoyu*. The history of women's *chanoyu* is long and complicated, and it remains partially obscured. In the peaceful tea rooms at this convent, however, the true meaning of *chanoyu* is preserved. ❧

part 3

The Tea Craze

IN THE WEST

Beatrice Hohenegger

FOR THOUSANDS OF YEARS, tea was regarded as one of the seven daily necessities in China—drunk at every occasion, celebrated in poetry and art, and offered as imperial tribute. In Japan it attained the status of sacred beverage and fostered the development of a national culture surrounding tea. All this transpired before Europeans had the faintest notion of "liquid jade," as tea was termed in China. They were also unacquainted with coffee and chocolate until maritime traders brought all three beverages to European tables at the beginning of the seventeenth century. Over time the impact of these new commodities proved enormous, not in the least because they all contain methylxanthine, also known as caffeine. Prior to the introduction of these exotic drinks, breakfast must have been a particularly dreary affair, especially considering that with water being unsafe, the morning beverage of choice in England was beer.

Initially, all three new beverages were rare and costly (figs. III.2, III.3), which limited their consumption to the wealthy few who could afford to keep up with current fashion. Tea was sold at apothecaries and was often purchased because of its health benefits—much touted in one of the most famous English broadsides[1] and later frequently discussed in the first European treatises on tea, which appeared in the second half of the seventeenth century (see Smith, this volume). Before its arrival in England, tea had become a trendy novelty among the Dutch, and they were the first to officially import it to Europe,[2] a half century before the English East India Company (EIC) realized the trade potential. Although the Company was chartered in 1600, it was not until 1669 that it began to import tea directly to England instead of buying it from the Dutch, and even then the amount of the first order was a paltry 143½ pounds (Ukers 1935, I: 29). By that time tea drinking had already spread beyond the English nobility and to the general population. If the EIC was slow to pick up on the tea phenomenon, however, the English government was not. It had begun taxing tea in 1660.

III.1 The Middle Clipper Ship *Derby* in Hong Kong Harbor
China, circa 1860
Oil on canvas
Framed: 88.3 x 125 cm
PEABODY ESSEX MUSEUM, GIFT OF BENJAMIN R. STONE, 1889, NO. M.210

This painting was executed by a Chinese artist or artists. The *Derby*, registered in Salem, was built in 1855 at Chelsea, Massachusetts, and weighed 1,062 tons. In the painting, the ship flies the house flag of Pickman, Stone, and Silsbee, the American firm for which it sailed. The *Derby's* maiden voyage commenced January 22, 1856, with stops in San Francisco, Hong Kong, Calcutta, and Cape Town—returning to Boston on July 7, 1857. She made several subsequent voyages to Hong Kong.

ABOVE

III.2 Edward Cornock (England, active after 1707)
Tea caddy box and key, London, 1730
Ivory, wood, metal, felt, pigment, scrimshaw
L: 28.7 cm
FOWLER MUSEUM AT UCLA, THE FRANCIS E. FOWLER, JR.
COLLECTION, X87.1018A-J

Some tea boxes, such as this one, contained two caddies, one for green tea, the other for "bohea" tea, as black tea was then known.

III.3   Hester Bateman (England, 1709–1794)
Tea Caddy, 1788
Silver
H: 14.6 cm

During the eighteenth century, tea was an expensive and exotic item that was kept under lock and key. The lady of the house retained the key, and servants were not given access to the contents of the caddy.

III.4   Richard Gurney (England, active circa 1721–1773)
and Thomas Cooke II (England, active circa 1721–1773)
Teakettle, 1753–1754
Silver
H: 29.5 cm

This type of kettle was not intended for the kitchen but for the tea table (or a small side table). During the serving of tea, water was kept hot with a spirit lamp positioned underneath the belly of the kettle. The heated water was then poured into the teapot as needed to brew more tea.

III.5   W. and P. Cunningham, Edinburgh, Scotland
Hot water urn (tea urn), 1791–1792
Silver
H: 59.7 cm

The hot water urns that appeared later in the eighteenth century were safer to use than teakettles with open spirit lamps below them. A solid metal core, heated in the open fire, was placed inside the urn to keep the water hot. The hot water in turn flowed into the teapot via a spigot on the body of the urn.

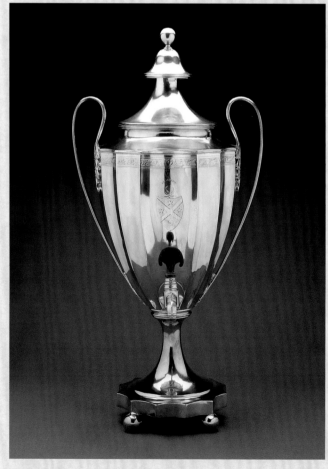

The primary locus of urban tea consumption in England was a new type of public establishment, the coffeehouse,[3] and access to it was limited to men. The first coffeehouse opened in Oxford in 1650. Within a few years, eighty of them had opened in London, and by the end of the century the number had reached five hundred. At these establishments one could order coffee, tea, chocolate, or a pipe; exchange the latest news and gossip, talk shop, or start a business; or get an education of sorts by being exposed to all manner of discussions, explanations, and diatribes (coffeehouses were referred to as "penny universities" for this very reason). It was here, where men congregated—to a great extent regardless of class, status, or rank—that tea grew to become the preferred beverage of Englishmen.[4]

At the beginning of the eighteenth century, tea drinking expanded even further, moving beyond the confines of male-only establishments and toward the female domestic sphere. This move was facilitated by the opening of a new category of shop, the tea shop. The first one, the Golden Lyon, was opened by Thomas Twining in 1706. There it was possible to purchase the dry leaf in order to brew tea at home. This development, in turn, spurred the production of special equipment designed for the purpose, including kettles and hot water urns (figs. III.4, III.5). The evolution of tea drinking from exotic novelty to domestic ritual is masterfully explored by Woodruff Smith in his essay in this volume, "Tea and the Middle Class." Although distinct from these middle-class developments, paintings known as "conversation pieces" are also instructive in

III.6 William John Huggins (England, 1781–1845)
East India Company Ship *Vansittart*, 1842
Oil on canvas
Framed: 148.6 x 207 cm
PEABODY ESSEX MUSEUM, NO. M3802

The East Indiamen were large, heavily armed merchant ships used by the Dutch and English East India Companies to bring enormous amounts of tea to Europe. They ruled Western maritime trade for more than two hundred years, braving pirate attacks and treacherous waters. East Indiamen were built for storage, not for speed.

examining tea and domesticity. Angus Trumble discusses this genre and the role of tea in the context of eighteenth-century art and social discourse in his essay "Tea and the Conversation Piece."

By the second half of the eighteenth century, tea drinking was a ubiquitous ingredient of daily life in English society. To support the habit, East Indiamen (fig. III.6)—the large, slow merchant ships of the EIC—sailed the seas and brought back ever-increasing quantities of tea. It took more than a year for the roundtrip from London to Canton, and the tea, which was mostly green at the time and had a shorter shelf life than black, often arrived in less than ideal condition. The East Indiamen would be replaced less than a century later by sleek clipper ships, which could make the voyage in half the time (fig. III.1).[5] Yet, while tea imports were on the rise, chinaware, which at first was brought to Europe in massive amounts—because it sold well on arrival and also functioned

III.7 Tea Bowl and Saucer
Staffordshire, England, circa 1755–1765
Earthenware, glaze, gilding
H (tea bowl): 4.13 cm
LOS ANGELES COUNTY MUSEUM OF ART,
GIFT OF DR. AND MRS. DENNY B. LOTWIN, NO. M.81.257.8A–B
PHOTOGRAPH ©2009 MUSEUM ASSOCIATES/LACMA

Early English tea-drinking vessels imitated Chinese tea bowls and were therefore smaller than the handled teacups that later came into vogue in Britain. The application of the handle became necessary due to the British habit of drinking hot black tea, which is consumed at higher temperatures than Chinese green.

III.8 Possibly painted by Richard Askew
(England, active ca. 1772–1795); Chelsea-Derby Factory
Tea bowl and saucer, circa 1775
Porcelain
H (tea bowl): 5.4 cm
LOS ANGELES COUNTY MUSEUM OF ART,
GIFT OF MRS. MARY P. WELLS, NO. 55.100.5A–B
PHOTOGRAPH ©2009 MUSEUM ASSOCIATES/LACMA

III.9 Chelsea-Derby Factory, England
One of a set of two tea bowls and saucers, circa 1775
Porcelain
H (tea bowl): 5.1 cm
LOS ANGELES COUNTY MUSEUM OF ART,
GIFT OF MRS. MARY P. WELLS, NO. 55.100.6A–D
PHOTOGRAPH ©2009 MUSEUM ASSOCIATES/LACMA

III.10 Jacob Petit (France, 1796–1868)
Traveling tea set, 19th century
Limoges porcelain with gold and silver overlay in a travel case
W (case): 47 cm
COLLECTION OF GLORIA AND SONNY KAMM,
COURTESY OF THE KAMM TEAPOT FOUNDATION

Jacob Petit was a master of hand-painted porcelain and created highly ornate pieces. He worked at the famed Sèvres porcelain manufactory and later, along with his brother, acquired his own porcelain manufactory.

as excellent ballast en route—was on the decrease. When tea was still a novelty, none of the necessary implements (tea bowls, saucers, teapots) existed in Europe, and they had to be imported mostly from China by the English and, to a lesser extent, from Japan by the Dutch. After Ehrenfried Walther von Tschirnhaus[6] discovered the Chinese secret of porcelain making in 1708, however, Meissen became the first European porcelain manufactory. Over subsequent decades, other factories in Germany, as well as France, England, and Italy, began producing original tea ware, at first imitating Chinese shapes (figs. III.7–III.9) and later coming into their own with a great variety of styles and designs, of which the traveling tea set in figure III.10 is only one of countless exquisite examples (figs. III.11–III.22). As a result of these developments, once-prized tea sets from China lay in overstock in East India Company warehouses. They were sold as "new" arrivals for a number of years until the Company discontinued bulk imports altogether in 1791.

By this time something else was overstocked in the Company warehouses as well: tea itself. This is often explained, at least in part, as the result of an increasing demand for tea—which pushed EIC tea imports to extravagant heights—and the competition from the burgeoning tea-smuggling industry, which made sales of expensive, legal, and heavily taxed Company tea more difficult. According to some estimates, the amount of tea smuggled into Britain was at times twice the amount of legal tea imported by the EIC (Bowen 1998, 167). Historian Huw Bowen has, however, added another important factor to the equation.[7] According to Bowen, the increase in volume of tea imports during the 1760s and 1770s had a very specific cause: when the East India Company became a revenue collector in Bengal (as well as Bihar and Orissa) in 1765, it was confronted with the quandary of how to transfer the revenue surplus from India to England. Not only was the direct transfer of bullion risky, but reducing the amount of coinage in circulation had the potential to ruin Bengal's economy. Considering that tea was in high demand, Company officials decided to redirect the surplus to the buying of greater amounts of tea in China, with the intention of using the purchases as a transfer of revenue to England in the material form of tea shipments. As such, the tea trade became "a 'national concern' because it offered one of the few channels through which revenue income could flow to Britain" (Bowen 1998, 163).

This course of action ultimately had disastrous consequences as the market was flooded. By 1772 the tea surplus had reached 17.5 million pounds, and it would soon become a powerful catalyst in the birth of the American nation. As Bowen notes "it can be argued that, far from underwriting British imperialism during the 1760s and 1770s, the tea trade did exactly the opposite and began instead to undermine it" (1998, 160). Every American schoolchild learns what happened to the 342 Company tea chests at Boston Harbor. Of less-common knowledge, however, is the widespread tea-related activism that occurred in colonies other than Massachusetts,

a topic insightfully addressed in Jane Merritt's essay in this volume "Beyond Boston: Prerevolutionary Activism and the Other American Tea Parties." Tea is inextricably linked to American independence, yet, it may be surprising for some readers to discover that before the Revolution gave tea a bad name, eighteenth-century colonists were even more avid tea drinkers than their English brethren and that, indeed, thanks to early Dutch colonization of New Amsterdam, one could say that Americans knew and appreciated tea even before the English. Barbara Carson's essay in this section of the book takes us on a journey through the eighteenth-century colonial world, acquainting us with early colonial tea habits. It also hints at postrevolutionary habits, correcting the common misperception that Americans became coffee drinkers as a result of the Revolution. ∽

II.11   Mounted teapot
        Chinese porcelain, circa 1662–1690; European mounts, circa 1700–1710
        Hard-paste porcelain, gilding; silver mounts
        H: 14.8 cm
        THE J. PAUL GETTY MUSEUM, LOS ANGELES, NO. 2001.76

The first teapots used in Europe were of Chinese manufacture. The addition of precious metal mounts was a common practice.

IIII.12   Johann Friedrich Böttger (German, 1682–1719)
        Teapot, Meissen Porcelain Manufactory, 1715–1720
        Stoneware, silver-gilt mounts and chain
        H: 14 cm
        THE J. PAUL GETTY MUSEUM, LOS ANGELES, NO. 85.DI.287

Chinese Yixing teapots first arrived in Europe in the 1670s, primarily intended for a Chinese clientele. Eventually, however, they came to be admired and imitated throughout Europe.

III.13   Trumpeter teapot
        China, circa 1750
        Porcelain
        H: 14.6 cm
        THE NEWARK MUSEUM, GIFT OF HERMAN A. E. AND PAUL C. JAEHNE, 1941, NO. 41.1999AB
        PHOTOGRAPH BY RICHARD GOODBODY

This teapot is part of a rare tea service that was commissioned by the Dutch East India Company.

III.14   House Teapot
        Staffordshire, England, circa 1750
        Salt-glazed stoneware
        H: 10.2 cm
        LOS ANGELES COUNTY MUSEUM OF ART,
        GIFT OF HERBERT AND ANNETTE LEWIS, NO. M.91.371.4A–B
        PHOTOGRAPH ©2009 MUSEUM ASSOCIATES/LACMA

Teapots in the shape of houses became popular toward the end of the 1750s.

III.15   Cauliflower teapot
        Staffordshire, England, late 18th century
        Creamware
        H: 13. 34 cm
        COLLECTION OF GLORIA AND SONNY KAMM,
        COURTESY OF THE KAMM TEAPOT FOUNDATION

Pottery in the form of fruit and vegetables (cauliflower, cabbage, lemon, quince, pineapple, and melon, among others) came into vogue during the mid-eighteenth century. The cauliflower pot with its green and cream-colored glazes was one of the most successful examples of this type.

EUROPEAN AND AMERICAN TEAPOTS

While tea has been around for thousands of years, the teapot—a much-loved household item—was invented only five hundred years ago. It came into being when the practice of steeping tea leaves displaced the use of boiled or whisked tea in China. It is commonly believed among tea scholars that teapot design is the result of adapting the previously existing lidded wine ewer to the requirements of steeped tea. Always subject to the fashion of the time, the teapot has continued to inspire artists to this day. Displayed here is a sampling of extraordinary European and American teapots that range in date from the seventeenth-century to the present.

III.16   Humphrey Chamberlain Jr. (England, 1791–1824)
Teapot with cover and stand, Chamberlain's Factory,
circa 1807–1810
Porcelain, enamels, gilding
H (teapot): 16.5 cm

Chinese potters had been making porcelain for more than a thousand
years before European manufacturers discovered the secret ingredients
(kaolin and petuntse) and techniques (high firing temperatures) in 1708.

III.17   Design by Bianchi (dates unknown); made by Carlo Landi
(Italy, active 1833–1846)
Teapot, circa 1840
Silver-gilt
H: 29.9 cm

With the increasing industrialization of tea ware production during the
nineteenth century, individually designed and executed pieces were less
frequently produced. This Italian work is unique not only because it is
one-of-a-kind but also because the ornament, instead of being cast, is
entirely chased.

III.18   Anne Kraus (United States, 1956–2003)
2 Dreams Last Night Teapot, 1988
Ceramic
H: 25.4 cm

Originally trained as a painter, Anne Kraus used her ceramic work to
explore the themes of consciousness and the human psyche, often through
detailed narratives involving image and text.

III.19   Kurt Weiser (United States, b. 1950)
Vitamin C, 1994
Porcelain
H: 29.8 cm

Kurt Weiser's work focuses on meticulously china-painted, luxuriant
jungle scenes with intense colors, often including figurative elements
suggesting disquieting themes.

III.20 Jay Musler (United States, b. 1949)
Beehhive, 1994
Mosaic glass, sandblasted and painted
H: 13.9 cm
COLLECTION OF GLORIA AND SONNY KAMM,
COURTESY OF THE KAMM TEAPOT FOUNDATION

Jay Musler is known for his innovative forms and techniques in glass.
These include employing layers of oil paint on glass to produce heavily
saturated color.

III.21 Sergei Isupov (b. USSR, 1963; active United States)
The Time Is Coming, 1997
Ceramic
H: 38.1 cm
COLLECTION OF GLORIA AND SONNY KAMM,
COURTESY OF THE KAMM TEAPOT FOUNDATION

Born in the Ukraine, artist Sergei Isupov came to the United States in
1993. Contorted, unsettling hybridizations of humans and animals commonly feature in his work.

III.22 Richard Marquis (United States, b. 1945)
Wizard teapot, 1985
Blown glass
H: 38.1 cm
COLLECTION OF GLORIA AND SONNY KAMM,
COURTESY OF THE KAMM TEAPOT FOUNDATION

Richard Marquis first studied glass techniques in Venice, Italy, in 1969.
He is considered one of the pioneers of the American studio glass movement.

Woodruff D. Smith

TEA AND THE MIDDLE CLASS

5

IN THE EUROPEAN WORLD, taking tea in company at home or in certain kinds of public establishments has long been identified as a particularly middle-class thing to do (Martin-Fugier 1990, 274–77). Why this identification should be made so automatically is something of a mystery. Social tea drinking initially became a fashion in Europe in the seventeenth century not among the "middle classes" but rather among aristocrats, among people who thought of themselves as fashionable and genteel, and among seekers after exotic experiences (Smith 2002, 75–76; Cowan 2005, 16–30). Well before the middle of the nineteenth century, at least in Great Britain, tea drinking had been adopted by a significant segment of the industrial and agricultural working classes (Mintz 1986, 141–50). The explanation that is usually given for the extension of tea throughout society—that the middle class imitated the upper class in the eighteenth century, while the working class imitated the middle class in the nineteenth—does not account for the peculiar identification of tea with the middle class.

The solution to the mystery lies in recognizing that, up until the late nineteenth century, much of the historical phenomenon we call the "middle class" consisted of a distinctive set of cultural patterns—meaningful practices attached in common understanding to particular sets of ideas, attitudes, and commodities—which were adopted by people of varied background as signs of their individual self-respect and their collective place in society. These patterns derived from many sources, but they were put together in a particular way in the Atlantic world in the late seventeenth and eighteenth centuries. The patterns were embodied quite consciously in an array of rituals of daily life that, despite their apparent ordinariness, were full of implied meanings—primarily moral meanings, but with multiple social and political implications. Tea was a central part of several of these rituals, and "respectability" was the term that, by the late eighteenth century, was typically used to refer to their meanings (Smith 2002, 189–221). If you took tea at the proper time and place, in the proper way, with the proper equipment, it meant more than anything else that you were respectable.

5.1 Robert Cruikshank (England, 1789–1856)
A Tea Party or English Manners and French Politeness,
London, 1835
Etching with hand coloring
16.5 x 21.4 cm
COURETSY OF THE LEWIS WALPOLE LIBRARY,
YALE UNIVERSITY, NO. 835.08.01.19

After thirteen cups of tea, the Frenchman at the left of this illustration finds himself in acute distress when offered a fourteenth. Unaware of English conventions, he has repeatedly returned his teacup to his hostess without the spoon across it. According to English practice at the time, the presence of the spoon would have indicated that no more tea should be served.

Did it also mean that you belonged to the middle class? If "middle class" refers to a distinct set of people following certain occupations and located in a social hierarchy somewhere between the landed aristocracy and the wage-earning classes (or if it refers to Karl Marx's "bourgeoisie," the owners of capital), not necessarily. Plenty of people outside the range of these rather vague boundaries thought of themselves as respectable and acted respectably, and their numbers increased in the course of the nineteenth century. But until the latter part of that century, it was people who could see themselves as fitting into the middle range of recognized hierarchies who perceived themselves as having the greatest need to manifest their respectability in ritual and who fashioned their notion of themselves as a class primarily around it.

A crucial aspect of middle-class culture was a set of implied claims about the social standing of the people who adopted the rituals of respectability and about their relationship to their nations. In certain regards, acting respectably could be taken as a statement that one belonged to a status group *morally distinct* from the typical members of other groups: a "middle" class that, because of its manifest virtues, because of its moderation (another quality suggested by "middle"), and because its members possessed sufficient income to ensure their moral autonomy, ranked above the various lower orders that supposedly did not possess these attributes and was entitled to real respect from the traditional upper classes, which possessed them in insufficient quantities (Smith 2002, 204–10). From this perspective, members of the middle class did not so much want to rise into the upper class as to establish an identity for themselves that was morally equivalent or superior. The rituals of respectability thus acted as markers of "distinction" in Pierre Bourdieu's sense of the term: they set the middle class apart in an honorable way (Bourdieu 1984). At the same time, however, respectability was portrayed throughout most of Europe and the Atlantic world as the ideal culture of the nation as a whole. On such a basis, the middle class could claim (and politicians could claim for them) the role of cultural and moral center of the nation. The British historian Thomas B. Macaulay did this, for example, in his speeches in 1831 supporting parliamentary reform (Macaulay 1980, II: 415–16).

These overlapping but not identical assertions incorporated, among other things, a request to participate in politics and a demand that the aristocracy acknowledge the grounds on which the middle class rested its respect for itself. By the nineteenth century, people describing the essential features of their nations—whether France or Britain or Germany, whether the United States or Australia—typically included the elements of respectability in their descriptions, with the further implication that one of the things that made their particular nation superior to others was the larger degree to which the national character embodied the moral values of respectability. This implication is suggested by a cartoon that contrasts a Frenchman's understanding of the practices of tea taking with those of his more competent (and more attractively portrayed) English hosts (fig. 5.1). In consequence, people who thought of themselves as belonging to classes other than the middle class and who wished either to retain a leading place in national politics (in the case of established upper-class groups) or to claim such a place for the first time (in the case of politically active segments of the modern working class) consciously adopted significant aspects of the culture of respectability—in the latter case producing the "respectable working class." In doing so, they were not claiming to belong to the middle class; they were asserting membership in the moral community of the nation and their right to share the national identity.

Why tea? Tea was far from the only commodity employed in the rituals of respectability, and its importance in this regard varied considerably from country to country. (It was especially prominent in Great Britain, where most of the practices of respectable tea taking in the late eighteenth and the nineteenth centuries appear to have developed.) What made tea particularly important was the wide range of ways in which its use could be understood within middle-class culture. That culture can be visualized as consisting of a number of different *contexts*: connections of practices and meanings that became linked to each other, mostly in the eighteenth century, to form a single entity. By looking at the apparent meanings of tea in each of them, it is possible to appreciate the role of tea in the culture of respectability and to understand the process by which the middle classes of the Atlantic world used tea to identify themselves, both individually and collectively.

Gentility

Tea became fashionable in Western Europe more or less simultaneously with coffee in the second half of the seventeenth century (see Hohenegger, p. 127 of this volume). What that meant was that tea, as a commodity consumed in a manner supposedly similar to the way it was taken by the upper orders of Chinese society, found a place in a distinct cultural context: the modes of behavior exhibited by people who consciously wished to signify that they were "gentlemen" and "ladies," that they possessed the manners of the hereditary aristocracy and pedigrees sufficiently distinguished to allow them to be accounted members of that class (if sometimes only on the fringes of it). One of the modes that made up this context of gentility was the adoption of changing fashions in dress,

5.2   Beauvais Manufactory, France, founded 1664
       Le thé de l'impératrice (*The Empress's Tea*), circa 1697–1705
       From the series L'histoire de l'empereur de la Chine
       (History of the Emperor of China)
       Wool, silk
       419.1 x 190.5 cm
       J. PAUL GETTY MUSEUM, LOS ANGELES, CALIFORNIA, 89.DD.62

The table depicted to the right of the empress holds glass and blue-and-white porcelain vessels. Despite attempts to suggest Chinese costume and setting, most of the portrait conventions in the tapestry are European. The woven coat-of-arms and monogram are those of Louis-Alexandre de Bourbon, comte de Toulouse and duc de Penthièvre (1678–1737).

5.3a,b Attributed to Pierre Golle (b. The Netherlands, circa 1620; d. France, 1684)
Tripod table with tea-drinking scene, France, circa 1680
Oak veneered with brass, pewter, tortoiseshell, walnut, and ebony with drawers of oak and rosewood, gilded fruitwood, gilt-bronze mounts
H: 76.8 cm
J. PAUL GETTY MUSEUM, LOS ANGELES, CALIFORNIA, NO. 82.DA.34

Pierre Golle moved to Paris at an early age and worked as an apprentice to a specialist in ebony furniture. By 1656 he had become a master furniture maker to the king. The top of this table folds open to reveal a central scene of tea taking (fig. 5.3b, opposite), after a design by Daniel Marot (1661–1752). The monkey and parrot in this depiction suggest an exotic locale. It is thought that the table was made for the eldest son of King Louis XIV of France.

literary interests, aesthetic tastes, and consumer goods. Gentility had been constructed in the sixteenth and early seventeenth centuries as a cultural pattern that highlighted qualities all members of the social elite were supposed to possess, regardless of their specific ranks, and that set them off collectively from other people (Bryson 1998). It was presumed by convention that most of these people possessed land and titles, but the pattern was sufficiently flexible that people at the upper ends of the professions, officials, the descendants of prosperous merchants, and the like could adopt it as well.

In the late seventeenth century, consuming tea in a moderately ceremonious and quasi-Chinese way, using, if possible, porcelain cups and teapots imported from China, was a very significant ritual of gentility. It was part of a broader fashion for material objects (especially expensive ones) that were Chinese in origin, pattern, or at least suggestion. This fashion for *chinoiserie* is illustrated by figure 5.2, a magnificent French tapestry of the late seventeenth or early eighteenth century (Honour 1961). It depicts the Chinese imperial family taking tea in high style, but also in the open air. Most of the conventions of portrayal are European, but most of the figures are dressed in a manner that lets the viewer know that the locale is the exotic and (at the time) greatly admired Empire of China. Here, tea is placed in a framework that refers simultaneously to its overseas origins, to its association with the most exalted social levels of the most prestigious monarchy in the world,

and to the combination of ritual and restrained informality (the domestic scene, the outdoor setting) that characterized the early modern culture of gentility.

Tapestries of this sort were specifically made for people of the highest rank in European society and could be afforded only by the very wealthy. This meant that although they were sometimes purchased by rich families who were not noble and by nonaristocratic institutions such as city governments, they were not practically available to merely well-to-do individuals. People at the middle levels of income could, however, buy other commodities related to genteel tea taking. Figure 5.3a shows a tripod tea table clearly made for the aristocratic market around 1680, at the height of the fashion for tea and at about the time at which European tea rituals were beginning to diverge from imagined Chinese models. This particular table was presumably quite expensive, although probably affordable for the families of moderately wealthy businesspeople and officials who wanted to announce their gentility. The style and decoration could, however, be readily reproduced at lower prices and on a larger scale by craftsmen working in substantial shops. In the eighteenth century, so-called populuxe renditions of tea furniture became a staple of Parisian high-quality industry, and less-expensive versions were produced in many parts of Europe—even in the Americas (Auslander 1996, 110–30). The same thing happened with the equipment needed to serve and consume tea. In the late

seventeenth and early eighteenth centuries, manufacturers in several European countries struggled to reproduce the porcelain that made Chinese pottery desirable as a sign of gentility. Eventually they did so, creating expensive and high-quality porcelain tea services intended for aristocratic customers. But in the early eighteenth century, good quality, very tasteful tea pottery was also available at lower prices, either produced in Europe or made to European specifications and imported from China, which met demand from a larger "middle-class" public (Hildyard 1999, 70–91).

Such products permitted families who could not even hint at aristocratic origins or great wealth to make a claim to gentility on the grounds of participating in the rituals of tea and adopting the fashions connected with tea taking in an appropriately tasteful way. But something happened both to tea and to gentility in this process (which was replicated with hundreds of other rituals and commodities between the mid-seventeenth and the mid-eighteenth centuries). Tea taking and the behaviors constructed around it ceased to be "fashionable" in their original sense, but instead of disappearing and being replaced by newer fashions, they became permanent features of European and Atlantic social life. Also, the network of meanings associated with tea as a sign of gentility changed—not completely, but substantially.

In essence, gentility came to be absorbed into the cultural framework of *respectability* (Smith 2002, 171–75, 204–10).

It retained some of its elements and language ("gentleman" and "lady," for instance), but these were reinterpreted to refer to a different array of meanings. Adopting genteel practices such as tea taking in a respectable context signified a demand for esteem based much more heavily on the obvious moral standing of the people who adopted them than on pedigree or even income. The latter retained some importance, which was, however, increasingly expressed in terms of the manifest virtue of families and the legitimacy of the way in which the income was obtained. (Of course, the older construction of gentility as indicating aristocratic status also continued to exist into the nineteenth century as a separate part of the European cultural repertoire, but tea played only a small role in it.)

Tea was particularly important among the cultural practices denoting respectable gentility because it possessed, from the time of its fashionable consumption in Europe in the seventeenth century, meanings in two other contexts that contributed to the formation of the culture of respectability in the eighteenth century: a context that treated the conscious maintenance of physical health as evidence of moral standing, and another that presented the family as the principal institution that framed and supported an orderly, sympathetic, and civilized society. Both of these contexts became essential features of middle-class life and values.

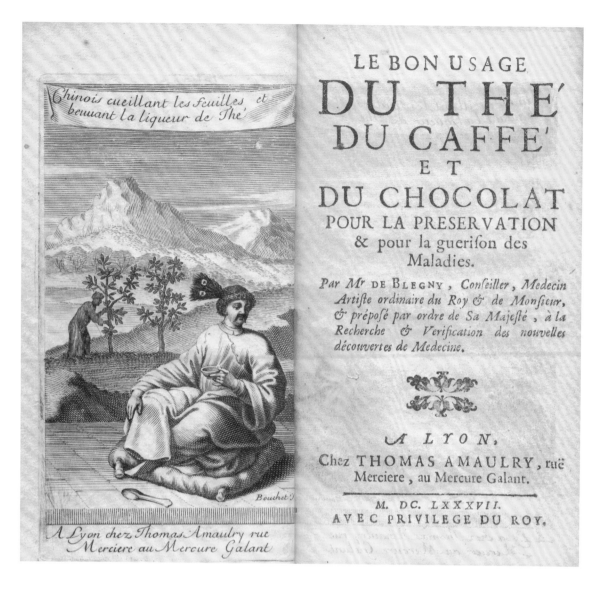

LE BON USAGE
DU THÉ
DU CAFFÉ
ET
DU CHOCOLAT
POUR LA PRESERVATION
& pour la guerifon des
Maladies.

Par Mr DE BLEGNY, Conſeiller, Medecin
Artiſte ordinaire du Roy & de Monſieur,
& prépoſé par ordre de Sa Majeſté, à la
Recherche & Verification des nouvelles
découvertes de Medecine.

A LYON,
Chez THOMAS AMAULRY, ruë
Merciere, au Mercure Galant.

M. DC. LXXXVII.
AVEC PRIVILEGE DU ROY.

Chinois cueillant les feuilles, et beuuant la liqueur de Thé

A Lyon chez Thomas Amaulry rue Merciere au Mercure Galant

Bouchet J.

Health and Well-Being

Tea became important in Europe in the seventeenth century mainly because it was fashionable and a sign of status, but it was initially imported and for many years sold as a drug: as a means of improving and maintaining health through diet. This remains, of course, one of tea's main selling points today. In the late seventeenth century, tea's medicinal properties were both exaggerated and denied. The Dutch physician Cornelis Bontekoe made himself famous by claiming that drinking thirty or more cups of tea a day would ensure perfect health, while others asserted that tea was unhealthy, among other reasons because it endangered masculinity (Bontekoe 1689). But by the eighteenth century, published opinion was generally favorable. Some saw tea as a means of counteracting the dangerous effects of consuming excessive sugar, which may have led to (and certainly justified) the growing tendency to take tea and sugar together.[1]

Two early examples of the large "health and diet" literature on sugar may be seen in figures 5.4 and 5.5, both popular treatises in French published in the 1680s. *Traités nouveaux & curieux du café, du thé et du chocolate* (*A New and Curious Treatise on Coffee, Tea, and Chocolate*; fig. 5.5) is particularly

5.4 Nicolas de Blegny (France, 1642?–1722)
Le bon usage du thé, du caffé et du chocolat pour la preservation & pour la guerison des maladies (*The Appropriate Usage of Tea, Coffee, and Chocolate for the Preservation of Health and the Cure of Illnesses*), 1687
Printed book
H: 15 cm
LIBRARY OF CONGRESS, WASHINGTON, D.C., TX415.B53

interesting because its author, a merchant named Philippe Sylvestre Dufour, explicitly relates tea not only to contexts of gentility and health but also to a view of society in which merchants can insist on respect from the aristocracy and from educated people on the basis of the knowledge of the world merchants have obtained and the personal virtue they have displayed while conducting the kind of trade that brings tea to Europe (Dufour 1685, preface). This demand suggests an assertive consciousness of class on Dufour's part, although its scope is limited to merchants in international trade. The process of constructing a broader conception of the middle class around the culture of respectability is shown by what happened to the context of health in the early eighteenth century:

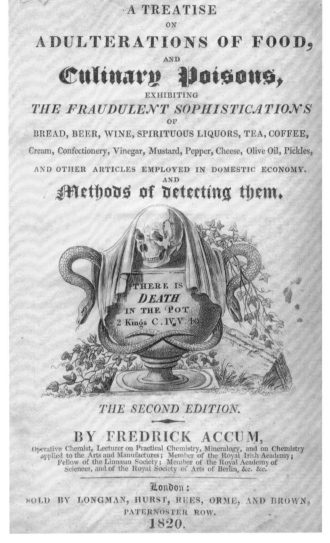

it became the center of a cultural framework in which the act of regularly taking care of one's own health and that of one's family served as evidence of general virtue, and therefore of fitness to be respected and trusted by the rest of society. If a merchant did business at a teahouse rather than a tavern, or if family members took tea together in an appropriate way at home, it showed not only that they laid claim to a species of gentility based on a presumption of moral standing but also that they had sufficient regard for their health and sobriety to be accounted responsible people.

The same factors also required that people who consumed commodities such as tea concern themselves with threats from harmful ingredients substituted for the real things by unscrupulous importers or manufacturers. A large pamphlet literature on the subject of adulterated foods found an audience not just because it purported to deal with a topic important in its own right but also because the act of demonstrating concern about dangers to health had meaning in the context of respectability (fig. 5.6).

5.5   Philippe Sylvestre Dufour (France, 1622–1687)
Traités nouveaux & curieux du café, du thé et du chocolate; Ouvrage également necessaire aux medecins, & à tous ceux qui aiment leur santé (New and Curious Treatises on Coffee, Tea, and Chocolate: A Work Equally Necessary for Doctors and for All Those Who Value Their Health), 1685
Printed book
H: 14 cm
LIBRARY OF CONGRESS, WASHINGTON, D.C., TX815.D82

Dufour wrote one of the most prominent seventeenth-century books on the subject of imported stimulant beverages. This illustration suggests the diverse "exotic" origins of coffee (from Arabia, figure at left), tea (from China, figure at center), and chocolate (from America, figure at right).

5.6   Frederick Accum (England, 1769–1838)
A Treatise on Adulterations of Food, and Culinary Poisons, Exhibiting the Fraudulent Sophistications of Bread, Beer, Wine, Spirituous Liquors, Tea, Coffee, Cream, Confectionery, Vinegar, Mustard, Pepper, Cheese, Olive Oil, Pickles, and Other Articles Employed in Domestic Economy, and Methods of Detecting Them, 1820
Printed book
H: 18 cm
LIBRARY OF CONGRESS, WASHINGTON, D.C., TX563.A2

Concern with adulteration of foodstuffs reflected the desire to maintain physical health linked with concepts of moral standing and respectability. Adulturating and smuggling tea were common at the time as legally imported tea was heavily taxed under a controlled monopoly.

5.7 James Gillray (England, 1757–1815)
*Anti-Saccharrites, or John Bull and His Family
Leaving off the Use of Sugar,* 1792
Etching
31.5 x 40.6 cm
VICTORIA AND ALBERT MUSEUM, NO. 15367

In this caricature, famed satirist James Gillray pokes fun at the royal family's lukewarm embrace of the sugar boycott in support of the anti-slavery movement (see fig. 5.16). His thinly veiled depiction of George III as "John Bull" was frequently copied by subsequent caricaturists.

Domesticity and the Family

One of the best-known characteristics of the culture of respectability and of the middle class in general was the concept of the nuclear family as the foundation of civilized society—as the social location at which people learned virtuous behavior and where sentiment and pleasure (even erotic pleasure) could be safely experienced in an appropriately moral setting (Hall 1990; Smith 2002, 171–87). Although the ritual performance that constituted the meal of "tea" in Britain was initially constructed in a context of gentility, it obtained most of its significance within this framework of domesticity. The ritual delineated the proper place of the respectable, adult, married woman in the world: she presided over the proceedings, organizing the distribution of sustenance and ensuring the maintenance of propriety and the use of appropriate language. Men, whether members of the family or guests, accepted symbolic secondary roles, whereas in other places they expected to be deferred to

TEA.

"My Wife had Tea ready for him which it is well known he delighted to drink at all hours, particularly when sitting up late, He shewed much complacency that the Mistress of the House was so attentive to his singular habit, and as no man could be more polite when he chose to be so, his address to her was most Courteous and engaging, and his conversation soon charmed her into a forgetfulness of his external appearance."

Vide. Journal p. 14.

E-146.
Publish'd May 15th 1786 by E.Jackson N.o 14 Mary-le-bone Street Golden Square.

by the other members of their families. Many illustrations of the time display variations on the theme of tea as a meal over which the lady of the family is supposed to preside, although in some cases the portrayal is satirical or comic (figs. 5.7, 5.8, and see fig. 5.1). Part of the rather cruel "humor" of a late eighteenth-century cartoon of an "old maid" drinking tea with only her cat for company (fig. 5.9) is that the lady does not have a family—particularly a husband—to give meaning to the ritual in which she is engaged.

Tea could also be consumed respectably in domestic settings without the presence of members of both sexes and without being explicitly a family ritual. It was, for example, the favored beverage for sociable gatherings of middle-class or aristocratic women in each other's houses, manifesting the moral and upright character of the event in a way that wine or spirits would not have done. Such gatherings could easily be satirized in the misogynistic mode of much of eighteenth-century

5.8   Thomas Rowlandson (England, 1756–1827)
Tea, London, 1786
Etching and engraving
25.2 x 27.7 cm
COURTESY OF THE LEWIS WALPOLE LIBRARY,
YALE UNIVERSITY, NO. 786.05.15.07

Thomas Rowlandson, like his friend James Gillray (see fig. 5.7), was a well-known English caricaturist. This is one of twenty prints, each of which was linked to a passage in James Boswell's *The Journal of a Tour to the Hebrides*. This print shows Boswell and his wife seated with Samuel Johnson (at the far right). Both Boswell and Johnson suffered from depression, but while Boswell anesthesized himself with alchohol, Johnson "cured" himself with legendary amounts of tea.

THE OLD MAID
The Lady here you see display'd,
By some is still an ancient maid,
But if her inward thoughts you'd view,
She thinks herself as young as you;
Oh! Puss forbear to lick the cream,
Your Mistress longs to do the same.

A CUP OF TEA AND A DISH OF CHAT.
1.—So they say Miss Stiff Rump is in the Straw!!   *2.—Why sure _____ is it a Girl?*
3.—No _____ guefs again.   *4.—A Boy.*
5.—Aye _____ Somebody told ye.

5.9   *The Old Maid*, England, 1777
Etching
33 x 22.2 cm
LIBRARY OF CONGRESS, WASHINGTON, D.C., NO. PC 3 1777

The "old maid" in this engraving sits alone with her cat drinking tea from a saucer. The poem below the print, however, indicates that she perceives herself as young. The last two lines allude to an association of milk, curds, and cream with sexual love. An early eighteenth-century collection of the "best merry ballads and songs, old and new" includes a song entitled "The Praise of the Dairy Maid," which claims that cream "makes an old Bawd like a Wench of fifteen" (Ganev 2007, 63).

5.10   Robert Cruikshank (England, 1789–1856)
A Cup of Tea and a Dish of Chat, London, circa 1830
Aquatint and etching with hand coloring
31.2 x 34.3 cm
COURTESY OF THE LEWIS WALPOLE LIBRARY,
YALE UNIVERSITY, NO. 830.00.00.122

OPPOSITE

5.11   *The Tea-Table*, London, England, circa 1766
Etching
20.8 x 15.6 cm
COURTESY OF THE LEWIS WALPOLE LIBRARY,
YALE UNIVERSITY, NO. 766.00.00.37

The association of women, tea, and gossip was commonplace, and Daniel Defoe (1659/1661[?]–1731) found a similar linkage between men and the coffeehouse. In his *Compleat English Tradesmen* (1725), he remarked, "The tea-table among the ladies, and the coffeehouse among the men seem to be places of new invention for a depravation of our manners and morals, places devoted to scandal, and where the characters of all kinds of persons and professions are handled in the most merciless manner, where reproach triumphs, and we seem to give ourselves a loose to fall upon one another in the most unchristian and unfriendly manner in the world" (cited in Cowan 2004, 356). The passage below this print would seem to confirm this sentiment in describing an environment where "Thick scandal circulate with right Bohea [a popular black tea]."

humor, a frequent theme of which was the irresponsibility and silliness of women. Figures 5.10 and 5.11, the first from the nineteenth century and the second probably from the early-to-mid eighteenth, show women at tea where, instead of engaging in appropriately modest conversation, they are gossiping. Many aspects of respectability lent themselves to comic representation and to satire—either on the grounds that actual behavior in rituals such as tea did not correspond to the meanings they were supposed to embody or because they were occasions for outright hypocrisy.

In the culture of respectability and in middle-class practice, a principal function of the family was educating children to become civilized adults able to take on their social responsibilities. One of the ways in which families performed this function was by trying to structure children's play as a kind of role-performance, a rehearsal for the rituals of adult life. A significant part of the expanding demand for toys in the eighteenth and nineteenth centuries resulted from such intentions (Plumb 1982). A miniature tea set (fig. 5.12) was thus possibly intended to be used as a toy by children to replicate adult tea taking or also employed by adults to teach children how to behave at tea.

Domesticating and Colonizing the Exotic
Initially one of the principal attractions of tea in Europe was the fact that, like many other desirable consumables such as coffee, pepper, sugar, and the major spices, it came from somewhere else in the world. The appeal of tea as an exotic import rested originally on its identification with the civilization of

5.12   William Chawner (England, d. 1834)
        Child's tea set, London, 1823
        Silver
        L (case): 23.8 cm
        FOWLER MUSEUM AT UCLA, THE FRANCIS E. FOWLER, JR. COLLECTION,
        X87.1019A–K

5.13   A. C.
        A Tea Leaf, London, England, circa 1834
        Lithograph with hand coloring
        21 X 31 cm
        COURTESY OF THE LEWIS WALPOLE LIBRARY,
        YALE UNIVERSITY, NO. 834.00.00.4

5.14   *Principal Tea Pots to the Celestial Court*, London, England,
        circa 1843
        Lithograph with hand coloring
        12.8 X 22.5 cm
        COURTESY OF THE LEWIS WALPOLE LIBRARY,
        YALE UNIVERSITY, NO. 843.00.00.27

China and with Chinese medicinal practice. These identifications made tea fashionable among the self-styled *virtuosi*: upper-class gentlemen who distinguished themselves through their interests in science and in non-European societies and through their possession and understanding of unusual objects from around the globe (Cowan 2005, 10–14). In addition to the other meanings they possess, the tapestry (see fig. 5.2) and the cover of the treatise (see fig. 5.5) clearly suggest the concerns of virtuoso exoticism—the former by representing appreciation on the part of its owner of Chinese civilization, the latter by advertising the esoteric knowledge divulged within.

In the eighteenth century, such concerns migrated into the culture of respectability, becoming an integral and extremely important part of the conceptual equipment of the middle class. Knowledge of the world overseas and the use of commodities that displayed such knowledge represented the claims of middle-class people of belonging to the "public"—the part of society that discussed matters of general importance and took a legitimate part in determining society's consensus on them (Habermas 1989). At the same time, exotic items needed to be suitably domesticated, to be made consistent with the values of respectable Western society (which were increasingly assumed to be superior in level of civilization to all others.) The exotic had, in other words, to be made in some sense ordinary.

The commodities and practices associated with tea show the process of domestication very clearly. Explicit, if not always accurate, depictions of Chinese people and settings tended to be replaced by representations of Europeans performing Western rituals. No one forgot that tea came from China (at least until the mid-nineteenth century), but it arrived in Europe under Western terms and fitted into patterns of usage that conformed to the culture of the Western middle classes—that is, to respectability. In a significant way, domesticating the exotic in Europe was part of the same process as the colonizing of exotic places overseas by Europeans.

The results of this connection can be seen by comparing the respectful admiration of what purports to be China in the tapestry from the seventeenth century (see fig. 5.2) with a belittling cartoon that mocks the ceremony of the imperial Chinese court by portraying it as a parade of teapots (fig. 5.14). The latter is typical of British representations of China in the aftermath of Britain's first (quite unsuccessful) official embassy to the Chinese emperor in 1793 (Spence 1991, 122–23). These representations ridicule Chinese pretensions to cultural and political superiority in the face of Europeans' certainty about the superiority of their own culture and power. The trade names of standard types of tea, which had once been part of its exotic attraction, became objects of humor, as in figure 5.14 and in the visual-verbal puns portrayed in another illustration (fig. 5.13). New types of tea introduced in the nineteenth century more often than not were given European, not Asian, trade names, for example, "Earl Grey."

5.15   Isaac Cruikshank (England, 1756–1811) after
George Murgatroyd Woodward (England, 1765?–1809)
View of the Tea Gardens at Bayswater, London 1796
Etching with hand coloring
26.3 x 20 cm
COURTESY OF THE LEWIS WALPOLE LIBRARY,
YALE UNIVERSITY, NO. 796.08.01.04

This illustration originally appeared as plate v, page 19, of *Woodward's Eccentric Excursions* (1796), a book detailing the travels of George Woodward around England and South Wales. As Woodward, the artist and author, was not formally trained, he typically collaborated with someone who could transfer his designs to copper plates. In this case his collaborator was Isaac Cruikshank, father of the famous Victorian caricaturist George Cruikshank. Woodward collaborated with Thomas Rowlandson as well.

The Public

The cultural context in which the exotic appeal of tea was domesticated featured a claim by self-consciously respectable people (mainly of the middle class) to participation in national *public* discourse. Much of the preceding discussion has focused on the role of tea in the construction of middle-class private life, especially within the family, but as we have seen, tea also had public functions. For one thing, respectable people consumed tea not only at home but also in public places, where behavior was no less ritualized and meaningful and where it was more readily observed. Respectable European gentlemen and ladies in the eighteenth and nineteenth centuries took tea at teahouses and coffeehouses, in conspicuous preference to places where alcoholic beverages were regularly served. In the eighteenth century, respectably dressed people could also take tea at large, open-air establishments near urban areas, such as the one near London humorously portrayed in a cartoon from 1796 (fig. 5.15). At such locations, individuals and families could display their status and, under appropriate circumstances, engage in conversation with others on topics of public interest ranging from the serious to the trivial.

On occasion, tea was significant in public discussions that were very serious indeed. A sugar bowl (fig. 5.16) and the satirical illustration that appears in figure 5.7 relate to the campaign in the late eighteenth and early nineteenth centuries to persuade the British public to confront the moral problem of slavery in Britain's West Indian colonies. This movement, which ultimately succeeded in 1807 in abolishing the British slave trade and then, in 1833 and 1838, colonial slavery itself, derived in many ways directly from the culture of respectability. Its success depended heavily on its ability to convince the respectable middle class that the moral imperative of ending slavery trumped all other political and economic considerations and that by leading the way to abolition, Britain would be proving its moral superiority over other nations—ideas based on and entirely consistent with respectability. By the early nineteenth century, supporting abolition had become one of the ways in which middle-class people asserted their perspective on politics as against that of many elite groups and against special interests that profited from slavery's continuance (Hochschild 2005).

Figure 5.7 is a cartoon from 1792 making fun both of one episode in the early history of abolitionism and of King George III, thinly disguised in the cartoon as "John Bull." Abolitionists had organized a campaign to convince people to stop adding sugar to their tea as a way to put economic pressure on the West Indian sugar industry so as to get it to stop opposing abolition. The campaign was not very successful, but at one point, Queen Charlotte was reported to have agreed to take part in the boycott. She and the king are shown trying to convince their reluctant daughters that tea tastes good even without sugar. (Almost everyone in Britain at the time took tea with large amounts of sugar.) An indirect object of the cartoon's humor is George III himself, not because the king was particularly sympathetic to abolition (he was not), but

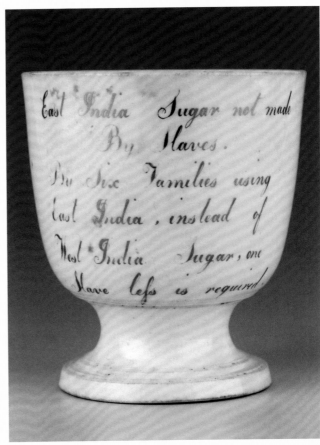

5.16a,b Sugar bowl, England, 1825–1830
Hand-painted bone china
H: 11.8 cm
COLONIAL WILLIAMSBURG FOUNDATION, NO. 1998.37

because he had deliberately and successfully tried to portray himself and his family (not counting his sons) as exemplars of respectability. This was the first conscious effort to create a link between the royal family and a middle class that conceived of itself in terms of respectability. It would not be the last (Smith 2002, 243–44).

The abolitionists later adopted tactics that required less self-sacrifice on the part of the public. The sugar bowl in figure 5.16 was manufactured around 1825–1830. It bears the standard abolitionist logo of a kneeling slave in chains on one side. On the other, it appeals to the public to use East Indian as opposed to West Indian sugar in its tea because the latter is produced by slaves and the former is not.

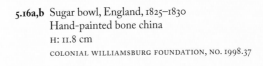

Tea carried a variety of meanings in the culture of respectability from the late seventeenth through the nineteenth centuries. Its ritual consumption was a sign of respectable gentility, fashion, and good taste; a means of supporting health and demonstrating moral virtue; a central symbolic focus of family life; a way to domesticate and colonize the exotic; and a demand for full inclusion in the public realm. Because of these meanings, tea played a significant role in the construction, definition, and practices of the middle class in the European and Atlantic worlds. Its relationship to the middle class was not the only factor that gave tea its world-historical importance, but it was a major one.

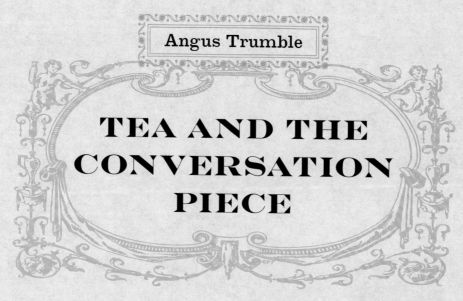

Angus Trumble

TEA AND THE CONVERSATION PIECE

CLOSE by those Meads for ever crown'd with Flow'rs,
Where Thames with Pride surveys his rising Tow'rs,
There stands a Structure of Majestick Frame,
Which from the neighb'ring Hampton takes its Name.
Here Britain's Statesmen oft the Fall foredoom
Of Foreign Tyrants, and of Nymphs at home;
Here Thou, great Anna! whom three Realms obey,
Dost sometimes Counsel take—and sometimes Tea.
Alexander Pope, *The Rape of the Lock*

THESE OPENING LINES from Part 3 of Alexander Pope's *The Rape of the Lock* (1712–1714) illustrate the seriousness of tea drinking in England in the second decade of the eighteenth century, only a few years after the Act of Union (1707) created the modern concept of "Britain." Here, in the final couplet, high matters of state and intimate domesticity converge in the person of Queen Anne at Hampton Court Palace. Although the point is satirical—implying a collision of pomposity with presumed triviality—it is telling that Pope chose tea as the fulcrum of his rebarbative wit, while the rhyme scheme incidentally reveals that in 1714 the English word "tea" still retained its French pronunciation (Jordan 1934, 220, 222). The brilliant antithetical conceit in the last line merely underscored what Pope's earliest readers already knew well, that taking counsel at court and taking tea were, more often than not, exactly the same thing. It is no accident therefore that an English portrait type soon developed in which tea and increasingly public sociability were often synonymous.

A "conversation picture" or "conversation piece" is a small-scale portrait consisting of two or more full-length figures, mostly but not always members of the same family, dressed informally in modern-day costume; grouped either indoors or outside in a park landscape; often accompanied by some of their favorite pets, furniture and other possessions, and servants—in that order. Developed in England in the 1720s and perfected by William Hogarth, Gawen Hamilton, Arthur Devis, Joseph Highmore, and others, the conversation piece reflected an increasing demand for small group portraits to suit more intimate early Georgian interiors than the picture galleries, great halls, and ceremonial corridors of Tudor and early Stuart houses of the sixteenth and seventeenth centuries. Indeed these older buildings provided the sociopolitical, semipublic forum, as well as the colossal amount of wall space, for large-scale, often full-length late Stuart portraits by Peter Lely, Godfrey Kneller, and others, a mode that persisted in non-British portraiture well into the mid-eighteenth century. By contrast, the conversation piece achieved remarkable popularity within a decade and persisted into the last quarter of the eighteenth century.

In its quiet way, the conversation piece represented more of a change to format and scale than to function or rationale, at least from the patron's point of view. Though quite different in size and format, in common with most earlier Stuart portraits, conversation pieces were generally commissioned to commemorate important dynastic events such as betrothals, marriages, the inheritance of property or titles, the assumption of a not particularly important seat in the House of Lords, or taking middle-level offices such as the lord-lieutenantship of a county. The genre was not one that appealed so much to Whig

B.1   Arthur Devis (England, 1712–1787)
Mr. and Mrs. Hill, circa 1750–1751
Oil on canvas
76.2 x 63.5 cm
YALE CENTER FOR BRITISH ART,
PAUL MELLON COLLECTION, B1981.25.226

Arthur Devis enjoyed considerable latitude in his approach to the interiors and park landscapes in which he set his many conversation pieces. Many incorporate real parks and houses, the properties appertaining to the members of the family in each portrait, while others were purely invented, the interiors especially. It has been suggested, therefore, that "Rather like the interiors of Hogarth's modern moral subject paintings, [the rooms and their contents] were to be understood as signifiers of abstract virtues—their generic quality enhancing their legibility" (Retford 2007, 291). Generic and legible though they may be, we also know that Devis employed miniature wooden artist's models or lay figures in his studio, which partly explains the stiffness and uniformity of his dramatis personae, mostly members of the Tory-leaning landed gentry.

B.2   *A Family Being Served with Tea*, British, circa 1740–1745
Oil on canvas
106.7 x 139.7 cm

This remarkable conversation piece is something of an enigma. The costumes suggest that it may be dated to no later than the 1740s. It was once tentatively attributed to Joseph Van Aken (ca. 1699–1749), the painter of draperies and decidedly workmanlike conversation pieces. Technical examination, however, suggests that whoever first tackled the subject, traditionally identified as "the Carter family," may only have finished the heads and hands of the ladies, the tea service, and the two male figures on the left, and that everything else was added much later and finished off much more crudely. Numerous pentimenti, which indicate, among other things, that the man in black was once much larger (previously concealing the left foot of the kettle stand, which now floats in mid-air), also reveal that certain layers of paint now obscured are of far greater quality than this extensive later surface re-painting, and for this reason certainly disqualify Van Aken. Whoever he was, the artist has bequeathed to us his tantalizing seated self-portrait as a reflection on the convex body of the silver kettle.

grandees and other powerful aristocrats; nor did it appeal to successive generations of Hanoverian royal patrons (Trumble 2007, 249–50). Arthur Devis, the most prolific painter of conversation pieces, produced more than three hundred examples, mostly for members of the rapidly expanding, largely Tory landed gentry and professional classes.

Although the conversation piece has long been considered a uniquely English contribution to the history of early eighteenth-century European portraiture, recent scholarship has served to demonstrate the extent to which the small-scale conversation piece at least partly emerged from certain conventions in nearly contemporaneous French genre painting, in which tea, coffee, and chocolate drinking are not merely conspicuous but to some degree explain or contextualize those social games that might safely be played in the boudoir and the closet (Eatwell 2008, 50–76). That French prompt arrived in London with artists such as Philippe Mercier, who did far more to inspire the development of the so-called Fancy Picture—"Pieces of some figures of conversation as big as the life: Conceited plaisant Fancies and habits," as George Vertue described the genre—than he gave rise to the conversation piece. Nevertheless, his impact upon Hogarth in particular did

much to insure that a fairly high proportion of English conversation pictures referred to tea.

Within the genre of the conversation piece, so evenly divided between outdoor settings and splendidly decorated rooms—which far more often reflect the future aspirations of the patron and his family than the actual appearance of existing dwellings—it is more often the informality of the scene that hinges upon tea than those tedious questions of manners and precedence, which through the course of the eighteenth century increasingly clustered around the tea table, gradually transforming its habits into complex ceremonial.

In other words, the conversation piece generally asks us to take tea at face value, which is not to say that its value was not high. Although the corner of the drawing room in which Devis portrayed Mr. and Mrs. Hill, circa 1750–1751 (fig. B.1) is unusually spare, it nevertheless contains a large oval italianate landscape, mounted high as an overmantel, and a Chinese blue-and-white covered export vase standing in the fireplace, suggesting almost certainly that it is summer. A Dutch red stoneware teapot (a type produced in imitation of Kangxi brown-glazed export "Batavian-ware" Chinese prototypes)

B.3   Jean-Etienne Liotard (Geneva, Switzerland, 1702–1789)
Still Life: Tea Set, Holland, circa 1781–1783
Oil on canvas mounted on board
Unframed: 37.8 x 51.6
J. PAUL GETTY MUSEUM, LOS ANGELES, NO. 84.PA.57

Liotard is perhaps best known for his exquisite and highly detailed pastel portraits. As a young man he began painting while traveling extensively throughout Europe and around the Mediterranean, at one point spending four years in Turkey. Although he had previously depicted fruit and porcelain in his portraits, he focused upon still lifes in the later decades of his career. This painting shows the disarray following the enjoyment of tea with six tea bowls and saucers attesting to the number of attendees. The large "slop bowl" at the back right was for used tea leaves and tea that had grown cold.

B.4   Artist unknown, possibly Richard Collins (England, d. 1732)
Man and Child Drinking Tea, circa 1720
Oil on canvas
Unframed: 71.1 x 62.2 cm
COLONIAL WILLIAMSBURG FOUNDATION, NO. 1954-654

Richard Collins was a portrait painter and topographical draughtsman.
He painted a conversation piece of a family taking tea, now in the Victoria and Albert Museum, London, and it is presumably some resemblance between that work and this that prompted the present attribution.
Certainly, the paintings do not seem too implausibly distant from each other, especially in the handling of the gentleman's face; nor indeed do they differ remarkably from the comparatively stiff manner of Collins's Swedish expatriate teacher, Michael Dahl (1659–1743). This painting does share something of the ebullience, though not the technical brilliance, of Dutch and Flemish food-and-drink portraits of the last quarter of the seventeenth century.

stands on the tea table, surrounded by an elegant porcelain service, which indicates that five guests are expected (Trumble 2007, 250). The cool precision with which these objects are drawn, and the daring spaciousness of the surroundings, here lay considerable emphasis on the accoutrements of tea.

But to what extent are those accoutrements intended to reflect the high status of the sitters, if at all? The question is complex as are the further questions: how high was the status of the Hills, or indeed how wealthy were they, or even how much this conversation piece cost. Mr. Hill adopts a position long recommended by etiquette manuals—not a habit made fashionable by Napoleon—with his feet positioned at an exact ninety-degree angle and his hand slipped inside his waistcoat. The attitude is aspirational. Mrs. Hill's exquisitely painted dress is expensive, but not excessively decorated. Mr. Hill's book, discarded on the mantel, tells us little except that it is apparently octavo and that there is only one of them. At best, many of these observations we may lay at the painter's feet, and not the patron's, but like many other conversation pieces that revolve around the tea table, and tea itself, the tea equipage was understood to be expensive and an increasingly indispensible mark of gentility. Similarly tea provided the logical narrative propulsion with which the as yet unidentified painter of *A Family Being Served With Tea*, circa 1740–1745 (fig. B.2) gathered his dramatis personae: mother presiding over the tea table as was the custom, father, two daughters, the family dogs, the artist himself—who appears seated at an easel in a deftly drawn reflection in the body of the silver kettle—and, finally, the servant who carries the kettle.

Representations of tea services—outside of the conversation piece genre—as subjects of still life on the continent, such as the example by Jean-Etienne Liotard (fig. B.3), or else as the dominant accoutrements of more tightly figured Dutch and Flemish half-length portraits (fig. B.4), perhaps carry the strongest possible indication that there is beyond the boundaries of each composition a radiating presence of human sociability, for which the tea things stand in. In this respect, continental paintings of each type—delicate French still lifes and robust Dutch food-and-drink portraits—share with those English conversation pieces that revolve around the tea table a capacity to see tea not only as leisure, but with some levelheadedness as money also.

Just as the English term "conversation piece" was originally taken to mean representations of people conversing,[1] there is also a strong hint, especially as regards the tea table, that it might also embrace representations of people that could, in turn, from the viewer's perspective prompt or stimulate real conversation. Certainly this was the view of an anonymous critic who in November 1820 identified himself in print as "W." and reflected a widespread and long-standing division of opinion (at least since the seventeenth century) as to the actual benefits of the plant, but not of meeting to drink cups of hot water infused with its leaves:

Tea, for a plant of doubtful properties, has extended its influence so widely, that either mankind have solved the doubt individually by their patronage of the tea-pot, or they have determined to swallow, for the sake of good company, what is "against the stomach of their sense." Now, I put it to some of your mathematical correspondents, what is the proportionable attraction of conversation at the tea-table, and of course, how much tea would remain unsold, and how much the [internal] revenue would lose, if every man should be compelled to drink his tea alone? That there is a peculiar tone given to conversation by tea, I will not pretend to assert; but we all know that there is no such agreeable commingling of sentiment, and equanimity of spirit any where, as we find at a tea-table [*Newcastle Magazine* 1820, 149]

As much as there were other voices regularly raised earlier, in the mid-eighteenth century, "accusing tea of impairing the digestion, unstringing the nerves, involving great and useless expense and inducing symptoms of paralysis" (Wesley 1748, 390), the conversation piece stands as persuasive evidence of its central role at the same time as a social lubricant and increasingly important status symbol among sitters who were amply prepared to run the risk, and to follow the prompts emanating from court, as in Pope's *The Rape of the Lock*. It raises the larger question as to whether the conversation piece could have achieved its wide currency in England without "the agreeable commingling of sentiment" afforded by tea.

Barbara G. Carson

DETERMINING THE GROWTH AND DISTRIBUTION OF TEA DRINKING IN EIGHTEENTH-CENTURY AMERICA

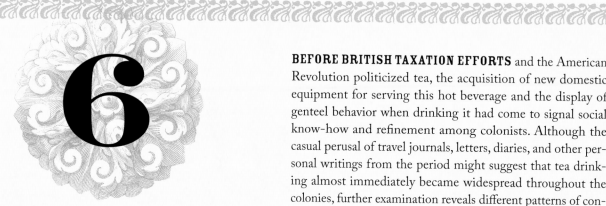

BEFORE BRITISH TAXATION EFFORTS and the American Revolution politicized tea, the acquisition of new domestic equipment for serving this hot beverage and the display of genteel behavior when drinking it had come to signal social know-how and refinement among colonists. Although the casual perusal of travel journals, letters, diaries, and other personal writings from the period might suggest that tea drinking almost immediately became widespread throughout the colonies, further examination reveals different patterns of consumption at various times and within differing populations.

Around 1750 Israel Acrelius asserted in his history of the Swedish settlement on the Delaware River that "[t]ea, coffee, and chocolate are so general as to be found in the most remote cabins, if not for daily use, yet for visitors, mixed with Muscovado [a partially refined sugar]" (Roth 1961, 66). The Virginian Devereaux Jarratt presented a different picture, however, when he reminisced about his childhood in the 1740s:

> Our food was altogether the produce of the farm, or plantation, except a little sugar, which was rarely used. We made no use of tea or coffee for breakfast, or at any other time; nor did I know a single family that made any use of them.... I suppose the richer sort might make use of those and other luxuries, but to such people I had no access. We were accustomed to look upon, what were called gentle folks, as beings of a superior order. [Jarratt 1952, 361]

Given the disparity between these two accounts, it is extremely useful to consult a variety of sources in attempting to determine the spread and pervasiveness of tea use in the colonies. This essay therefore employs a personal diary, works of art, archaeological finds, documentary accounts, and several sets of probate documents from estates representing different regions and degrees of wealth in order to identify the types of objects associated with tea drinking in America and to test the extent of their distribution throughout the general population.

6.1 The Gansevoort Limner (America, active 1730–1745),
possibly Pieter Vanderlyn (New York, ca. 1687–1788)
Susanna Truax, 1730
Oil on bed ticking
95.9 x 83.8 cm

Susanna Truax was a descendant of Dutch settlers, and her dress and
the interior depicted in this painting are typical of Dutch taste and fashion in early eighteenth-century New York. The four-year-old Susanna
appears to be eating sugar from a spoon. The report of a Swedish visitor
to the Dutch colonies around this time may explain this behavior, as
he observed that the colonists "never put sugar into the cup, but take
a small bit of it into their mouths while they drink" (Chotner and Aronson 1992, 145). Controversy exists concerning the authorship of this
painting with some scholars maintaining that the artist described as the
"Gansevoort Limner" was actually Pieter Vanderlyn, and others disputing
this attribution.

Early Eighteenth-Century Tea Drinking:
The Diary of William Byrd (1674–1744)

In the early eighteenth century, the uses of tea in the American colonies were largely medicinal and ceremonial. The so-called secret diary kept in shorthand code by William Byrd allows us to look at the early use of hot beverages by one of Virginia's wealthiest men (Byrd 1941). For nearly four years, from February 1709 to September 1712, Byrd made entries in his diary almost every day. The entries are repetitive in their mention of his personal habits, and it is therefore likely that the diary offers a somewhat accurate record of his use of hot beverages. Byrd recorded only a few details relative to his drinking behavior and did not identify the household items relating to it. Fewer than 10 percent of his daily entries mention tea, chocolate, or coffee drinking, with tea being noted most frequently. In other words, for this very wealthy, early Virginia gentleman, who clearly could have afforded to make a habit of tea drinking, it does not appear to have been a daily ritual.[1] The few mentions of tea in the diary are, however, revealing.

Tea, as noted above, was often associated at this time with the treatment of illness or with formal ceremonies of official greeting and not as refreshment offered to guests after dinner or in the evening. Nor was it a breakfast beverage. Byrd's usual breakfast consisted of milk, served boiled rather than cold. On the infrequent mornings when he drank tea, which he often referred to as "milk tea," taken with bread and butter, he sometimes mentioned being sick. He seems to have suffered from malaria for which he also drank sage tea and a bark infusion. Although he hosted many overnight guests at Westover, his

6.2 John Brevoort (New York, 1715–1775)
Teapot, 1775
Silver
H: 19 cm
FOWLER MUSEUM AT UCLA, THE FRANCIS E. FOWLER, JR.
COLLECTION, X87.914

This small pear-shaped teapot and the round one in the portrait of Susanna Truax (see fig. 6.1) are relatively simple compared to later Rococo and Neoclassical tea wares (see figs. 6.3–6.5).

plantation on the James River, he rarely mentions tea offered for breakfast on these occasions. The major exception is the visit of Governor Spotswood in June of 1710. Byrd offered tea to the governor on three mornings and chocolate on the fourth. When in Williamsburg on business, Byrd met with the governor and other officials in the morning. Tea, or occasionally chocolate, was served at these times. It seems to have been presented as a kind of salute, a formal recognition of status or membership at the beginning of their discussions.

Unlike tea, Byrd does seem to have thought of chocolate as a breakfast beverage. He mentions it about two-thirds as often as he does tea. He records that he drank chocolate with the women who were attending his wife when she gave birth to a son in June 1709. Otherwise his references are not connected with specific occasions. He mentions drinking coffee only four times: with the governor (July 5 and 6, 1710), with women (March 30, 1711), and at home with visitors (April 9, 1711). He notes visits to Williamsburg's coffeehouses, however, on more than sixty days. Although he played cards, gambled, and frequently lost money in these establishments, he may not have been drinking coffee. On October 29, 1710, he wrote, "Walked to the coffeehouse where I drank two dishes of tea."[2]

At the time when Byrd was writing, tea was about to begin its slow climb to dominance among hot beverages. Although merchants had sporadically imported tea from China to England and then to the American Colonies in the late seventeenth century, the East India Company only secured partial access to the Port of Canton in 1713. Direct and regular shipments of tea from China began in 1717 (Chaudhuri 1978, 388). Shortly thereafter, British artists depicted elite and middle-class families gathered around tea tables (see Smith, this volume). These scenes tell us much of what we know about behavior surrounding tea drinking. For the American colonies, however, visual depictions of tea equipment are rare. The earliest, dated around 1730, is a portrait from New York of Susanna Truax at the age of about four (fig. 6.1). This painting, attributed to the artist known as the "Gansevoort Limner," possibly Pieter Vanderlyn, reflects the early presence of the Dutch in New York. The Dutch were in fact among the first to bring tea to North America. In the painting, the young girl is shown standing beside a tea table. A small teapot rests on a protective stand or pad with a cup and saucer and a sugar dish nearby. Susanna, who seems to be eating sugar with a spoon, drank her tea with a minimum of equipment. One can only assume that somewhere in her family's house was a kettle or container for boiling the water and some sort of canister or box for holding tea.

Tea among the Chesapeake Elite:
Objects in Sixty-Eight Inventories, 1741–1760

An analysis of sixty-eight probate inventories dating from 1741 to 1760 expands the picture of the equipment considered essential for social tea drinking. These documents are the earliest in a larger group of 325 representing the top 5 percent of wealth holders in selected areas of northern Virginia and Maryland.[3]

Only one of these sixty-eight decedents, Jeremiah Greenhan of Richmond, Virginia, who died January 1, 1753, did not own equipment relating to hot beverages. A few show possession of miscellaneous items suggesting that the service of these new drinks was either unlikely or hardly expressive of a set social ritual. For instance, John Glasscock of Richmond listed "1 Coffy Pot" at 5 shillings in July 1756. In the same year John Spann Webb owned "½ Dozn silver Teaspoons" valued at 20 shillings. Nearly every other decedent owned significant equipment for tea, as well as some for coffee and chocolate. For example, the inventory of Hugh West, entered in Fairfax, Virginia, in 1755, was valued in two parts. Personal property or household furnishings, slaves, an indentured servant, and livestock at the home plantation totaled £399 17s.7d. Property at the slaves' quarters came to £299 8s.6d for a total value of £699 6s.1d. Hot beverage items were scattered through the list for the home plantation only.

½ Dozn. Cups and sausers Slop Dish & Sugar pot	0.16.0
4 Cups sausers & 2 plates 1 Chiney Tea pot 6	0.7.6
6 Glass sausers & 4 glass cups 2/	
6 Coffee cups 2 sausers & 1 Bowl	0.2.6
2 Tea pots 1/6	
1 Tea chest 6/	
7 silver tea spoons & 1 pr of tongs £1.3.6	
1 Tea kettle 5/	
1 Tea Table 8/. 1 Do 15/	
1 Tea Kettle	
1 earthen pan & Tea pot 1/	

The values immediately following the items are subtotals, which are added with other items to yield the total given at the far right. West's hot beverage service amounted to a tiny fraction of his total estate, £3 8s or less than half of 1 percent. Fourteen slaves and a servant woman accounted for £355 10s. Among the furniture, a clock appraised at £9 was the single most valuable item. West did not own much plate, only "11 silver table spoons" valued at £8 in addition to the teaspoons and tongs. Beds, because of the labor-intensive textiles that furnished them, were assigned high values ranging from £2 to £6. In contrast "2 Negro's beds and Furniture" were a mere 10 shillings. Entries of a Bible at 5 shillings and "2 old Baskets" and "1 Frying pan" both at 1 shilling 6 pence illuminate the relatively small amounts of cash required to purchase hot beverage equipment.

Of note, teakettles of the sort referred to in the West inventory were rather plain flat-bottomed vessels, usually made of copper with hinged handles suspended from above the spout to the opposite side. They could be placed directly on a hearth or grate or hung over an open fire. It is likely that a servant or slave would have performed the controlled pouring required to direct the boiling water into the teapot either in the kitchen or at the tea table. The hostess then poured the tea from the teapot into cups and offered it along with sugar and milk or cream to her family or guests. Any tea or leaves remaining in the cups were poured into a slop dish before more tea was served. West's ownership of four teapots is fairly typical. Very few decedents owned just one. The only essential item missing is a jug for milk or cream.

Appraisers seem automatically to have separated tea and dinner services, as the two almost never appear listed together in inventories. They were used for different events, and the equipment for each seems rarely to have matched. Tea items made of silver may be grouped with all other silver items, ranging from shoe buckles to soup tureens, and sometimes the objects themselves are not identified with only the total weight of the silver and its value cited. Although West's appraisers did not identify the rooms where they found his personal property, other documents from the late 1750s on are more likely to associate tea wares with dining rooms and parlors than with private chambers. Kettles often show up in kitchens or with other cooking equipment.

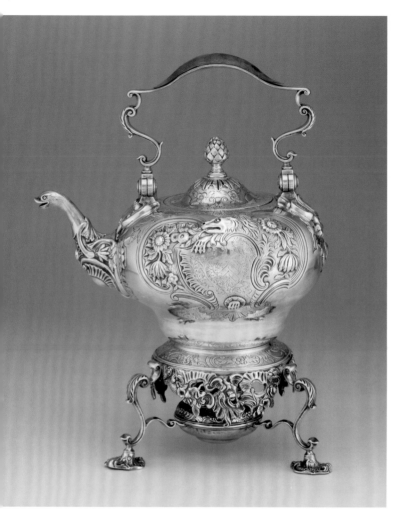

6.3   Joseph Richardson (Philadelphia, 1711–1784)
Teakettle, stand, and spirit lamp, 1745–1755
Silver
H (including stand and handle): 38.9 cm
YALE UNIVERSITY ART GALLERY, MABEL BRADY GARVAN COLLECTION

This teakettle is a superb example of the Rococo elegance that was much appreciated among the upper classes in England and its North American colonies in the mid-eighteenth century.

6.4   Richard Humphries
(b. Tortola, West Indies, 1750; active Philadelphia; d. 1832)
Grand presentation urn, 1774
Silver
H: 54.6 cm
PHILADELPHIA MUSEUM OF ART, PURCHASED WITH FUNDS CONTRIBUTED
BY THE DIETRICH AMERICAN FOUNDATION, 1977, NO. 1977.88.1
PHOTOGRAPH BY WILL BROWN

This urn is the earliest known example of the Neoclassical style in American silver. It is inscribed to Charles Thomson and was a gift to him from the Continental Congress, of which he was the secretary.

6.5   Paul Revere (Boston, 1734–1818)
Sugar urn, circa 1790
Silver
H: 23.5 cm
FOWLER MUSEUM AT UCLA, THE FRANCIS E. FOWLER, JR.
COLLECTION, X87.907A,B;

A work by noted Boston patriot and silversmith, Paul Revere, this fluted sugar urn reflects the Neoclassical style that became increasingly popular following the American Revolution.

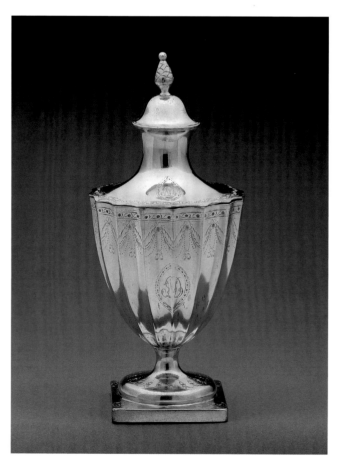

The Maryland lawyer Daniel Dulaney (1685–1753) became one of that colony's wealthiest officials and largest landowners. At his death he left personal property worth £10,921 9s.8d, including 187 slaves, substantial loans, and about ten thousand acres of land in five counties. Personal property in his Annapolis mansion was valued at £3,062 2s.10-1/4d and included 2,594 ounces of silver with a total value of £415 2s.6d. His hot beverage service—itemized in the rooms where it was kept and used—was impressive, elegant, and in a few instances unusual.

IN THE GREAT DINING ROOM

10 Ditto [China] Coffee Cups 9 Ditto Saucers	
3 Ditto Chocolate Cups	1.4.0
2 Ditto Tea pots, 2 Canisters, 12 Cups, 12 Saucers	1.5.0
One Sett of China Containing One Tea Pot and Stand,	
12 Cups and Saucers, 6 Coffee Cups, 1 Butter Plate,	
1 Spoon Boat, 1 Bowl and Saucers, 1 Sugar Dish,	
1 Cream Pot, 1 Canister 1 Spoon Boat and	
1 Stand	5.10.0
3 old Tea Cups 9 Ditto Saucers and Tea Pot	
1 Spoon Boat and 1 Stand	0.5.0
One Set of Old Fashioned broken China	
on the Japan Tea Table cont' 3 Tea pots 3 Bowls	
2 Butter Plates, 1 Stand, 1 Spoon Boat 1 Cream Pot,	
7 Tea Cups, 8 Saucers & 11 Coffee Cups	1.5.0
One Japan Tea Table Silk Covering for Ditto	1.0.0
1 Tea Chest Silver Mounted	1.10.0
1 Tea Kettle Lamp. And Stand [silver]	
22 Tea Spoons [silver]	
2 Pr. Tea Tongs [silver]	
2 Chocolate Pots, 1 Ditto Smaller [silver]	
1 ditto Strainers [silver]	
1 Coffee Pot [silver]	
1 Tea Pot [silver]	
2 Milk Pots [silver]	
3 Casters [silver]	
2 Tea Canisters and Sugar Dish [silver]	

IN THE PARLOUR

1 Japan'd Tea board 3/ 1 Do. Mahogony 3/	
28 Tea and Coffee Cups. 17 Saucers 1 Tea Pot	
1 Bowl & 1 Cream Pot	1.17.0
1 Japan'd Tea table and Covering for Ditto	0.15.0
9 Tea Table Cloths	4.10.0
5 Ditto old	1.0.0
4 Ditto very small	0.8.0
8 Tea napkins 9 old do very small in all 17	0.17.0
13 Tea napkins	0.16.3
1 Japan Tea Table	0.10.0

IN THE DINING ROOM CHAMBER

A box of Hard Sugar No.59 wt. Net 111	5.11.0
1 box Ditto 48 102	5.12.0
A Canister with 16 lb of brown sugar	9.0
5 Loaves Single fine Sugar wt. Net 26 lb	1.19.0
2 lb old Congo & 2 old Bohee Tea	1.0.0

ROOM AT THE HEAD OF THE STAIR CASE
Tea Cups and Saucers

2 Stone Tea Pots 1 Ditto Milk Pot	0.1.0

IN THE KITCHEN
2 Tea Kettles

[almost at end after fabric, etc.]

1 Coffee Roaster	3.6
1 {Copper} Tea Kettle	1.2.7
2 lb Hyson Tea	2.11.4
172 lb Loaf Sugar	12.13.3
126 lb Single Do	6.9.8

Spoon boats or saucers or rests for spoons do not often appear in American inventories. References to table linens associated with tea are even less common. Dulaney's "9 Tea Table Cloths" are unprecedented, especially since they are accompanied with an additional five old and four very small cloths and thirty tea napkins. In addition there was a cover for the "Japan'd Tea table."

Because the silver items are assigned a collective value, a total for the hot beverage service is not possible. Appraised values for items other than silver amount to £23 18s.1d. They range from "2 Stone Tea Pots 1 Ditto Milk Pot" at 1 shilling to "1 Japan'd Tea table and Covering for Ditto" at 15 shillings. For comparison, "11 Mouse Traps and 5 Ratt Ditto" came to 4 shillings 6 pence and two "Ivory fans carved & painted" were worth £3 7s.6d. Furniture had greater value, an "Eight Day Clock" at £10, "Twelve Silk damask bottom's Mahogany Chairs with Linnen Covers" at £18, and "Three Dotto [pictures] by Wollaston" at £28 7s.

Among Dulaney's silver tea wares was "1 Tea Kettle Lamp. And Stand." Two other decedents in this group of sixty-eight owned less-valuable examples of this form.[4] These kettles were not kitchen equipment (fig. 6.3). During the serving of tea, water kept hot with a spirit lamp positioned underneath the belly of the kettle, was poured into the teapot to brew more tea. The stands were usually low, intended to rest on the tea table itself or on a small stand or table just big enough for the kettle. Among these decedents Henry Fitzhugh (Stafford County, Virginia, 1742) was the second owner of a "tea kettle & lamp." His was brass valued at sixteen shillings. No American paintings depict a tea kettle of this type. In British scenes of tea drinking, servants attend them, possibly because the open spirit lamps and hinged handles were potentially dangerous. Safer were the hot water urns that appear later in the eighteenth century. Instead of an open lamp, a solid metal core that had been heated in the open fire was placed inside the container to keep the water hot. It flowed from a spout into the teapot (figs. 6.4, 6.5).

Food of any sort is uncommon in probate documents. Tea and sugar, nonetheless, appear in Dulaney's inventory. It mentions three types of tea—hyson (a Chinese green tea made from twisted leaves that are long and thin), bohea (a Chinese black tea that derives its name from the Wuyi mountains in

Fujian Province), and congo (or congou, a finer type of Chinese black tea, the name of which is derived from *kong-hu*, meaning "well-worked" or "pains taken"), along with several grades of sugar. Other miscellaneous items from this group of inventories include a "Glass Tea canister" (Jessie Ball, 1747) and "6 small Silver hafted Tea Knives" (Henry Holland Hawkins, 1751). Most tea wares were ceramic, not glass. Tea knives are very rare, and those with solid silver handles would have been expensive.

Expanding Distribution
of Tea Drinking and Its Equipage

If roughly five percent of the richest decedents in the Chesapeake owned impressive equipment for serving tea and other hot beverages between 1741 and 1760, what can be learned about its distribution among the rest of the population? Anecdotal evidence suggests interest in tea equipment and tea drinking was spreading throughout the social order. In 1744 Dr. Alexander Hamilton of Annapolis headed north on a pleasure trip hoping to improve his health. From New York, he and Mr. Milne, formerly a churchman in Albany, traveled up the Hudson River. When their sloop tied up on the west bank to collect water, the men entered a small log cottage that was home to a husband, wife, and seven children. While the parents were otherwise occupied and the children gathered blackberries, the visitors rather ungraciously passed judgment on the family's

6.6   Tea set, Jingdezhen, China, circa 1755
Hard-paste porcelain, enamel, gilt
H : 22.86 cm
THE MOUNT VERNON LADIES' ASSOCIATION COLLECTIONS

This set is an example of Chinese export porcelain. It is believed to be the "Compleat Sett [of] Fine Image China" that was shipped from London to George Washington at Mount Vernon in 1757. Washington was very particular about furnishings and decorative items, and we know from his records that he frequently served hyson tea to visitors.

furnishings. Mr. Milne thought a pail with water would make a satisfactory substitute for the looking glass with its painted frame and that wooden spoons and plates should replace the worn out but bright pewter. The stone tea dishes and teapot were "quite unnecessary" (Bridenbaugh 1948, 55).

Clearly, however, the family had other ideas about the role of tea equipage in their lives, and they were not alone. Throughout the colonies Americans were buying teapots, cups and saucers, and other items. Those made of silver, hard-paste porcelain from China (fig. 6.6), or soft-paste porcelain from England were expensive, but similar items, made of lead- or tin-glazed earthenware or stoneware (fig. 6.7), were available at low prices.

As the century progressed, innovations in ceramic production further expanded the range of available wares in terms

of price and appearance. Poorer customers with only small amounts of cash or limited credit could, therefore, participate in this new consumer revolution. Hot beverages represent only a small fraction of the consumer goods that began to make the lives of people in Europe and America more pleasant, comfortable, and aesthetically pleasing. A major transformation in both demand and production was well underway by the middle of the eighteenth century. The list of industrial inventions exploded. Nearly every category of household furnishing was affected—textiles, metal cooking wares, table knives and forks, other dining equipage, looking glasses, prints and paintings, and so forth. Previously only the wealthy were entitled to display fancy clothes and indulge in luxuries. Gradually, however, ordinary people assumed the right to spend a little money and express personal taste. As they bought new equipment and learned to use it, they abandoned traditional folkways and became early consumers.

Modern historians estimate that by the time of the Revolution about two-thirds of white adults could have had tea every day (Shammas 1990, 64). Some years earlier in 1759, Ezra Stiles, the president of Yale, traveled to Cape Cod where he counted 1,940 families of whom 1,500, or 77 percent drank tea (Stiles 1916, 31). There is also limited evidence of interest in tea drinking among African Americans and Native Americans. A few African American and Native American potters were sufficiently familiar with tea wares to have copied European

6.7   William Rogers
(active 1720–1739, Yorktown, Virginia; d. 1739)
Fragments of stoneware with teapot lid and partial body,
Yorktown Virginia, circa 1720–1739
Salt-glazed stoneware
Estimated H (teapot): 10.2 cm
COURTESY NATIONAL PARK SERVICE, COLONIAL NATIONAL
HISTORICAL PARK, YORKTOWN COLLECTION, NOS. COLO Y: 37515,
9813, 9815, 9816, 9817
PHOTOGRAPH COURTESY OF *CERAMICS IN AMERICA*, PHOTOGRAPHER
GAVIN ASHWORTH

William Rogers of Yorktown, Virginia, known in records as the "Poor Potter," was a businessman and entrepreneur who owned a successful earthenware and stoneware pottery from approximately 1720 to 1739. His output included tea wares as suggested by these fragments. No instances of his tea wares have, however, been found outside the settlement site in Yorktown where these were located.

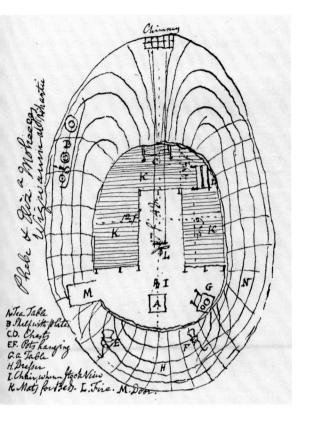

6.8   Ezra Stiles (Connecticut, 1727–1795)
Sketch of a Wigwam, Niantic, Connecticut, 1761
Ink on paper
REPRODUCED FROM STILES (1916, 155)

Ezra Stiles, the president of Yale, indicated the presence of a tea table, labeled with the letter "A," in his sketch of the interior of a wigwam belonging to the Native American sisters Phebe and Elizabeth Moheege in Niantic, Connecticut.

6.9   Partially reconstructed teapot, South Carolina, circa 1750–1780
Unglazed earthenware
H: 29.21 cm
COURTESY OF THE SOUTH CAROLINA INSTITUTE OF ARCHAEOLOGY
AND ANTHROPOLOGY, UNIVERSITY OF SOUTH CAROLINA, COLUMBIA,
NO. 38CH241-77C-1

Although unglazed earthenware of this type is often referred to as "Colono Indian ware," this teapot is attributed to an African American potter and was found on the Hampton plantation in Charleston County, South Carolina. European forms in such low-fired, unglazed earthenware are very rare.

shapes in ordinary earthenware.[5] In 1761 Stiles sketched the location of a tea table that he observed in the Niantic, Connecticut, wigwam of the Native American sisters Phebe and Elizabeth Moheege (fig. 6.8). Their dwelling was also furnished with a shelf with plates, two chests, a second table, a dresser, and six chairs. There were mats for beds (Stiles, 1916, 155). There also exists evidence of African American tea use and tea ware manufacture (fig. 6.9). When Jullian Ursyn Niemcewicz from Poland visited Mount Vernon in 1797, he wrote:

> We entered one of the huts of the blacks, for one can not call them by the name of houses. They are more miserable than the most miserable of the cottages of our peasants. The husband and wife sleep on a mean pallet, the children on the ground; a very bad fireplace, some utensils for cooking, but in the middle of this poverty some cups and a teapot. [Niemcewicz 1965, 100–101]

Probate Evidence from the Chesapeake and from Pennsylvania, 1774

Two other groups of inventories, all taken in 1774, help to refine these views and suggest a more limited pattern of ownership of hot beverage service items. These samples are statistically accurate and range from the poorest to the richest decedents in two geographic locations, several counties in Maryland and Virginia and three areas in Pennsylvania.[6]

The 143 inventories from Anne Arundel and Queen Anne Counties in Maryland and eight counties in Virginia serve as a counterbalance to the group of documents that focus on wealthier decedents in the Chesapeake from 1741 to 1760.[7] Hot beverage items appear in just over half of the inventories (seventy four). Fourteen decedents owned equipment for serving both tea and coffee, three for both tea and chocolate. Only two mentioned coffee without tea. The dividing point falls at the estate value of about £500, but the poorer people were not ignoring all the new refinements associated with the emerging desire for and acquisition of consumer goods.

The three areas of Pennsylvania represented include two rural counties and Philadelphia. In Northampton County to the north along the Delaware River nearly everyone farmed and no one was wealthy. Of twenty-one decedents, there was one widow, one laborer-weaver, and one farmer-cooper. In Westmoreland County, well toward the west along the border with Maryland, the eight decedents were a mix of yeomen, farmers, and a single weaver. Eight of the total twenty-nine documents contain some mention of coffee or tea, but none suggests social consumption. For instance, T. Jamison of Westmoreland owned a single "coffey mill" and S. Wilson "a tea pot" valued at 3 shillings 5 pence. In Northampton the widow Frederick's estate included "1 coffee mill" at 4 shillings 6 pence and a "tea pot."

In Philadelphia County the 134 decedents were mainly artisans and merchants with a few farmers. Not surprisingly, equipment for the service of hot beverages was more widespread and differed according to wealth groups. The useful breaking point is again £500. Above that, nearly all decedents owned some object associated with tea, coffee, or chocolate.

6.10 John Eckstein (b. Germany; active United States 1794–1817)
The Samels Family, circa 1788
Oil on canvas
64.8 x 76.2 cm
MUSEUM OF FINE ARTS BOSTON,
ELLEN KELLERAN GARDNER FUND, NO. 59.194
PHOTOGRAPH ©2009

This family portrait prominently features a tea service arranged on a tilt-top table. Tables that could tilt so that the top was vertical when not in use were valued for their ability to save space. After tea had been served, such a table could be moved to the periphery of the room.

Below that amount, roughly half were so equipped. It is reasonable to read these numbers as confirmation of Devereaux Jarratt's experience and even of Ezra Stiles's somewhat higher numbers for tea drinkers on Cape Cod. While Pennsylvania, especially during the 1750s and early 1760s, was sometimes called the best poor man's country, by the 1770s it is likely that between one-fourth and one-third of its free population lived precariously. Poorer people struggled to meet basic expenses for food, shelter, and clothing. Even the modest price of a kettle, teapot, and a few cups exceeded their budgets (B. Smith 1981, 202).

Eighty-two of the 134 Philadelphia County inventories list some hot beverage item—seventy-eight for tea, forty-eight for coffee, and five for chocolate. The overlap is significant. Only two inventories mention chocolate without tea or coffee, and another two note coffee without tea. The seventy-eight tea takers (58 percent) were far from uniform in what they owned. Three quarters listed teakettles (60 of 78) and crockery of some sort (59 of 78), often specified as Chine, blue and white, Queensware, Burnt, stoneware, earthenware, tea cups and saucers, or tea ware. Teapots, sugar bowls, milk or cream jugs, and slop basins may have on occasion been lumped with the ceramics, but they also appear separately. Teapots are mentioned in only twenty-eight inventories. Two were specified as silver and came with stands. In addition, there were three tea

6.11   Richard Brunton (active Connecticut, late 18th century)
Mrs. Reuben Humphreys, circa 1800
Oil on canvas
113 X 102.9 cm
THE CONNECTICUT HISTORICAL SOCIETY, HARTFORD,
CONNECTICUT, GIFT OF THE JOSLYN ART MUSEUM
THROUGH MRS. FRANK M. WILLS, NO. 1970.2.2

Anna Humphreys (ca. 1759–1827) was the wife of the superintendent of Newgate Prison in East Granby, Connecticut. She poses here cradling her baby while sitting next to a tea table displaying fashionable white tea ware with floral decorations in pastel enamels. Richard Brunton, the painter of the portrait, was an inmate at Newgate Prison from 1799 to 1801. He was a metal engraver and had been arrested for counterfeiting.

6.12   Jacob Frymire (America, 1765–1822)
Portrait of Mrs. Calmes Holding a Cup of Tea, 1806
Oil on canvas
Framed: 85.1 x 712.1 cm
CHICAGO HISTORY MUSEUM, NO. 1922.4

Mrs. Calmes in this picture holds what appear to be two tea bowls. Like the tea ware in figure 6.11, these are white with floral decoration.

6.13   John Lewis Krimmel (b. Ebingen, Germany, 1789;
d. near Germantown, Pennsylvania, 1821)
The Quilting Frolic, 1813
Oil on canvas
42.5 x 55.4 cm
WINTERTHUR MUSEUM

Born in Germany, John Lewis Krimmel immigrated to Philadelphia in
1809 and is regarded as one of America's first painters of genre scenes.
Although by the second decade of the nineteenth century the young
African American girl he depicted in the *Quilting Frolic* may have been
serving the assembled family members and guests coffee, it is just as likely
that she would serve tea.

urns. Cream jugs appear in seventeen inventories and ten of
them were of silver. Sugar bowls (8) and slop basins (2) were
less likely to be identified. Nearly half the decedents owned
tea tables (39 of 78) and teaspoons (37 of 78). About a quarter
owned sugar tongs (22 of 78). More than half the spoons (20 of
37) and the tongs (12 of 22) were of silver. Canisters or chests
(29) appear in more than a quarter. Trays, often itemized as
"waiters" or "salvers," show up less frequently (16 of 78). There
were very few stands (8 of 78). The blizzard of objects, materials, and prices reveals buyers taking advantage of the wide
range of similar goods available in shops. Even so, while many
took tea, few had the equipment to impress their guests with
a complete service for a large company.

Tea drinkers also drank coffee. By about 1750 European
growers had secured fertile seeds from Yemenite traders and
were growing coffee in the mountains of the South American
coast and the Caribbean islands. The relative importance of
the tea and coffee trades and the preference for the beverages
during these decades is, however, obscure. Only two of the
inventories of 1774 mention coffee or its equipment without

any reference to tea. Both are mentioned in 46 inventories. Two documents simply refer to coffee or a "coffee can." Two others specify coffee cups. More frequent in their appearance are mills for grinding (24) and pots (26). Materials are rarely specified. Four coffee pots were made of copper and two of silver.[8] Roasters were scarce, appearing in only three estates, but beans might have been either purchased roasted and ground or roasted at home in a sauce or frying pan.

Five inventories list chocolate. Two of the decedents were shopkeepers who sold the commodity but did not own any equipment for its preparation. Three men, a merchant, an innkeeper, and an apothecary owned chocolate pots. The merchant's and apothecary's estates were valued at well over £500; the innkeeper at less than £100. All three also owned equipment related to both tea and coffee.

Tea's dominance over coffee and especially chocolate seems to have persisted into the very early nineteenth century. This is of note because it is a commonly held belief that today's preference for coffee over tea in the United States stemmed directly from the role of tea in the Revolution (see Merritt, this volume). The affluent Samels family, for example, chose to be painted at a tilt-top tea table (fig. 6.10). Similarly, portraits of Mrs. Reuben Humphreys (ca. 1800) and Mrs. Calmes (1806) feature elegant tea ware prominently (figs. 6.11, 6.12). There is no way to tell conclusively what beverage the young African American serving girl is offering to those in John Lewis Krimmel's painting of a quilting party (fig. 6.13). By the

second decade of the nineteenth century coffee had begun to dominate the hot beverage market in the United States. Just as the opportunity to trade at Canton after 1713 led to the preference for tea in Britain and her colonies, when the interests of American merchants expanded into the coffee trade of the Caribbean islands and South America, the buying and drinking public eventually began to follow. By 1827 the African American butler Robert Roberts was instructing young servants to fill their trays with "one cup of tea between every two of coffee, as they [the guests] generally take more coffee than tea at the first round" (Roberts 1827, 62). The switch was assured by the 1840s when American merchants came to control the international buying, roasting, grinding, packaging, and selling of coffee to an international market (MacDonald, forthcoming). This did not, however, indicate the demise of tea.

As the foregoing evidence suggests, while tea, tea wares, and social tea drinking were important in the eighteenth century, they were not universal. Wealthy urban families in Europe and America initially began to serve tea on social occasions. They bought significant quantities of equipment and used it according to precise rules of conduct and performance. About 1750, however, people with less money began to express their social ambitions and took advantage of the wares that producers were supplying in many materials and designs and at a wide range of price levels. Even so, many poor families (generally those with estates valued below £500) chose not to indulge in the luxury of hot tea. ❧

Jane T. Merritt

BEYOND BOSTON

*Prerevolutionary Activism
and the Other American Tea Parties*

THE BOSTON TEA PARTY holds a revered place in the history of the American Revolution and is often cited as key to our political independence and emerging national identity during the postwar period. Tourists today still make pilgrimages to Boston Harbor to see reenactments of the patriots' actions. At least four major Massachusetts archives claim possession of a small bottle of "Tea Party" tea. Donated in the early nineteenth century, these relics boast authenticity and lend sanctity to Boston as the birthplace of patriotic activity and American independence.[1] The unprecedented destruction in December 1773 of 342 chests of English East India Company tea (valued at £25,000 sterling according to one observer's estimate) sent shock waves through the British public and Parliament, leading to a backlash that economically crippled Boston (Tudor 1773; Newell [1773] 1878, 346). The Port Act of 1774 in fact closed the harbor to all commerce, putting both middle-class merchants and maritime laborers out of work.

It is important to acknowledge, however, that tea and consumer taxation were no less important to debate and political action in other parts of the colonial Atlantic world. New York, Philadelphia, and Charleston, all set to receive commissioned tea from the East India Company in late 1773, wrestled over their initial responses. Beyond the large port cities, smaller colonial communities were also drawn into the political deliberation over whether tea, as a symbol of British economic dominance, should be bought, sold, or even used by their citizens. Thoughtful debate based on impassioned Enlightenment ideals of liberty and rights to self-government engendered many a local boycott of English trade goods. Several towns chose more extreme measures to express their displeasure, and like Boston, they threatened or engaged in direct action against merchants, transporters, purchasers, or consumers of tea. While we might dismiss these other communities as mere imitators (and, indeed, most of the destruction of tea outside of Boston occurred after its Tea Party), in the long run, the political pamphleteering and economic boycotts initiated in Philadelphia and New York probably did far more than commonly believed to propel a united group of colonists toward revolution.

7.1 Daniel Berger (Germany, 1744–1824)
Die Einwohner von Boston werfen den englisch-ostindischen Thee ins Meer am 18, December, 1773 (The Inhabitants of Boston Throw the English-East Indian Tea in the Sea on the 18th of December, 1773), 1784
One of a continuous strip of six etchings
43.2 x 12.7 cm
LIBRARY OF CONGRESS, WASHINGTON, D.C.,
PGA BERGER-AMERICANER PCI5490

German artist Daniel Berger created a series of American Revolutionary prints, including this example (one of six individual images on a continuous etching). It depicts a small crowd on the Boston pier waving triumphantly at the Sons of Liberty who dump East India tea into the harbor. Two young black men (servants, slaves, or sailors) sit prominently at the left of the scene (as they do in other of Berger's prints), alluding to the broader implications of revolution on the American social landscape.

Indeed this essay aims to explore why the less-celebrated protests of American colonists were necessary catalysts for prerevolutionary activism both before and after the Boston Tea Party. Boston may be best remembered for its activism because the town bore the brunt of British economic sanctions (fig. 7.1), eventually provoking military confrontation in 1775, but the "other tea parties" beyond Boston help us understand a less-familiar, even subversive, colonial America and its relationship with a new world of consumption. The best-known example of such activism came from Edenton, North Carolina (fig. 7.2), where an unlikely group of "Patriotic Ladies" swore on October 25, 1774, "not to Conform to that Pernicious Custom of Drinking Tea" nor to "promote to wear of any Manufacture from England untill such time that all Acts which tend to Enslave this our Native Country shall be Repealed" (Sweeney 1998, 21). These women are depicted as of mixed class and race; some are plainly dressed, others wear elaborate wigs. An African American servant holds a tray with an inkpot and pens for the women to use in signing a petition laid out on the table. On one level, the print appears to mock women as frivolous and fickle consumers, a common practice among many eighteenth-century critics. These are, after all, careless, even disorderly, women in the company of leering men; a child sits neglected on the floor. Yet, the women also display their political acumen. Some dump tea from their canisters, others sign the petition. Even the child throws a small tea set on the floor in a fit, while a dog urinates on another pile of tea canisters nearby.[2] Whether the Edenton "tea party" really happened in this manner or not, the image and its implication that female consumers had great power to protest the sale of Chinese tea by British companies for American tables raises interesting questions concerning revolutionary activism. Did Americans fear that boycotts and political protests might lead to gender and racial disorder? Or did they welcome the social dislocation that broader economic choice and republican ideals sometimes produced? Indeed, by the early 1770s the rest of the world watched Americans with fascination to see where a seemingly trivial conflict over tea and taxation would take them.

A SOCIETY of PATRIOTIC LADIES,
AT
EDENTON in NORTH CAROLINA.

Plate V.

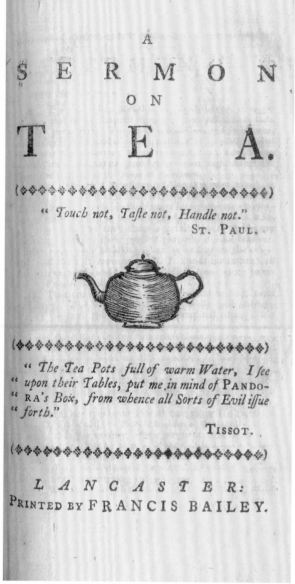

7.2   Philip Dawe (England, 1730s–1832)
A Society of Patriotic Ladies at Edenton, North Carolina,
published by Sayer and Bennett, London, March 25, 1775
Mezzotint
36.8 x 27.3 cm
LIBRARY OF CONGRESS, WASHINGTON, D.C., PCI5284B

Like the print by Daniel Berger (see fig. 7.1), Philip Dawe's cartoon depicts a nontraditional view of revolutionary activism. Although originally meant to poke fun at American consumer protests of tea, the engraving suggests that political activity was not bound by gender, class, race, or region.

7.3   Title page, *A Sermon on Tea*, printed by Francis Bailey,
Lancaster, Pennsylvania [1774]
Printed, eight-page pamphlet
H: 21 cm
LIBRARY OF CONGRESS, WASHINGTON, D.C., C901.H3, VOL. 36, NO. 6

This pamphlet combines the physiological, social, and political criticisms of tea common in the eighteenth century.

To understand the American political response to tea, and the role of the Edenton Ladies in protest, we must first consider the place of tea within the cultural debates of the early modern period. The standard of living for the English-speaking world had risen significantly by the mid-eighteenth century as a consequence of growing trade and prosperity, which brought the increasing availability of imported luxury items and manufactured goods. Tea in particular emerged as an important commodity of global trade, tying Britain and its colonies to Asia and providing a medium of exchange in the empire. Because it was light and easy to transport, merchants could sell tea for "ready money" or on short credit (one to three months), which helped them maintain a needed cash flow (Kidd 1752; James and Drinker 1764). In 1690, a mere 38,390 pounds of tea was imported to England and priced accordingly, making it a wealthy man's drink. By the mid-eighteenth century, however, the East India Company imported more than 2.5 million pounds of tea annually into Great Britain, of which 20 percent was re-exported to the American colonies (Samuel Wharton 1901, 140; see also Drake 1884, 192–93). In addition, Americans purchased and drank a good deal of smuggled tea. In 1771 Massachusetts Governor Thomas Hutchinson lamented to Lord Hillsborough that the "consumption of Tea in America exceeds what any body in England imagines. Some persons capable of judging suppose 5/6 of what has been consumed the two last years has been illegally imported" (Hutchinson 1771).

Whether legally imported or not, the price of tea dropped in the eighteenth century, making it available to a broader range of people in England and America. Elites, shopkeepers, and the "lower sort" began to drink tea on a regular basis, their tastes and preferences shaping the course of the tea trade and also reflecting the emergence of a new consumer class. This trend was particularly evident in the American colonies. Although historians have placed the annual consumption of tea at under one pound per person, eighteenth-century observers estimated that some two million Americans drank more than five million pounds of tea a year, at least one cup apiece per day (Samuel Wharton 1901, 139–40).[3] With 489,180 pounds legally imported to the North American colonies in 1764 and 515,477 pounds shipped the following year, there could be no doubt that Americans had come to love Chinese tea and had grown dependent on British companies and merchants to provide it (Thomas 1987, 28).[4]

Even as it surpassed other beverages in popularity, tea, more than any other consumer item, became controversial and raised debate over its properties and impact on health and moral virtue. A few extolled the invigorating physical benefits that tea afforded the individual. According to one essayist, tea was considered a panacea for head colds, stomach disorders, lethargy, and "well adopted for consumptive, thin, and hectic Persons, or that have Coughs, or profuse draining Ulcers, or an acrid Humour in their Blood" (Short 1750, 40–41). To critics of tea, however, women, children, and the poor were especially susceptible to the negative impact of the beverage. Some thought it a narcotic like opium, which would overstimulate those of smaller physique. Besides its physical effects, others feared that tea, as a luxury item, would have a corrupting influence on morals. Social commentator Jonas Hanway, in his tome *Letters on the Importance of the Rising Generation*, devoted a dozen or more pages to "Interest of Money paid to Strangers, and the Consumption of Tea, some of the Causes of the Beggary and Distress of a Part of the People." Referring to tea as "this Chinese drug," he asserted "if we may judge from the nature of tea, and the universality of the fashion, the expence it creates to the poor, and the contraband trade it occasions, it will…prove extremely hurtful to this nation" (Hanway 1767, 2: 179).

In the English-speaking world, tea and tea drinking, especially the negative aspects, were almost exclusively linked with the female domain. Popular and literary culture painted a picture of idle, elite, or social-climbing women gathered around the tea table, gossiping and dishing out scandal with tea and cakes. Poetry was particularly catty. Allan Ramsay, who devoted an entire volume of verse and song to *The Tea-Table Miscellany*, warned men of women's agenda:

> Then Coffee and Tea,
> Both green and bohea,
> Are serv'd to their tables in plate,
> Where tattles do run,
> As swift as the sun,
> Of what they have won,
> And who is undone,
> By their gaming and sitting up late.
> [Ramsay 1763, 286–87]

It would come as no surprise, then, that the critique of tea in prerevolutionary America drew on the assumption that mostly women bought and drank the brew, and therefore women, such as those gathered in Edenton, were called upon to set a patriotic example by refusing it. *A Sermon on Tea* (Anonymous [1774?]) exhorted women to "taste not the forbidden fruit" and to be wary of the physical and moral effects on the female frame (fig. 7.3). As early as December 1767, colonial newspapers carried news from Boston that "Bohea tea [a popular Chinese black tea] is now wholly laid aside or used but very sparingly in many of the best families in this town" (*Pennsylvania Journal* 1767). Even before American patriots destroyed an ounce of tea, a "Number of Ladies of the highest Rank of Influence" from Boston had pledged to "totally abstain from the Use of it (Sickness excepted)" (*Pennsylvania Gazette* 1770a).

Besides the cultural critique of tea, or perhaps inspired by it, a heated pamphlet war took place during the late 1760s and early 1770s focusing on the political implications of tea consumption and the place of tea and other British goods in the life of colonial consumers. Despite the patriotism of "Ladies of the highest Rank," most of the intellectual discourse, instigated by men, came from everywhere but Boston. Pamphleteers sounded the *Alarm* from New York, and John Dickinson's pseudonymous "Mechanic" roused Philadelphians to think of the broader repercussions of their daily economic choices. Merchants in most major port towns were pressured to sign nonimportation agreements in response to the Stamp Act (1765) and the Townshend Acts (1767–1770). Many agreed to forego purchase and sale of certain trade items, including East India Company tea. Even after Parliament agreed in April 1770 to rescind the Townshend duties on enumerated trade goods, it retained the tax on tea, compelling traders in America to agree in principle—as did the New York committee of merchants—that the colonies should extend nonimportation of British goods (*Advertisement* 1770; Thomas 1987, 176).

The united resolve of American merchants, however, soon unraveled. In June 1770, Joseph Galloway of Philadelphia informed Benjamin Franklin, then envoy to London, that whereas the "People of Boston and Maryland are of the same

Opinion until the Duty on Tea is taken off. The Yorkers and Rhode Islanders seem to be divided among them selves, but I think they will soon concur to support the Cause of Liberty" (Joseph Galloway 1770). Tensions grew rapidly between New York, Philadelphia, Rhode Island, and Boston in the years preceding 1773. Philadelphia blamed Boston for breaking their nonimportation agreement too quickly. In September 1770, the *Philadelphia Gazette* published a list of "Total Importation late the Port of Boston, by 27 Vessels, from Great-Britain, from January 1770, to 19th June, 1770, Contrary to AGREEMENT," including items such as raisins, saltpeter, linens, brass, stationery, books, calicoes, cambrics, playing cards, shoes, china, woolens, silk, glass, and 152 chests of tea (*Pennsylvania Gazette* 1770b). Indeed, between 1769 and late 1773, it was clear that Boston imported 1,863 full chests and 186 half-chests of duEed tea against the general nonimportation agreement (Pigou and Booth 1773d).[5] Boston, in return, complained that Philadelphia and New York could afford to maintain the boycott because the cities had better access to Dutch smuggled goods than Boston, which housed the King's Board of Custom Commissioners and their attendant security force. Boston's position on the remaining tea tax was ambiguous at best; despite the brief two-thirds drop in American tea sales, Boston inhabitants continued to demand and purchase duEed tea (Labaree 1966, 32). By late 1770 merchants in Philadelphia and New York allowed their nonimportation agreements to expire, and American markets were once more flooded with English goods. Ironically, perhaps, the desire to access free markets drove the initial struggle to assert colonial leadership in countering British policy (*Pennsylvania Gazette* 1770b, 1770c; Oaks 1977, 421; Doerflinger 1983, 220–22).

Free markets and the demands of American merchants and consumers meant little to the English East India Company, which had enjoyed a monopoly on trade since the early seventeenth century. Still, by the eighteenth century, the Company directors faced bankruptcy. Financial mismanagement, the cost of territorial expansion in Bengal, an economic downturn in Europe, and internal divisions among shareholders over retention of unsustainable dividend payments all precipitated a crisis of confidence and growing debt by the 1770s. The American boycotts and the proliferation of tea smuggling into England and the colonies only exacerbated the problems of an already ailing company (Labaree 1966, 58–73). Parliament passed the Tea Act in 1773 as part of broader legislation meant to regulate the Company and keep it solvent. The bill eliminated all customs duties on teas brought into England for re-export to the colonies, while maintaining the hated American Townshend duty of three pence per pound. By effectively lowering the price of tea, the East India Company hoped to sell some of the seventeen million pounds of tea accumulated in its warehouses and fund its debt. The Tea Act also allowed the East India Company, which relied heavily on the sale of tea for its revenue, "to export tea, on their own account" directly to merchants in America, instead of through British wholesalers.[6] The directors immediately commissioned local firms in Boston, New York, Philadelphia, and Charleston to receive and sell large consignments in late 1773 (Thomas 1987, 18; Chaudhuri 1978, 97).[7]

American merchants, including some chosen to receive the tea consignments, however, were apprehensive of the new terms of trade and worried that the Company might take advantage of its foothold in America after dumping tea on the colonial marketplace. New York merchants Pigou and Booth wrote their Philadelphia counterparts James and Drinker, speculating that "if the India Company succeed in establishing a Monopoly of one Commodity, they will also attempt a second and a third, till the whole foreign Trade of this port falls into the hands of a few monopolizers" (Pigou and Booth 1773a). Others feared the loss of business less but viewed the Company's monopoly on tea as a sign of larger problems within the British empire of trade. Philadelphia pamphleteer John Dickinson's "Mechanic" warned that the "designing, depraved, and despotic" East India Company, "well versed in Tyranny, Plunder, Oppression, and Bloodshed.... have enriched themselves,—thus they are become the most powerful Trading Company in the Universe" (Mechanic 1773). Thus on the eve of the tea's arrival, the greatest misgivings came not from Boston but from merchants in New York and Philadelphia who voiced concerns about the consequence of granting great power to one British trade company and its impact on an American world of business.

When American colonists learned that the first shipments of East India Company tea were scheduled to reach American ports in late 1773 under the sponsorship of American merchants, local patriot committees took action (fig. 7.4). Although it is the turbulence of Boston that we remember, as news of the tea consignments spread along the coast, it was the inhabitants of Philadelphia who first responded to the impending arrival of the cargo and began to take sides. One faction, a self-appointed "Committee for Tarring and Feathering," threatened any Delaware River pilot who assisted the Philadelphia-bound tea ship with "A halter around your neck, ten gallons of liquid tar scattered on your pate, with the feathers of a dozen wild geese laid over that to enliven your appearance" (Etting 187[?], 6). But in mid-October 1773 a more staid group of citizens called a meeting of the populace to discuss a measured response. They resolved that "the duty imposed by Parliament upon tea landed in America [was] a tax on the Americans, or levying contributions on them without their consent" and within a week selected members began to pressure the tea commissioners to resign their posts (Etting 187[?], 4–5). The Philadelphia agents, hoping to avert a crisis, "behav'd in a soothing Manner to the People, and...declar'd without Reserve they would not have the lest Share in executing a Commission so disagreeable to their Fellow Citizens" (Cooper 1773). Indeed, by the time Captain Ayres, the commander of the *Polly*, arrived in port with 568 chests and 130 quarter-chests of tea in mid-December, all the consignees—Thomas and Isaac Wharton, Abel James and Henry Drinker, Jonathan Brown, and Gilbert Barclay—notarized affidavits refusing to accept the tea or its freight charges. Although one firm offered a compromise to receive and store the tea but not sell it, ultimately Captain Ayres returned peacefully to England with the controversial commodity still aboard (fig. 7.5; James and Drinker 1773; Drake 1884, 256).

The diplomatic nature of Philadelphia's deliberations in October and November set the tone for two other port responses. Merchants in South Carolina and New York also wanted to reach a compromise between their sense of responsibility to the East India Company and the demands of the urban crowds with minimum conflict. In early December 1773 after the *London*, under command of Alexander Curling, arrived with 257 chests of Company tea in Charleston, laborers, artisans, and planters called a general assembly. In a letter of December 4, 1773, James Laurens told his brother Henry that "a Select Committee Mr. Gadsden, &ca. are going about to demand a Subscription from the Merchants to Import no more of that Article [tea] untill the Duty shall be taken off," but they were also "determined if it be possible, so far as honor & conscience will permit, to keep peace with all Men" (cited in Rogers 1974, 159; *Connecticut Journal* 1773). The Charleston tea agents, Roger Smith, Peter Leger, and William Greenwood, finally agreed "not to import, either directly or indirectly, any teas that will pay the present duty, laid by an act of the British Parliament for the purpose of raising a revenue in America" (*Pennsylvania Gazette* 1773; Rogers 1974, 158). The consignees publicly resigned their commission, and rumors circulated that the tea ship had returned home. It soon came to light, however, that "a difference had arisen between the merchants and the planters," and instead of sailing, after a twenty-day period had expired, the shipment was confiscated by customs officer John Morris on December 21, 1773, and surreptitiously unloaded and stowed in the Merchant Exchange cellar (*Essex Gazette* 1774; Thomas Wharton [1773] 1909; Rogers 1974, 164). Morris told his brother that since the committee had not come to a clear decision and the consignees refused to receive the tea, "We then gave the captain a permit to land it by sunrise. In the morning I went on board, and called the captain out of his bed, begged he would begin to get the tea out of his vessel.... There was not the least disturbance; the gentlemen that came on the wharf behaved with their usual compliance and good nature to me, and I believe the same to the rest of the officers that were there."[8] Still, when news of Philadelphia and Boston reached the Charleston merchant committee in January 1774, they rued their inability to keep the tea from port.

New York also managed to resolve its initial conflict over commissioned Company tea nonviolently—by happenstance, if not by choice. During the fall, merchants and the patriot committees of New York were in constant correspondence with Philadelphia. There appeared to be little open resistance to the shipment, however, until October 1773, when a series of five pamphlets written under the pen name "Hampden" issued an *Alarm* to New York inhabitants about the "dreadful machinations" of the East India Company and its attempt to force dutied tea on an unsuspecting public (Hampden [pseud.]

The BOSTONIAN'S Paying the EXCISE-MAN, or TARRING & FEATHERING

Plate I.

7.4   Philip Dawe (England, 1730s–1832)
The Bostonians Paying the Excise-Man, or Tarring and Feathering,
published by Sayer and Bennet, London, October 31, 1774
Mezzotint
35.6 x 24.1 cm
LIBRARY OF CONGRESS, WASHINGTON, D.C., PCI-5232B

By 1773, the British public thought of American patriots as little more than thugs bent on violence against government agents. This political cartoon, published by a British newspaper, depicts the attack on unpopular customs commissioner John Malcomb, who was tarred, feathered, and forced to drink tea by a group of Bostonians. The Stamp Act, a tax on printed paper, hangs upside down on a Liberty Tree, which also sports a noose. In the background, patriots dump tea into the harbor. Other colonial communities, such as Philadelphia, also used tarring and feathering as unofficial punishment for a variety of offenses.

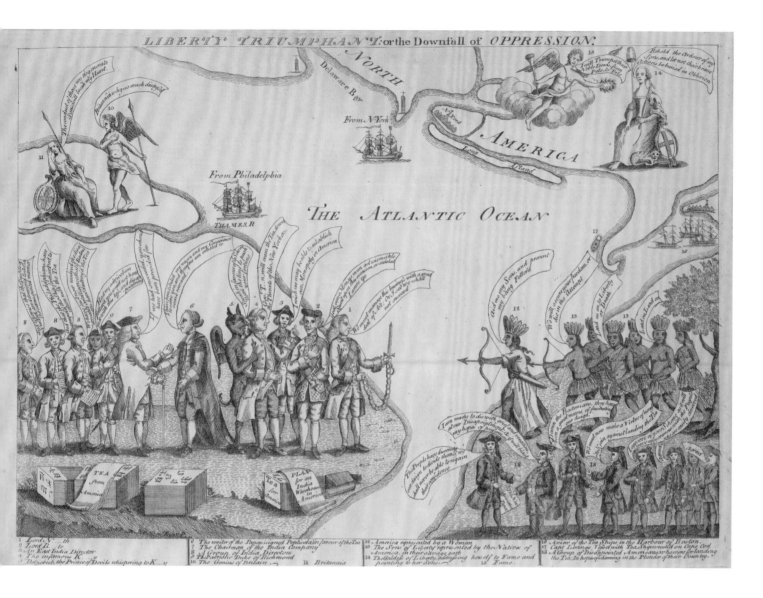

7.5 *Liberty Triumphant; or the Downfall of Oppression,*
Philadelphia, 1774
Etching
26 x 37 cm
THE LIBRARY COMPANY OF PHILADELPHIA, 5760.F.1

Although metaphorical Native American figures (Sons of Liberty) on the right call for assistance from their fellow Americans, the Philadelphia engraver downplays the role of Boston during the 1773–1774 tea crisis. The tea ships returned from Philadelphia (at the mouth of the Thames) and New York are clearly marked, and the machinations between the East India Company, the British ministry, the popular press, and the devil take center stage. (For a more detailed explanation of the figures see Richardson [1974, 36]).

1773, 4). Pigou and Booth, one of the consignee firms, at first insisted that "if any application is made to us [to resign] before the Tea comes, our reply will be that, we have not a line from the India Company, and can give no answer till the Tea arrives and we receive our instructions from them" (Pigou and Booth 1773b, 1773c; Matson 1998, 306). On November 29, 1773, when it became clear that both Philadelphia and Boston intended to refuse their shipments, the New York Association of the Sons of Liberty met "to prevent a Calamity." Like the Philadelphia resolves, New York patriots also feared that the tea and its attendant tax duties would "sap the foundation of our freedom, whereby we should become slaves to our brethren and fellow subjects." Ominously, the Sons of Liberty warned that anyone "whoever shall aid, or abet, or in any Manner assist, in the Introduction of Tea from any Place whatsoever, into this Colony, while it is subject by a *British* Act of Parliament, to the Payment of a Duty, for the purpose of raising a Revenue in *America*, he shall be deemed an Enemy to the liberties of *America*" (Sons of Liberty of New York 1773).

New York also watched Charleston closely. Upon hearing of the Charleston meeting of early December and its resolution

The able Doctor, or America Swallowing the Bitter Draught.

to send its shipment of tea back to London, New York patriots were determined to follow suit (*Connecticut Journal* 1773). Although prepared to stop the tea from landing, the committee was probably disappointed when news arrived in late December that the New York-bound tea ship *Nancy,* under command of Captain Lockyer, had encountered a storm and lost its mizzenmast and anchor. Stuck on Sandy Hook at the mouth of New York Bay, the captain entered the city to resupply. The 698 chests of East India Company tea, however, remained in limbo until April 20, 1774, when Lockyer contacted the New York consignees (Abraham Lott and Company, Henry White, and Pigou and Booth). He "left the ship and cargo at Sandy Hook for their safety," but he desperately wanted to "deliver the said cargo according to the bill of lading" (cited in Tea Association of the United States of America [1924], 6). Wisely, the New York consignees sent Lockyer home, after briefly considering a plan to forward the tea to Halifax (Booth 1774a).

The initially measured response of major American port cities slowly gave way as news of Boston's capsized tea spread. A number of New England towns showed their solidarity and approval by passing resolutions either during the tea crisis in

7.6   *The Able Doctor, or America Swallowing the Bitter Drought,*
London, May 1774
Etching
12 x 17.8 cm
LIBRARY OF CONGRESS, WASHINGTON, D.C., PCI5226A

The allusion to the rape of America by Lord North, who pours tea down her throat with a copy of the Boston Port Bill in his pocket, and Lord Bute, who peeks up her skirt, is hard to ignore in this popular engraving, which was frequently reprinted at the time. Britannia can only weep as Spain and France leer nearby and "Military Law" has "Boston cannonaded." The imagery and the American response to British economic policies became more violent by spring of 1774.

December or immediately following. Lexington, Massachusetts (December 13, 1773), and Portsmouth, New Hampshire (December 16, 1773), resolved not to receive or sell tea, perhaps for fear that the Boston consignments might be diverted to their towns (Lextington Resolves 1773; *Portsmouth Resolves* 1773). On December 27, Lincoln, Massachusetts, promised not to "purchase nor use any tea nor suffer it to be purchased or used in their families so long as there is any Duty Laid on Such tea by an act of the brittish parliament" (Lincoln Resolutions 1773). Watertown and Newport, Rhode Island, followed with resolutions in January; the former included its belief that Bostonians had not conspired to destroy the tea "but on the contrary were very Desirous and used their utmost indeavours that Said Tea might be safely return'd to the owners thereof—that the Destruction of the Tea was Occationed by the Custom house Officers and the Governours Refusing to grant a Clearance and Pass for the Vessell that was designed to carry said Tea back to the owner from whence it came" (Watertown Resolutions 1774).

Resolutions, however, hardly expressed the strong feelings of many communities. The cocky behavior of Boston soon emboldened other American patriots to devise their own "tea parties." Beyond the decision not to use tea, in late December the inhabitants of Lexington "brought together every ounce contained in the town, and committed it to one common bonfire."[9] On December 31, 1773, John Rowe noted that the people of Charlestown, Massachusetts, "collected what Tea they could find in the Town & burnt it in the view of a thousand Spectators" (Cunningham [1903] 1969, 259). According to another witness, they also "publicly burned a barrel of tea, which was found passing through the village to a country trader. It was undutied, but they would not submit to the suspicion of tolerating even the transportation of that through their borders" (Thatcher 1835, 189). Into early 1774, tea up and down the Atlantic coast was at risk of being destroyed, though the demonstrations were sometimes nominal. In January 1774, while at the College of New Jersey in Princeton, Charles Clinton Beatty recorded that he and a group of students, "to show our patriotism…gathered all the Steward's winter store of Tea, and having made a fire on the campus…there burnt near a dozen pounds tolled the bell, and made many spirited resolves. But this was not all. Poor Mr. Hutchinson's Effigy shared the same fate with the Tea; having a Tea canister tied about his neck" (Beatty [1774] 1920, 196).

By early 1774, Americans faced the broader political implications of Boston's actions. Many communities, horrified by the potential repercussions of the Port Bill of March 31 and fearful of parliamentary control, rallied together. Tea remained the major target of their anger. Indeed, New York and South Carolina enjoyed a second chance to demonstrate support of Boston and their own burgeoning patriotism. In April 1774, Captain Chambers, already rebuffed by Philadelphia, arrived in New York on the *London* with eighteen boxes of tea. Chambers had been "one of the first who refused to take the India Company's Tea on Freight the last Summer," for which he

had been highly praised (*New-York Journal* 1773). The New York Committee of Observation boarded his current vessel to check the manifest and found not only the eighteen boxes of tea, but the captain's own small stash of "20 small Boxes of fine Hyson tea," which were also dumped into the harbor by an impatient crowd (Booth 1774b; Newell [1774] 1878, 351; Cunningham [1903] 1969, 269; Matson 1998, 305). That fall, when several Charleston merchants attempted to import seven chests of tea aboard the *Britannia*, "an Oblation was made to NEPTUNE," according to the *South Carolina Gazette*. The consignees "with their own Hands respectively stove the Chests belonging to each, and emptied their Contents into the River, in the Presence of the *Committee of Observation*, who likewise went on board, and in View of the whole General Concourse of People, who gave three hearty Chears after the emptying of each Chest, and immediately separated as if nothing had happened."[10]

Perhaps the most dramatic demonstration against tea importation came not immediately after the Boston incident but in late 1774, once the First Continental Congress convened and passed the Articles of Association. In Maryland's colonial capital and largest port, Annapolis, merchants and patriots struggled with the implications of a general trade boycott. Although merchants had resolved in June 1774 to "stop all exportations to, and importations from, Great-Britain" until the Boston Port Bill was repealed, the Annapolis tea crisis came in mid-October, when Captain Jackson arrived on the brigantine *Peggy Stewart* from London with 2,320 pounds of "that detestable weed Tea," in violation of the general non-importation passed by Congress (Meeting of the Committees 1774; *Pennsylvania Gazette* 1774; *Boston Evening Post* 1774). Jackson, who scrupulously refused to ship any tea, had been unaware of the cargo when British merchant Joseph Williams placed seventeen chests on board, which Jackson only discovered at sea (John Galloway 1774, 248). Once at Annapolis, a crowd threatened to tar and feather the shipowner, Anthony Stewart, and to destroy his home. The Annapolis Committee of Association, which had unanimously voted to bar the tea from port, agreed that "if the tea was destroyed by the voluntary act of the owners, and proper concessions made, that nothing further ought to be required" (*Pennsylvania Gazette*

7.7   Francis Blackwell Mayer (United States, 1827–1899)
The Burning of the Peggy Stewart, 1896
Oil on canvas
182.8 x 134.6 cm
MARYLAND COMMISSION ON ARTISTIC PROPERTY, MSA SC 1545-1111

Created in the late nineteenth century, and bought by Annapolis for display in the Maryland State House, this painting rehabilitates the memory of Anthony Stewart's actions in 1774. At the time, some speculated that a debt of £12,000 drove Stewart to burn the ship, assuming that Great Britain would reimburse him for the damage. The Mayer painting, however, shows a proud, even heroic Stewart unflinchingly raising a torch to start the fire. Mayer spent much of his adult life devoted to the civic improvement of Annapolis and may have seen himself in the image of Stewart, acting on behalf of the citizens of the city (Steinberg 2004).

7.8   Carl Guttenberg (German, 1744–1790)
The Tea-Tax Tempest, or The Anglo-American Revolution, 1778
Engraving
43.8 x 53.3 cm
LIBRARY OF CONGRESS, WASHINGTON, D.C., PC15490

Carl Guttenberg's engraving reminds us that anti-tea protests were key to the explosion of revolution in the British colonial world but also points toward broader unrest during the late eighteenth century. As allegorical figures representing the continents look on, a Native American woman leads colonial troops (including sepoys from South Asia) against a fleeing British force. The exploding teapot, central to the image, became shorthand for the American Revolution. The two medallions at the bottom depict the Spanish Inquisition and the persecution of Protestant heretics under the Auto da Fe in Holland during 1560 and the William Tell-inspired uprising in Switzerland against Austrian rulers dated 1296. Alternate versions of this engraving are in the collections of the Library of Congress and the Historical Society of Pennsylvania.

1774; John Galloway 1774, 250–51). After some urging, Stewart "volunteered" and with "Messrs. James and Joseph Williams, owners of the tea, went on board said vessel with her sails and colours flying" and set fire not just to the cargo but to the ship as well.[11]

Not only did the conflagration in Annapolis inspire a late nineteenth-century painting (fig. 7.7), from which we get a vivid view of prerevolutionary protest against tea, but it brings us back to the interconnectedness of colonial political activity. A few local and seemingly insignificant consumer boycotts, sometimes led by those on the margins of society, fanned the flames of revolution. We know, for instance, that one contemporary Annapolis visitor, Philip Vickers Fithian, took the "patriotic Fire" of the *Peggy Stewart*, which he witnessed in Maryland (Farish 1943, 274), back home to Greenwich, New Jersey, where on December 22, 1774, he joined "a number of persons in disguise" to haul out and burn a cache of recently delivered tea (Andrews 1908, 22). We can also envision the news of a vessel burning in the Chesapeake quickly reaching the small town of Edenton, North Carolina, where a group of self-proclaimed patriotic ladies met a few weeks later to ceremoniously dump their tea. Just as it took more than Bostonians and a Tea Party to make an American Revolution, the symbols of the teapot, tea parties, and marginalized "others" who fomented rebellion resonated beyond 1773 and North America's shores. In 1778 German engraver Carl Guttenberg used the image of *The Tea-Tax Tempest* to comment on the potentially explosive anger of colonial peoples under the domination of imperial Europe (fig. 7.8). Another German, Daniel Berger depicted celebrating African American figures in his illustrations of prerevolutionary protests, implying that white Americans acting to free themselves from British control would eventually have to embrace the core principles of abolition and emancipation of slaves (see fig. 7.1). What began as a drop in a teacup—as an internal issue of taxation, representation, and consumer cost—turned into inspiration for greater upheavals about to shake up European nations and their colonial power over regions of a world far beyond Boston. ∽

part 4

Tea and EMPIRE

Beatrice Hohenegger

A TEAPOT DECORATED WITH A WARTIME IMAGE of a city in flames is highly unusual. Susan Thayer's *Opium Wars Teapot* (fig. IV.1), however, proves to be a compelling and thought-provoking work of art that raises the question: How can tea be so profoundly and universally representative of bliss and harmony, domestic serenity, and spiritual depth and at the same time be associated with such violence? The paradox in this case is explained by the intersection of two commodities—opium and tea—a crossing that represents one of the darkest chapters in the British colonization of Asia.

During the eighteenth century, British tea imports grew exponentially. This was in part due to increasing consumer demand, but it was also because the British government relied on the significant excise duties it imposed on tea and, perhaps more importantly, because the English East India Company used tea imports as a system of revenue transfer (see p. 132). A growing problem existed for the British in that Chinese merchants were not interested in trading tea for any other goods, with the exception of some handwoven Indian cotton cloth, and instead required payment in silver. Concerned about the outgoing cash flow and the increasing trade imbalance, as well as its own staggering debt, the Company turned to the one trade item that was guaranteed to remedy the issue: opium.

The Dutch and the Portuguese had been exporting opium to China for decades, but it was the British who took the trade to unprecedented levels of international drug trafficking. As John Wills explains in detail in his insightful essay, in 1773 the Company established an opium monopoly in Bengal, setting up mass-production facilities and a sophisticated distribution system through independent agents, or "country traders," as they were known. As a result China was flooded with opium, despite a valiant attempt at resistance by Imperial Commissioner Lin Zexu, who confiscated and destroyed 2.5 million pounds of the drug. The ensuing Opium War (1839–1842) and the humiliating defeat of the Chinese by the more powerful British navy secured the continued flow of the drug into the country, along with the opening of more ports; the ceding of Hong Kong; enormous war restitutions; and the repayment for the opium

shipments destroyed by Lin. The Chinese would not, however, concede to the British demand that they legalize opium.

From the British standpoint, the trade imbalance was unquestionably addressed by the opium trade. In *The Fall of Imperial China*, Frederic Wakeman Jr. states: "During the first decade of the nineteenth century…China's balance of trade was so favorable that 26,000,000 silver dollars were imported into the empire. As opium consumption rose in the decade of the 1830s, 34,000,000 silver dollars were shipped out of the country to pay for the drug" (1975, 126). And, as far as the tea bills were concerned, Wakeman comments a little later that "it was opium which bought the tea that serviced the E.I.C.'s [East India Company's] debts and paid the duties of the British crown, providing one-sixth of England's national revenue. Moral scruples bent easily before this kind of cost accounting" (1975, 127). It took a second Opium War (also called the Arrow War, 1856–1860), however, to legalize the opium trade, which expanded even further. By then, China had been pried open and trading vessels of all nationalities docked at Chinese ports (fig. IV.2). In *China Watch*, John King Fairbank aptly referred

OPPOSITE

IV.1   Susan Thayer (United States, b. 1957)
Opium Wars Teapot, 2001
Porcelain
H: 24 cm
THE NEWARK MUSEUM, PURCHASE, 2002 FRIENDS
OF THE DECORATIVE ARTS, NO. 2002.9.4

Susan Thayer's teapot depicts a battle scene during the Opium Wars in China. These wars (1839–1842 and 1856–1860) represented China's last desperate attempt to stem the flow of opium into the country and were triggered by the destruction of a very large consignment of British opium.

ABOVE

IV.2   *City of Victoria, Hong Kong*, China, 1860–1865
Gouache on paper
70.5 X 134.8 cm
PEABODY ESSEX MUSEUM, GIFT OF LEWIS A. LAPHAM, 1984, NO. E81235

The artist presents a panoramic view of Hong Kong Island with foreign ships in the harbor trading tea and other commodities.

After a hundred years of Empire tea production in India, China, which had been cultivating tea for thousands of years, is not even listed in this map of 1940 under the heading "chief TEA suppliers to the world."

Up until the mid-nineteenth century British officials stationed in India drank Chinese tea, as Indian tea production had not yet begun.

to the opium trade as "the longest-continued systematic international crime of modern times" (1987, 13).

Building an empire, however, is a multipronged affair. While doing brisk business addicting millions of Chinese to opium, the Company was also intent on eliminating China as sole tea supplier by setting up its own plantations in India. Although today the image of the ubiquitous "*chai wallah*" roaming the Indian metropolis with metal teapot and sweet chai is a common one, up until the mid-nineteenth century tea drinking was limited to the elite in India (fig. IV.4). The fact that *Camellia sinensis* grew wild in Assam was a crucial piece of information that was acquired by Company officials only in the 1820s. Until then the whole world—with the exception of the local populations and a few Western naturalists—believed that the tea plant grew only in China (*Camellia sinensis* var. *sinensis*) and to a smaller extent in Japan. Although the indigenous Indian plant was of a different variety (*Camellia sinensis* var. *assamica*), the Company swiftly and skillfully exploited its existence in order to create an alternative supply after the loss of its China trade monopoly in 1834. What followed was the massive development of British Empire tea cultivation—Assam became and still is today the largest tea-growing region in the world—along the model of the large-plantation system used for growing sugarcane. In less than a century Indian tea all but obliterated Chinese tea (fig. IV.3) The tragic human cost of this development is explored in Elizabeth Kolsky's brilliant and much-needed essay on Indian tea labor.

After operations in northeastern and southern India as well as Ceylon (present-day Sri Lanka, now a major tea exporter) had turned British Empire tea into the dominant commodity on the world market, British planters and tea companies sought new territory in their African colonies. This

IV.5   Miss Bishop/Dresses Mantle Maker… (label)
Woman's tea gown, England, late 1870s
Light blue silk satin, light blue and white figured silk
satin, cream-colored lace, starched beige cotton gauze
L (of center back): 199.4 cm
LOS ANGELES COUNTY MUSEUM OF ART,
GIFT OF LOEWI-ROBERTSON INC., NO. M80.293
PHOTOGRAPH ©2009 MUSEUM ASSOCIATES/LACMA

By 1914 the British Empire was comprised of eighty territorial units, eleven million square miles, and four hundred million colonial subjects. The ability of some Londoners to live in luxury was enabled by the creation of an interconnected imperial world in which the freedom to consume at home depended on the domination of others abroad.

The tea gown, which came into use between the 1870s and the 1920s, was a hybrid between a comfortable house garment and a more formal ball dress. It could be worn for afternoon tea or even for dinner at home, but it was not considered formal enough to wear on evening outings. As Emily Post's 1922 *Etiquette* later instructed, "One does not go out to dine in a tea-gown except in the house of a member of one's family or a most intimate friend."

expansion began toward the latter part of the nineteenth century and intensified when it became apparent that India and Ceylon would gain independence. The first African tea plantations were established in Nyasaland (present-day Malawi; figs. IV.6a-d) and cultivation later expanded to other African countries such as Tanganyika (present-day Tanzania) and Uganda, and most importantly Kenya. The latter is today one of the main tea exporters in the world, principally producing black tea used for blending and for tea bags. African and Indian as well as Ceylon tea are based on cultivation of the Assam, not the China, variety (although today there are no longer pure varieties, but mostly hybrids). The differences between the varieties, as well as the ways in which they are grown and processed, explain why *assamica* yields a rich, malty, dark liquor rather than the lighter, more yellow-green liquor of Chinese teas.

Whether in Africa or on the Indian Subcontinent, in spite of technological progress, life on the tea plantation remains very difficult for those who do the hard work of plucking and tending the soil. Unless low-quality machine-harvested tea is produced, tea remains a very labor-intensive crop that requires hand-plucking of the young shoots at the tip of the bush. All day long tea pluckers walk up and down the rows of bushes, filling their baskets with the fresh leaves and bringing them to the weighing and collection point, just as they used to do a hundred years ago (figs. IV.7, IV.8). While the horrific abuses described in Kolsky's essay are rare today, the poor health and living conditions, the limited access to education, and the endless cycle of debt and poverty keep the tea workers imprisoned in a grim reality without much prospect for improvement. In some extreme cases, tea companies that found it was more cost effective to buy tea crops from countries with even lower labor costs than India (such as Vietnam, for example) abandoned their tea plantations altogether, leaving thousands of workers and their families, who are entirely dependent on plantation infrastructure, to a terrible fate, which has included starvation in several cases.[1]

The fair trade movement (fig. IV.9), which has grown to considerable proportions during the last few decades, reflects an attempt to address some of the inequities in the producing countries. With the goal of turning tea from an exploitative crop to an opportunity for social empowerment, fair trade organizations have set up the monitoring of fair labor practices, health and living conditions, and environmental standards on the plantations; they also collect fair trade premiums in the consuming countries and send them back to the plantation communities to be used according to their needs. While this work represents a worthy effort in the right direction and has achieved some important goals, critics contend that it caters mostly to large-plantation owners—ironically subsidizing a dysfunctional structure left over from exploitative colonial practices—and fails to address the needs of small-scale growers, who are increasingly being squeezed out in the global economy and are therefore the ones most in need of help. Others note that it is too easy to acquire the status of "fair trade retailer" by adding just a few fair trade teas to

TEA from Nyasaland

ISSUED BY THE CENTRAL OFFICE OF INFORMATION, LONDON

TEA FROM NYASALAND.
4. The bushes are pruned every three years to keep the leaves succulent and the bush size convenient. Some of the pluckers, here bringing their baskets in for weighing, pick 30,000 shoots in a day's work of eight to ten hours.

TEA FROM NYASALAND.
7. After rolling, the tea passes to the cool, humid fermentation rooms. When fermentation is completed the tea is 'fired' by being passed through volumes of increasingly hot air. Here girls are sorting coarse stalks from 'fired' tea.

TEA FROM NYASALAND.
9. Here an expert tea-taster is sampling blends. Grades are mixed to get the most palatable teas which can be uniformly produced at a uniform price.

IV.6a–d *Tea from Nyasaland*, Portfolio on African tea plantations
issued by the Central Office of Information, London, 1948
LIBRARY OF CONGRESS, WASHINGTON, D. C., LOT 3577,
BOX 3 OF 4, COVER AND NOS. 4, 7, 9

The first tea plantations established in Britain's African colonies were located in Nyasaland (present-day Malawi).

the general catalog and that some retailers take advantage of this, motivated by the desire to capture the fair trade market and not by a true respect for ethical practices. In some cases, the plantation communities complain that they never see the premiums.[2] Still others contend that the fair trade system does not accomplish much that progressive and fair-minded tea estate managers and owners have not already implemented without the bureaucracy, paperwork, and fees required for fair trade certification.

Clearly, more work needs to be done to create satisfactory living and working conditions for those who toil to produce the tea we enjoy; to build market access for small- and medium-scale tea growers and make the certification system accessible to them; to encourage the development of cooperatives among small farmers working in remote areas without infrastructure; and, last but not least, to develop and enforce regulations for truly sustainable environmental practices, so that nature's cycles may be preserved and respected instead of exploited and drained.

IV.7   Tea industry: Weighing of tea leaves
India, circa 1900
PHOTOGRAPH ©BRITISH LIBRARY BOARD. ALL RIGHTS RESERVED,
PHOTO NO. 703 (10)

IV.8   These tea workers gather at a weighing and collection point at
Satrupa, a tea plantation in Assam, much like tea pluckers did a hundred
years ago (see fig. IV.7). PHOTOGRAPH BY BEATRICE HOHENEGGER, INDIA, 2006.

IV.9   Fair Trade Tea poster, Transfair, San Francisco,
United States, 2004
Print on paper, poster
58.4 x 40.6 cm
PRIVATE COLLECTION

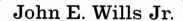

John E. Wills Jr.

TEAPOTS, OPIUM PIPES, GUNS

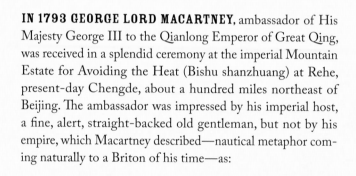

From the Canton Trade to the Opium War, 1700–1842

8

IN 1793 GEORGE LORD MACARTNEY, ambassador of His Majesty George III to the Qianlong Emperor of Great Qing, was received in a splendid ceremony at the imperial Mountain Estate for Avoiding the Heat (Bishu shanzhuang) at Rehe, present-day Chengde, about a hundred miles northeast of Beijing. The ambassador was impressed by his imperial host, a fine, alert, straight-backed old gentleman, but not by his empire, which Macartney described—nautical metaphor coming naturally to a Briton of his time—as:

> an old, crazy, first rate man of war, which a fortunate succession of able and vigilant officers has contrived to keep afloat for these one hundred and fifty years past…. but whenever an insufficient man happens to have the command upon deck, adieu to the discipline and safety of the ship. She may perhaps not sink outright; she may drift some time as a wreck, and will then be dashed to pieces on the shore; but she can never be rebuilt on the old bottom. [Wills 1994, 232]

In 1839 war broke out between Great Britain and Great Qing. It is referred to as the Opium War, and in most ways it was about opium, but it was also part of a major effort to compel China to open itself to the forces of "progress"—nation-state diplomacy, free trade, Christianity. Some Qing troops fought to the last man, and there were some first signs of popular resistance to foreign aggression, but superior guns and steamships produced a military rout and an enforced settlement in the Treaty of Nanjing (1842), changing the terms of trade, opening four more ports in addition to Guangzhou, and beginning the enmeshment of China in a growing web of treaty-made foreign power that would not be fully broken until the Communist victory of 1949.

Was Lord Macartney prophetic? Did the Opium War represent the fatal shipwreck of an antiquated system? The Qing Empire was under great strain by the time of the Opium War, but this was in many ways the result of growth, and the empire had no shortage of able officials working hard to reform

8.1   Opium smokers, rich men and women—group of women
China, late 19th century
Photographic print on stereopticon card
8.9 x 17.8 cm

The image in the background of this photograph is identified as Con-
fucius, who is transformed into something like a god of Chinese popular
religion, quite a long way from the austere teacher who urged that we
should "respect the ghosts and spirits but keep them at a distance."

basic components—the examinations, the salt monopoly, the Grand Canal—of a system that ruled in peace over a quarter of humanity. We will not ignore the strains, but we should begin by noticing that by the 1840s the Qing were confronting for the first time the results of unprecedented developments, "revolutions," in the North Atlantic world. The steamships used by the British in the Opium War represented the first time the Qing Empire had faced the new forms of power unleashed by the Industrial Revolution. The empire-building, war-making British state, forged in a very long century of war and near-war with France (1689–1815), was as unprecedented as the steamship in its ability to deliver violence at a very great distance. Over the course of a century of foreign domination and humiliation, from 1842 to 1949, the secrets of industrialization would be easier for the Chinese to learn than those of nation building.

The objects and images illustrated in this volume, and in collections in North America, Europe, and China, tell an even more complicated tale involving a number of "consumer revolutions." The story of the Industrial Revolution has usually been told in terms of processes of production and organization of capital. Historians, however, have come to understand that changes in consumption patterns, "consumer revolutions," first visible in Great Britain in the 1700s, helped to stimulate and sustain economic growth. In any society before our own, and perhaps even today, there are limits on how many people feel comfortable owning goods that are more than simply useful—more beautiful, more comfortable, of more exotic origin. How many can own such things without suffering the disapproval of their social superiors for their presumption? As numbers of willing and able consumers increase, widened circles of demand and distribution, fueled in part by advertising, stimulate production and help to sustain economic activity through other uncertainties.

One of the important eighteenth-century masters of demand-creation was Josiah Wedgwood, whose beautiful designs and canny promotions created a nationwide middle-class demand for fine earthenware, not porcelain, not cheap earthenware, not pewter. If you think about it, you can follow these themes of stimulated demand and consumer revolution right on to the Model T, Starbucks, and a global economy precariously dependent on the continued demand of American consumers for things they don't really need. In this essay we will examine how at least two consumer revolutions, in tea and in opium—interacting in a growing and increasingly connected global economy with large intercontinental flows of silver—contributed to massive changes in the positions of China and the North Atlantic world, especially Great Britain.

This particular set of consumer revolutions began with tea. In 1650 relatively few Europeans had ever had a cup of tea. By 1750 a great many, especially in Great Britain, drank it every day. All the tea drunk in London and Edinburgh, all the tea thrown into Boston Harbor in 1773, was grown in China. The increasing taste for it paralleled and interacted in interesting ways with the growing consumption around the North

Atlantic of Indian fabrics, which gave us chintzes, calicoes, and many other Indian names and wares; coffee from the seaport of Mocha in Yemen and later from Java; and sugar, produced by slave labor in Brazil and the West Indies, which was consumed in large quantities with tea or coffee (Wills 1993). For some time coffee retained a sense of its exotic Middle Eastern origins and created a masculine sphere of political argument and business activity in the coffeehouses of London. Tea eventually became more domestic, more respectable for ladies, and not as much was made of its exotic origins. The ladies' tea party became so common that it elicited satirical commentary in both England and Holland (see Smith, this volume). By the second half of the eighteenth century, London had several famous tea gardens, where couples and families might stroll in the open and enjoy the music and refreshments in a relatively respectable atmosphere. Drinking tea with milk and sugar produced a good source of reasonably hygienic stimulation and nourishment, which by 1800 was part of the daily routine even of some urban workers.

The British state, always looking for new modes of financing the next war with France, taxed legal tea imports at about 100 percent, quite predictably stimulating a huge and widespread smuggling trade and providing a key source of demand for the tea imports of Amsterdam, Ostend, Copenhagen, and even the hated French. Smuggling made good tea available all around the island, not just through the legal London distribution channel. Competition, expanding supplies, and shifts to cheaper varieties kept prices low and thus made tea accessible to more and more ordinary people.

All the knitting together of the continents by maritime trade between 1500 and 1800 was small and fragile compared to that of the world of steam, steel, and colonies around 1900, which today has been surpassed many times over by the trains and trucks carrying container after container arriving from the Canton Delta and rumbling out of the Port of Los Angeles every day. Early modern growth was nonetheless continuous and irreversible; I estimate that tea exports from China doubled between 1720 and 1740, doubled again from 1740 to 1765, and doubled yet again from 1765 to 1795. The great English East India Company (EIC) was a very effective coordinator of purchases, shipping, and sales, but it continually faced competition from other Europeans. Interested in stability in the trade, the English, the Dutch, and others did not expect to get their own way at Canton, and they made the necessary compromises and adjustments in their practices that allowed them to carry on their businesses. Cooperation with Chinese merchants and officials thus often proceeded smoothly for years at a time.

The Chinese side of the trade represents just as great a triumph of organization. The Manchu rulers of the Qing dynasty had been brutal in some episodes of their conquest in the mid-1600s, but thereafter they provided good order and tolerable government across their immense realm, where the population farmed and produced and traded fine craft goods in peace. Frontier areas were settled, and the population of the empire doubled between 1700 and 1800. The bureaucracy, however,

8.2   Folding fan depicting Canton, China, circa 1850
Paper, wood, lacquer, silk, ivory, metal
H: 27.9 cm
PEABODY ESSEX MUSEUM, MUSEUM PURCHASE, 2000, NO. AE85719

This Chinese export fan depicting the waterfront at Canton was painted after the construction of the Anglican church in 1847 and before the fire of 1856. The back of the fan is decorated with groups of Chinese figures.

expanded much more slowly than the population, and was thus stretched thin. Ethnic mistrust between the Manchu rulers and the Han (ethnic "Chinese") majority, especially the population of the far south, strengthened a wariness, deeply embedded in Chinese traditions of statecraft, of foreign connections that might aid subversion and rebellion. Foreigners could come to stay in the empire, as some Roman Catholic missionaries and some frontier Russians did, but those who came and went would be strictly confined to border outposts like Kiakhta, where the Russians traded, or Guangzhou, the port for the maritime Europeans, which foreigners called Canton (from the local pronunciation of the name of the province, Guangdong). The steady growth of the tea trade was managed within these rules. Although attempts were made, we know of no foreigner who visited the tea-producing areas before the 1850s.

At Guangzhou, Europeans made contracts and advanced silver to big Chinese merchant houses that were approved by the government to engage in foreign trade and that were also responsible for the collection of duties on the trade and for keeping the foreigners under control. During the summer trading season the foreign ships were towed up the Pearl River and anchored at Huangpu (or "Whampoa," as the name appears in European records of the time), where a small European cemetery may still be seen, a few miles down the river from the city of Guangzhou. Movement between Huangpu and the Guangzhou waterfront was in smaller

8.3 Folding fan with view of Whampoa (Huangpu), Guangzhou,
China, circa 1790
Paper, ivory, pigment
H: 27.9 cm
PEABODY ESSEX MUSEUM, MUSEUM PURCHASE, 2003, NO. AE86457.1–2A,B

This fan features a view of the island of Whampoa (present-day Huangpu)
with British, Danish, Swedish, and American vessels at anchor. Whampoa, where Western ships docked during their stay in China, lies in the
Pearl River seventy miles north of Macao and ten miles south of Guangzhou. The American vessels at anchor are of note, as the new nation only
began directly trading with China in 1784.

craft, completely controlled by the Chinese authorities (Van
Dyke 2005).

By 1800 some of the big Chinese merchants owned tea
plantations and processing facilities in the tea-producing
areas, but the coordination and fulfillment of the foreigners'
orders was largely accomplished through many small trans-
actions among growers, processors, and merchants (Gardella
1994). The foreign buyers tasted a sample of a particular variety of tea before ordering it, and if the tea delivered did not
match the sample, they would reject it and get their money
back. There were even cases when tea found unsatisfactory
upon arrival in London or Amsterdam was returned to Canton for full refund. As the volume of the trade expanded, the
merchants performed prodigies of organization, providing
boats equipped with rowers to tow the big Western ships up
to Huangpu and furnishing sufficient food, water, and naval
crews for their stays in the trading season and their homeward
voyages. Drink and sexual pleasure were fairly readily available around the Huangpu anchorage, and of course there were
some nasty brawls between French and English sailors, but in
general the trade continued to run smoothly as it expanded.
Trading was wound up, and ships full of tea dispatched on
the "north monsoon," starting in November. Thereafter, all foreigners were supposed to leave Guangzhou; some went home
on the ships, quite a few wintered in Portuguese Macao, and a
few stayed behind in Guangzhou to collect remaining debts.

A little semi-quarantined world of Sino-foreign contact grew up on the Guangzhou waterfront. Each national group had its own "Factory" (i.e., warehouse and residence of commercial agents, or "factors," not a place of production) with its own piece of river frontage and flagpole. Local artists and craftsmen developed a nice business painting this waterfront scene on silk, porcelain, and even fans for sale to the foreigners. On a few streets near the Factories it was possible, in the late 1700s, to buy off the shelf or to custom order items like the elegant fans illustrated in figures 8.2 and 8.3 and the punch bowl in figure 8.4. Also available were paintings of the shops, warehouses, and the orderly procedures of the trade (figs. 8.5a-f, 8.6, 8.7), urban and rural scenes in China, and much more.

Although Chinese artists produced what the foreigners wanted to buy, their images of shops, workshops, and tea warehouses also convey a vivid sense of their own pride in Guangzhou's large-scale craft and trade activities. Cultural interchange did not run very deep, but it could be cordial. The Chinese were not supposed to teach their language to foreigners, and few of them got further in learning a European language than a "pidgin" of European vocabulary items in Chinese syntax, which was useful for business but not much more. William Hickey described a pair of banquets in the 1770s in which the foreigners watched the Chinese try to handle knife and fork; the next day the Chinese watched the foreigners try to eat with chopsticks; and the true highlight was a Chinese

8.4   Punch bowl depicting foreign Factory sites at Canton,
China, circa 1788
Porcelain
H: 14.9 cm
PEABODY ESSEX MUSEUM, GIFT OF THE ESTATE OF HARRY T. PETERS, JR.,
1984, NO. E81407

Commonly called "Hong bowls" today, punch bowls of this sort decorated with the image of a foreign Factory site were popular during the period 1760–1800. Multiple Factories are depicted on this bowl in a continuous scene, a style that came into fashion around 1780. The flags of each nation are visible in front of their respective Factories with the American, Swedish, and British flags appearing in this photograph. Various Westerners are depicted observing the waterfront from balconies or strolling the walkway.

PAGES 196–198

8.5a-f   Six studies of tea production from a series of twelve,
China, circa 1805
Gouache on silk laid on paper
Each: 35.5 x 44.4 cm
©2009 THE KELTON FOUNDATION

These six gouaches from a set of twelve, produced in China for the Western market, depict distinct stages in the processing of tea from growing to sale: (a) Hoeing the ground, (b) Picking the tea, (c) Roasting the tea, (d) Sorting the tea (e) Tasting and negotiating a sale to a tea merchant, (f) Packing the tea for the Western market.

8.5a

8.5b

8.5c

8.5d

8.5e

8.5f

theatrical in which a Chinese actor appeared as a British ship captain, shouting "Maskee can do! Goddam! Goddam!" to general merriment. Some of the ships at Huangpu had small brass bands, and when they played a number or two at twilight the effect was quite lovely (Hickey 1913–1925, 1: 196–232).

Despite such encounters, the situation was by no means a static idyll. The trade grew, and the financial capacities of the licensed Chinese merchants came under great strain. The merchants had to send money up-country to the tea production areas to keep the trade moving, so credit was an essential part of doing business, just as it is today. Qing prohibitions against borrowing from foreigners were unenforceable. Many foreigners, especially the increasing number of British private traders not employed by the East India Company, loaned Chinese merchants money at high interest. When some of the merchants consequently went bankrupt, Chinese officials and other merchants worked very hard to repay the principal owed on these loans but not the constantly compounding interest. Many of the foreign private traders that arrived in China were fresh from the orgy of extortion in the first years of the British political and fiscal control in Bengal where British thugs and their Bengali clients thoroughly corrupted the systems of taxes and transit tolls inherited from the Mughal Empire. They were less inclined to settle for the system of steady, long-term relations that had worked so well earlier in the century. Nonetheless, the expansion and adaptation of the system was very impressive.

The porcelain items that foreigners bought from China to use in preparing and drinking tea rarely represented more than 5 percent of their export cargo by value, but the importance of this trade in the history of Chinese-European cultural exchange is immense, and we can learn much from it because so much of it has been preserved. Porcelain does not decay, even when submerged for centuries in Southeast Asian shipwrecks—from which many thousands of pieces have been recovered in the recent past. Europeans had seen and prized a few pieces of porcelain, brought by overland routes, as early as the time of Marco Polo. Chinese kilns also did some custom production for the European market very soon after the coming of the Portuguese, and one example bears the arms of Portugal reproduced upside-down (Le Corbeiller and Frelinghuysen 2003, 6). Museums in Europe and the United States contain many pieces of Ming and early Qing blue-and-white ware, sometimes with European metal fittings added. Many more examples are to be seen in seventeenth-century European still lifes.

The porcelain trade took on new dimensions as the tea trade expanded with its settled center at Guangzhou after 1700. This is reflected in the presence of Chinese export porcelain in old merchant or plantation houses—now open to the public—from Massachusetts to Virginia. There are staggering collections of Chinese ceramics at the Peabody Essex Museum in Salem, Massachusetts, and at the Metropolitan Museum of Art, New York (see Mudge 1986; Sargent 1991; Le Corbeiller and Frelinghuysen 2003). Both institutions have large matched

services for many guests, including sugar bowls, creamers, and other vessels for which there were no Chinese precedents. All the ordering party had to do was to provide a sample of the desired shape in pottery or wood, which would be sent up to the great kilns at Jingdezhen in Jiangxi and very carefully copied. Family coats-of-arms were meticulously reproduced. More than one set of special porcelain was made for the Order of the Cincinnati, the elite society of George Washington's former officers. One of these contains a splendid punch bowl, decorated on its outside with a marvelously clear copy of a certificate of membership in the Cincinnati, executed by an artisan who cannot have known a word of English (Le Corbeiller and Frelinghuysen 2003, 45).

These numerous American examples are exceeded many times over by those in European collections. Rulers procured splendid, matched vases of huge proportions, which were made to order in China, and they filled their palaces with porcelain. Chinese figures and landscapes painted on these pieces found many imitators in the European "chinoiserie" movement, and some of the results were sent back to China and copied yet again. But in the early 1700s Europeans had discovered the secrets of the manufacture of porcelain and were soon making fine products to the European taste without delay or distortion at Sèvres, Meissen, and many other manufactories. Wedgwood's fine earthenware was setting yet another competing standard of elegance. The moment of chinoiserie and *rêves chinois* was soon past.

The continuing expansion of the tea trade intersected in the late 1700s with another consumer revolution: that of opium. The drug had been taken by mouth since ancient times and produced an addictive sense of euphoria, as well as relief from the internal distresses attendant on bad food and tropical marching. By 1700 or 1750, however, some Southeast Asians, probably in western Java, had come to use a new mode of delivery: heating pure opium over a spirit lamp until it started to vaporize and then inhaling the vapors through a specially designed pipe. This practice probably originated in the Middle East or Central Asia. The opiate taken in this manner entered the pulmonary system, as opposed to the digestive, and produced a much sharper spike of opiate level in the blood, acute pleasure, and a much greater addictive potential.

A fair amount of Dutch colonial evidence dating to around 1670 suggests that an additional practice, that of mixing tobacco and opium and lighting the mixture in a pipe, was widespread in western Java. If Middle Easterners were mixing tobacco and opium in their water pipes about this time, this could account for the coincidence of the Malay/Indonesian word for the opium-tobacco mixture, *madat*, with one of the colloquial Arabic words, used in Yemen, for the water pipe, *mada'a*. One German employee of the Dutch East India Company in the late 1600s left a very odd description of Javanese mixing opium and tobacco, lighting up a pipe, and inhaling the mixture *through a mouthful of water*; if not simply confused, this account may represent some awareness of the existence of the Middle Eastern water pipe and an attempt to

8.6 The Tea Warehouses, Canton, China, circa 1820
Oil on canvas
48.3 x 72.4 cm
©2009 THE KELTON FOUNDATION

This is one image in a set (see also fig. 8.7) and depicts workers carrying tea to be mixed and packed. With their dark, somber atmosphere these paintings convey a more realistic view of the harsh labor conditions endured by tea workers than most of the idealized portrayals of tea manufacture of the period, which were produced for Western customers by Chinese artists.

improvise something analogous to cool the smoke. At some point a small "Chinese water pipe," just a pipe with a little extra chamber full of water, became very common in China.

Resident Chinese in Java were great tax-collecting, labor-organizing allies of the Dutch dating from the early 1600s. In the late 1600s, we find these same Chinese buying increasing quantities of opium, imported from Bengal. In the 1700s Dutch records yield ample evidence of the increase of opium consumption by Javanese and by resident Chinese across the great island. It stands to reason that some of these Chinese took the habit back to their homeland. Official Chinese concerns about opium imports and their effects on people are recorded as early as the 1720s.

The Chinese opium pipe pictured in figure 8.10 is an elegant and expensive creation, not intended for a poor man but rather meant for a consumer culture where display is of concern. Modern testimony suggests that vaporizing opium requires considerable practice and a high-quality grade of the drug. This was not, therefore, typical end-of-day relaxation for a tin miner or a boat puller. Late nineteenth-century stereopticon photographs of Chinese opium smokers are good examples of a very popular genre: striking images of "Oriental decadence" intended for the European and American markets. Where two female smokers recline facing each other with their pipes, working to get the right result from the spirit lamp between them, we seem to be witnessing a strongly social occasion (fig. 8.1), not the solitary and obsessive withdrawal of

some of our images of addiction. In another image (fig. 8.8), Chinese water pipes are clearly visible.

Most of the opium that was sold throughout Southeast Asia and all the way to China was grown and processed in Bengal (see Kolsky, this volume). After it became the dominant power in Bengal, following the Battle of Plassey in 1757, the English East India Company took control of opium production and cultivation; studied carefully the records of opium quotas owed by farmers in various districts to the previous Mughal administration and, unlike the Mughals, made sure the full quotas were collected; and finally asserted its monopoly on opium trade in 1773. The Company did not carry on its own opium trade in Southeast Asia, and especially not in China, where the trade was illegal and open EIC involvement might have interfered with the thriving tea trade. Instead it sold the opium at auction to private "country traders," the same network of bullyboys, fresh from the pillage of Bengal, who were causing so much trouble in Guangzhou. The preparation, storage, and sale facilities of the Company and the later English government in Bengal suggest a large, efficient operation and a major source of revenue for the Raj.

In the 1800s other colonial administrations—the Dutch in Java, Bali, and the outer islands; the French in Vietnam; and the British at Singapore—would make a government monopoly of the sale of opium a major source, perhaps the major source, of revenue supporting the colonial venture (Trocki 1999). Chinese residents were frequently the major

8.7   The Tea Warehouses, Canton, China, circa 1820
Oil on canvas
48.3 x 72.4 cm
©2009 THE KELTON FOUNDATION

In this painting, which forms a pair with figure 8.6, workers stomp on the tea to pack it into transport chests.

8.8   Opium smokers, rich men and women—group of men
        China, late 19th century
        Photographic print on stereopticon card
        8.9 x 17.8 cm
        KEYSTONE-MAST COLLECTION, UCR/CALIFORNIA MUSEUM
        OF PHOTOGRAPHY, UNIVERSITY OF CALIFORNIA RIVERSIDE

8.9   An opium storage ship
        Shanghai, China, late 19th century
        Photographic print on stereopticon card
        8.9 x 17.8 cm
        KEYSTONE-MAST COLLECTION, UCR/CALIFORNIA MUSEUM
        OF PHOTOGRAPHY, UNIVERSITY OF CALIFORNIA RIVERSIDE

licensees for wholesale and retail sales. On the China coast, away from Guangzhou, wholesale sales to Chinese dealers took place at highly visible rafts or hulks of sailing ships (fig. 8.9). There was very little overt mixing with the legal export of tea from Guangzhou. Nonetheless, it was here that tea and opium joined with silver in the intricate enmeshing of China in a growing global economy. From before 1600, China had run a positive balance of trade in its relations with Europeans, who wanted to buy first silks and then tea in far greater quantities than they could sell any of their own goods to the Chinese. The opium trade changed all that. The opium importers were paid in silver, deposited their earnings in the treasury of the East India Company in Canton, drawing bills on Calcutta or London, so that the proceeds of the opium trade in fact paid for the continuing growth of tea imports to Europe.

The Qing court issued many prohibitions against the use of and trade in opium, but to little effect. In some remote areas the Chinese began growing their own or importing overland from Burma and Central Asia, but a massive share of total consumption still came by British shipping from Bengal (Bello 2005). A final worry after 1830 was an apparent net outflow of Chinese silver, reversing the positive balance of payments run by the silk and tea trades for the previous two hundred years. That seems to have pushed the Qing into the serious efforts to cut off the trade that led to their cataclysmic defeat in the Opium War of 1839–1842. Many Englishmen were opposed to the opium trade, but in the dominant perspective, the opium issue was trumped by the imperative of forcing the Qing Empire to deal with the Western world on the terms of that world's multistate diplomatic order.

It seems appropriate to end an essay that has moved from the refined pleasures of tea and porcelain to the darker pleasures of opium with a reminder that India and Southeast Asia were not quiet places in the late 1700s. A huge trade in firearms to warring powers in South India and to Burma, the Malay Peninsula, and Siam was dominated by English private traders. The Danes tried to get a share of this market, but the guns they supplied were of very poor quality (Feldbæk 1969, 17–18). In South India, the rise of competing, mobilizing states out of the wreckage of the Mughal Empire ended in the victory of one of those states, the British Raj. Civil wars broke out in Siam in 1767 and in Vietnam in 1773. The gunrunners must have found good markets. In and around the Malay Peninsula, where sales were especially strong, the local power holders found themselves outgunned by the British. By 1790, however, strong new regimes were established in both Siam and Vietnam, closely tied to commercial ports and with a notable presence of Chinese émigré advisers and administrators. In many cases—think of Somalia today—an excess of guns can make settled government impossible. In Siam and Vietnam, however, the guns were imported through a few ports, and they had to be paid for. They may well have strengthened the new monarchies against less well-connected rivals and thus bolstered the trend toward political centralization. If we end with guns, which were in a way consumer goods for which there was a demand—and with the crosscutting and contradictory effects of the trades in tea, porcelain, opium, and guns on the growing links all around Asia and even to the Americas circa 1800—we will have some sense of the ways that this volume and the exhibition that accompanies it provide food for thought as well as a feast for the eyes. ⌒

8.10 Opium pipe, Yunnan, China, early 20th century
Bamboo, copper, brass, silver, stoneware, jadeite
L: 64.1 cm
QIN XUAN COLLECTION, SAN FRANCISCO

Elizabeth Kolsky

TEA, LABOR, AND EMPIRE IN INDIA

9

WHAT COULD BE MORE QUINTESSENTIALLY ENGLISH
than a cup of sweet tea? At any fine London hotel, one can
delight in the pleasures of high tea, a decadent affair offering not only exotic brews from faraway places like Darjeeling,
Ceylon, and Assam but also finger sandwiches, butter scones,
clotted cream, and strawberry jam. And yet, the two key ingredients that make high tea such a delectable experience—the
tea and the sugar—are not homegrown. When you think
about it, this makes the very names of Britain's most popular
teas, "English Breakfast" and "Irish Breakfast," rather curious.
How did the British establish a core national tradition based
on goods imported from outside the nation? In short, through
the expansion of its empire.

Tea and sugar initially entered the British marketplace in
the mid-seventeenth century as rare and exorbitantly expensive commodities available for use only by the elites (see Mintz
1986; Hohenegger 2006). Within two hundred years, sweet
tea displaced beer and malt liquor as the national beverage
of choice. By 1900 tea consumption in the United Kingdom
comprised 40 percent of the entire global market share (International Tea Committee 1946).[1] Every man, woman, and child
consumed approximately 90 pounds of sugar along with their
5.9 pounds of tea per capita per year (Gupta 2009). The success
of tea was intimately tied to the success of sugar, as sweetened
tea was consumed with other sugar-based goods such as jams,
condiments, and pastries.

The enormous growth of Britain's tea market must be
understood in the context of two historical developments. The
first is industrialization: the increased consumption of sweet
tea was linked to the dietary needs and changing work patterns
of a new class of British industrial workers. As these workers
turned from agricultural and artisanal jobs to labor in urban
factories, they were separated from traditional food sources
(like the family cow and the small garden plot). Locally grown
foodstuffs were displaced by new foreign imports including
sugar, tea, and coffee, all former luxury goods that were now
widely consumed to help meet their daily caloric needs—one-
sixth of which were supplied by sugar by 1900. Tea workers

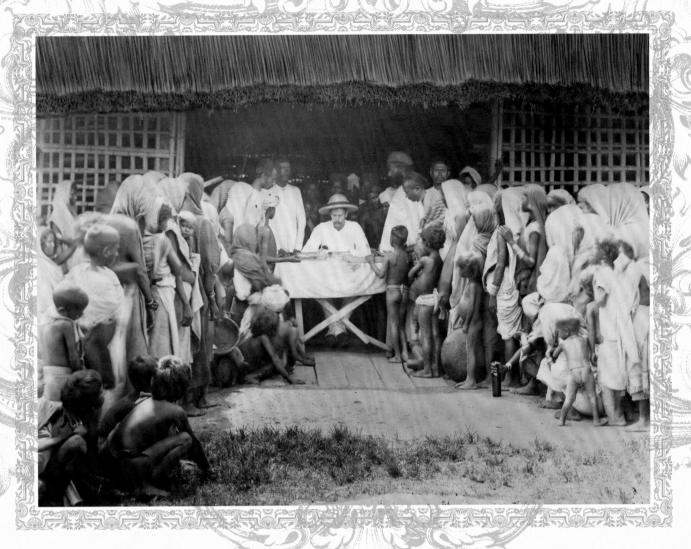

also helped British industrial workers stay awake and alert on the job (Hannah and Spence 1997; Mintz 1994).

An advertising poster of 1939 from the Victoria and Albert Museum, depicting a handsome young couple leisurely sipping tea under an umbrella, cleverly masks the class question at the heart of tea's history (fig. 9.2). For while tea was certainly desired by the working masses as a stimulant, the expansion of the British tea market was not caused by young beauties rushing to sip it seaside. The increase in tea consumption related rather less glamorously to a growing population of poorly paid British factory workers desperate for calories and a short respite from a long hard day.

The growth of Britain's overseas empire provides the second historical framework for understanding the expansion of the domestic tea market. In drinking tea to take comfort from the harsh conditions of industrial life, British workers became tied to an imperial system of production that was even more brutal and exploitative. In Britain's Caribbean colonies, more than one million Africans worked under conditions of chattel slavery to produce "King Sugar." The death rate on Britain's sugar islands exceeded the birthrate with overwork, malnutrition,

9.1   Tea plantation workers waiting to be paid, India, circa 1900
Photograph
22.6 x 29.2 cm

Child labor was extremely common on tea plantations. To be paid, pluckers had to meet a daily harvesting quota and often needed the help of their children to reach it. Today Indian laws prohibit child labor, but they are often ignored.

9.2   *Tea Revives You*, England, circa 1939
Advertising print on paper
76.2 x 101.6 cm
©V&A IMAGES/VICTORIA & ALBERT MUSEUM, LONDON, NO. E.128-1973

By 1900 British Empire tea constituted 40 percent of the world's tea market. This promotional poster, issued by the Empire Tea Market Expansion Bureau, associates the drinking of tea with leisure, youth, health, and sophistication. The immense expansion of Britain's tea market was, however, actually driven by the Industrial Revolution and the consequent increase of poorly paid British factory workers. These working people used tea with large amounts of sugar, another popular imported food item, to help meet daily caloric needs and to stay awake for long hours at often boring and repetitive jobs.

OPPOSITE, PP. 208–210

9.3a–g Captain Walter S. Sherwill (England, 1815–1890)
Illustrations of the Mode of Preparing the Indian Opium Intended for the Chinese Market from Drawings by Captain Walter S. Sherwill (London: J. Madden, 1851)
Engravings
H (book): 37 cm
CORNELL UNIVERSITY LIBRARY,
CHARLES W. WASON COLLECTION ON EAST ASIA

This series of engravings depicts the stages involved in processing opium. The East India Company established a monopoly on its production in India in 1773. The processed opium was shipped from Calcutta to China through independent traders.

and disease reducing the average work life of a slave to three years or less (Littlefield 1991, 67). The demand for sweet tea was facilitated by the possession of colonies where cheap land and labor made once-exotic products available and affordable to those at home with little more than a few pence in their pockets. It was through these interconnected processes of industrialization and colonization that tea became embedded in daily life on the British Isles.

Interrelated tales of pleasure and pain are a striking feature of the past and present history of tea. It is no coincidence, for example, that the London Ritz was built in 1906 at a time when Britain's global power was near its apex. To enter the tea room at the Ritz in London even today is to be transported by the sights, sounds, and smells of opulence and grandeur: the gold-gilded walls, the classical music, the soaring floral arrangements, to say nothing of the specially blended teas, the freshly baked pastries, and the perfectly trimmed sandwich wedges served on three-tiered silver trays. Tea at the Ritz has been an English institution since the hotel opened over a century ago.

By 1914 the British Empire was comprised of eighty territorial units, eleven million square miles, and four hundred million colonial subjects. The ability of some Londoners to take tea at the Ritz was enabled by the creation of an interconnected imperial world in which the freedom to consume at home depended on the domination of others abroad. Thus, there is a dark side to the magical pleasure and sumptuous elegance of the high tea experience. That dark side, revealing a brutal history of hardship and exploitation, is the central focus of this essay.

Until the mid-nineteenth century, the global tea trade was dominated by Chinese exports. East India Company traders, who possessed a royal monopoly on British trade in China until 1833, initially purchased Chinese tea with precious metals as they had nothing else of interest to offer to local Chinese merchants. Although tea turned a handsome profit at home, the shareholders of the East India Company were concerned about this "drain of bullion" and eager to find a renewable resource to exchange for their precious "liquid jade." The Company eventually settled on a system through which they could acquire their desired soft drug (tea) by trading a more dangerous hard one: opium.

Opium was first introduced to the Indian Subcontinent by Arab traders in the eighth century. In 1708 the East India Company joined an existing network of European opium dealers selling to the Southeast Asian and Chinese markets. In 1773, the Company established a state monopoly that allowed it to control the production and sale of all opium in India. Prohibiting the private cultivation of opium, the Company forced licensed peasants to grow, harvest, and sell poppy plants to government agents at fixed prices. In government-run factories, the unadulterated opium was pressed, shaped, and wrapped into one-kilogram (2.2 pound) balls and packed into 140-pound wooden chests, which were loaded onto ships in the port of Calcutta and sent off to China through independent traders (figs. 9.3a–g). Opium proceeds were then used by the

9.3a

9.3b

THE BALLING ROOM,
OPIUM FACTORY AT PATNA, INDIA.

9.3c

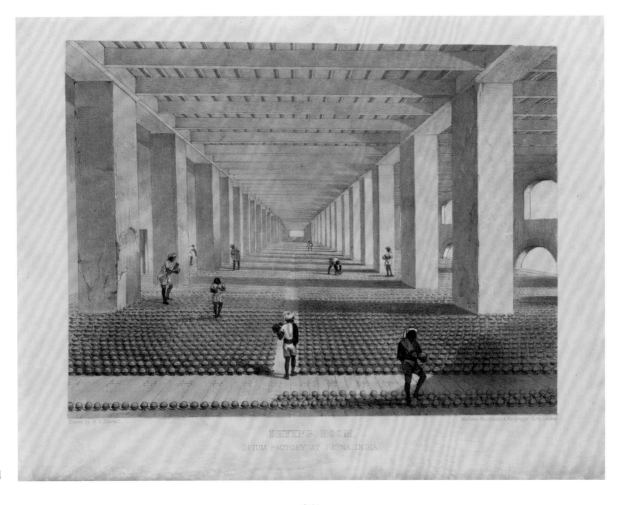

DRYING ROOM,
OPIUM FACTORY AT PATNA, INDIA.

9.3d

THE STACKING ROOM,
OPIUM FACTORY AT PATNA, INDIA

9.3e

THE OPIUM FLEET
DESCENDING THE GANGES EN ROUTE TO CALCUTTA

9.3f

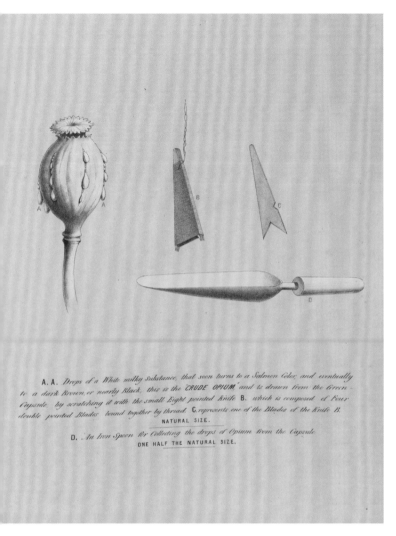

A. A. *Drops of a White milky Substance, that soon turns to a Salmon Color, and eventually to a dark Brown, or nearly Black, this is the* CRUDE OPIUM, *and is drawn from the Green Capsule, by scratching it with the small Eight pointed Knife* B. *which is composed of Four double pointed Blades bound together by thread.* C *represents one of the Blades of the Knife* B. NATURAL SIZE.

D. . *An Iron Spoon for Collecting the drops of Opium from the Capsule* ONE HALF THE NATURAL SIZE.

9.3g

Indian Tea Exports

YEAR	QUANTITY (POUNDS)	VALUE (RUPEES)
1870–1871	12,700,000	10,800,000
1880–1881	38,400,000	30,700,000
1890–1891	110,200,000	55,000,000
1900–1901	192,000,000	96,800,000
1910–1911	255,000,000	124,600,000
1920–1921	285,000,000	121,000,000

9.4 This table reveals the tremendous growth in Indian tea exports between 1870 and 1921 (Kumar 1983, 855).

Company to finance the tea trade. In 1837, shortly before the first Opium War broke out, the Company sent 15,000 chests, or 2,100,000 pounds, of Indian opium into the Chinese market.[2] By 1880, opium sales constituted 15 percent of the total revenues of the Government of India, as Britain's central government in India was called (Richards 1981).

As lucrative as the opium trade in China was, British capitalists sought out alternative sites to produce "their own" tea. India with its vast population of peasant cultivators presented just the right opportunity. The formal colonization of India began in 1757 with the conquest of Bengal. In 1826 the East India Company annexed the neighboring region of Assam, where a handful of Europeans began to experiment with the cultivation of tea. To assist in the colonization of Assam, the colonial government offered favorable landholding conditions to attract foreign planters. By 1901 European tea planters held more than a quarter of the total settled area in the Assam Valley, 85 percent on privileged terms that greatly disadvantaged indigenous entrepreneurship (Sharma 2002, 15).

Early efforts to expand the tea industry were hindered by labor shortages and the high cost of local workers. In 1859 the planters began to press the colonial government for a law to secure the recruitment, transportation, and employment of tea workers from outside Assam. Six years later, they achieved their goal when the Government of India established an indenture system that recruited and bound tea laborers to the plantations under what was called a penal contract. The penal contract—so-called because of the criminal rather than civil penalties for its breach—gave planters the right to fine, imprison, punish, and forfeit the wages of workers who failed to work and to arrest those who attempted to leave the plantation.

The use of the indenture system in Assam mirrored its application elsewhere in the British Empire. After the abolition of slavery in 1833, Indian indentured laborers sustained Britain's imperial plantation economy in Mauritius, Fiji, the West Indies, Southeast Asia, and East Africa. The lives of indentured Indian laborers in this "new system of slavery" were scarcely better than those of the African slaves whose places they took (Tinker 1974).

Under the indenture system, Indian tea (most of it produced in Assam) quickly supplanted Chinese tea as the dominant force in the global tea market. In 1860, tea produced in China constituted nearly 100 percent of world exports. Forty years later, that number fell to 26 percent as Indian tea assumed 41 percent of the total market share (with the remainder largely coming from Ceylon; see Gupta 2009). By 1920 more than one million Indian laborers were producing two hundred and eighty five million pounds of tea for export.

The colonial government's justification for the indenture system in Assam was that in return for secure pay and working conditions, and to protect the planter's economic investment, a tea worker should be bound to the plantation. In defense of the penal contract, Charles Alfred Elliott, Chief Commissioner of Assam, observed in 1885: "As to the tea-coolie, the protection he gets, the excellent cottage he lives in, the good

water-supply, the fairly cheap food, and the fairly reasonable wage he gets are a *quid pro quo* granted in return for the penal clauses which compel him to carry out his part of the contract. He would not get the one without the other and he certainly would be worse off if he had to part with both" (Elliott 1885). G. W. Lawrie's staged photograph of "tea-making in Chowbattia" offers a visual representation of Commissioner Elliott's pristine and orderly tea plantation (fig. 9.5).

The idyllic images offered by Elliott and Lawrie, however, did not square up with the reality of daily life on the inaptly named "tea gardens." While the new legislation did increase the labor supply—by 1883, 95 percent of the labor force on the tea plantations came from outside Assam—it certainly did not protect the workers or guarantee them decent living conditions. If anything, the new labor laws were directly linked to widespread criminal fraud, abduction, and inhumane abuse of workers. In Assam, thousands of Indian men, women, and children worked under harsh and crowded conditions for low wages where food was scarce and deadly diseases such as cholera and typhoid spread like wildfire. Between 1863 and 1866, thirty-two thousand of the eighty-four thousand laborers brought to Assam died (Jha 1996, 145). The penal contract placed the laborer in a deathly double bind, for while mortality rates on some plantations ran as high as 30 percent, the

9.5   G. W. Lawrie and Company
Chowbattia, tea making, 1880s
Photograph
20.9 x 27.2 cm

This photograph was staged to present a highly idealized picture of the tea industry in India. In reality, however, indentured workers were bound to tea plantations under a penal contract. Given this arrangement any attempt to leave the plantation or avoid work could be met with a criminal penalty. Most of the workers lived and worked in abominable conditions—faced with low pay, lack of proper nutrition, rampant disease, and frequently cruel treatment at the hands of British plantation owners.

9.6 Robert Phillips (British, dates unknown)
Manufacture of Tea at Darjeeling, Plucking Leaf, 1870s
Photograph
20.9 x 27.5 cm

9.7 Robert Phillips (British, dates unknown)
Manufacture of Tea at Darjeeling, Plucking Leaf, 1870s
Photograph
9.2 x 16.7 cm

indenture system made leaving the garden a criminal offense. As one official observed, "they have to choose between the risk of death if they stay or imprisonment if they desert" (Ganguli [1872] 1972, 8). Two laborers attempting to flee their plantation expressed a tragic awareness of this die-if-you-stay, die-if-you-go predicament when in response to their manager's warning that he would shoot them if they did not stop, they replied, "Shoot away" (Ganguli [1872] 1972, 39).

Exacerbating the crushing effects of this morbid physical environment was the excessive brutality of the planter himself. British tea planters worked on the geographical fringes of the empire, and the vicious violence exhibited by many of them reflected both their virtually unrestrained authority to control the lives and movement of laborers and their acute sense of their own vulnerability. Tea planters were always vastly outnumbered by tea workers and fear of insurrection and reprisal was always on their minds. In 1904 the 143 tea gardens in operation in upper Assam employed 100,849 Indians and only 199 Europeans (Jha 1996, 20). Robert Phillips' photographs of tea workers plucking leaves in the 1870s demonstrate the remoteness of the plantation and the supervisory role played by white planters and managers (figs. 9.6, 9.7).

Tea planters perpetrated extreme acts of violence and inflicted exemplary public punishment to create a culture of terror that kept workers working and deterred them from deserting. Routine forms of violence on the plantation included floggings, canings, confinement in subterranean lock-ups, cuffing, kicking, and assault. Because the colonial government depended on the planters to produce wealth from this increasingly profitable industry, little was done to curb their behavior.

As one Indian critic cynically observed: "The primary object of British rule in India is to benefit the European capitalist and merchant, even, if necessary, at the sacrifice of justice and humanity"(*Bengalee* 1901). The portrait of civility captured in the photograph of a tea party in Calcutta entirely occludes the barbarity under which the tea itself was produced in the nearby hills (fig. 9.8).

British tea planters exerted tremendous influence over the colonial government. Unlike their workers, who were poor, disenfranchised, and divided along lines of region and language, the planter class was extremely powerful, organized, and well connected. Most of the local political organs and committees in Assam were dominated by the planters, and all municipalities in Assam had ex-officio European chairmen until 1912. The planters also worked through influential lobbying groups, such as the Indian Tea Association, to exert formal and informal pressure on the governments in London and Calcutta. The intimate links between the planters and local officials were evident in their social interactions, such as when they dined, hunted, and played polo together. These social affinities enabled and aggravated the brutality and injustice committed by the planters as British magistrates were unlikely to prosecute or punish their friends and fellow countrymen on the local plantations.

The colonial government was intimately aware of the systematically brutal conditions under which the system functioned, and its annual "Reports on Labor Immigration into Assam" paint a chilling portrait of life on the tea plantations. These labor reports provide extensive documentation about life and living conditions, including data on: immigration and fraudulent recruitment; age and gender composition of the labor force; contracts and wages; desertions and other criminal offenses; birth and mortality rates; health, disease, and sanitary conditions; relations between employers and laborers; and the working of the general system. As most administrators in Assam favored the planters, the ghastly statistics presented by these reports did not receive much official notice or censure until Henry Cotton became Chief Commissioner. In 1901, a deeply distressed Cotton wrote to India's Viceroy Lord Curzon about his moral obligation to reign in the planters:

as my knowledge of the actual state of things extended and especially when it became my duty to probe this wages question to the bottom I learnt many matters which an officer in my position may very easily remain, and often has remained in ignorance. I was distressed beyond measure at the innumerable abuses which came to my notice and I felt it to be my duty not to conceal the truth. I have stated facts in my last report without the glazing which usually marks these productions but I have written with moderation and have indulged in no exaggeration or pictorial description. There is no bias here: far less indeed than there was in favor of the industry in my earlier reports. I cannot deny that I have gradually become convinced that the system of tea planting in Assam is thoroughly bad and that the penal contract arrangement is detestable. [Cotton 1901]

Perched at a remote frontier of British India, Assam sat on the geopolitical edge of empire and possibly beyond the pale of justice. Due to the social ties that bound the planter class to the colonial bureaucracy, the legal restrictions placed on the laborers' physical movement, and the planters' right to discipline their own employees, it was rare that planters were ever charged with crimes. The plantations were generally located far from the nearest police station, and tea workers were prohibited from lodging complaints both by the vast distances they had to travel and by the environment of intimidation that enveloped the plantation. The fact that leaving the plantation was itself a crime created the possibility of double jeopardy for a laborer who wanted to initiate criminal proceedings against a planter. To disastrous effect, the planters themselves often acted as police, judges, and juries on their own plantations. Though not a courtroom scene, an image of tea workers waiting to be paid evokes a sense of the planter's unitary position of power and authority (fig. 9.1).

Critics of the judicial system in Assam disparagingly referred to it as *safed insaaf* (white justice), noting that the scales of justice were consistently imbalanced by the weight of race. The strength of racial solidarity in the region produced startlingly biased judgments as those planters who did stand trial were inevitably booked on lesser charges that resulted in little to no punishment. Indeed, the tea planters functioned in a zone of illegality inside of which they could literally get

away with murder. As Viceroy Curzon noted with disgust in 1901, "What is called 'grievous hurt' in India often bears the more uncompromising title of 'murder' at home."

Although tea workers labored in extremely unsanitary conditions with little to no access to hospitals or basic medical care, medical evidence figured centrally in almost all criminal trials of planters. In most cases, a European doctor (who was generally a friend or acquaintance of the offending planter) would offer testimony that attributed the cause of a worker's death to internal rather than external causes—weak insides, poor health, enlarged spleens. Sympathetic juries packed with fellow planters would then conclude that a planter whose coolie appeared healthy on the outside could not be held responsible when death ensued from a "light beating."

One of the first Indian cartoons to make a major political impact depicted a European doctor conducting a perfunctory postmortem examination on the body of a dead laborer. In the background, the accused European stands nonchalantly smoking a cigar (Mitter 1997, 16). A good example of the collusion between planters and doctors involved the case of Charles Webb who was charged with repeatedly raping a female laborer overnight in his cabin, ultimately causing her death. As the postmortem report stated that the woman died of natural causes, however, Webb was convicted only of wrongful confinement, for which he was fined 100 rupees and released (Ganguli [1872] 1972, 72).

Medical evidence about the weak coolie constitution offered a purportedly objective account of the vulnerable Indian body that exonerated Europeans from criminal liability and punishment and made a flogged coolie responsible for his or her own death. As British statesman and author George Trevelyan vividly remarked: "The performances of these thin-legged, miserable rice-fed 'missing links' are perfectly inexplicable according to our notions of muscular development.... The physical conformation of these men is so frail, that a blow on the body is liable to cause instant death. It is commonly believed that this proceeds from the large size of the spleen" (Trevelyan [1864] 1992, 62).

Sometimes, however, tea workers did strike back. And when they did, they could turn the oppressive plantation environment on its head as they had the advantage both in terms of their numbers and their instruments. Laborers tended to act collectively, using their work tools—knives, hoes, and pick-axes—as weapons to threaten and attack their superiors. As planter J. H. Williams recalled in his memoir, "It is quite startling to be surrounded by a gang of 100-odd pruners armed with their pruning knives."[3]

As the nineteenth century drew to a close, members of the Indian public, local Christian missionaries, and parliamentary reformers increasingly called upon the colonial regime to bring offending planters to justice and to reform the tyrannical conditions under which Assam tea was produced. Reverend Charles Dowding was particularly tireless in his efforts to expose the physical, economic, and social abuses on the plantations and the irresponsible behavior of the government

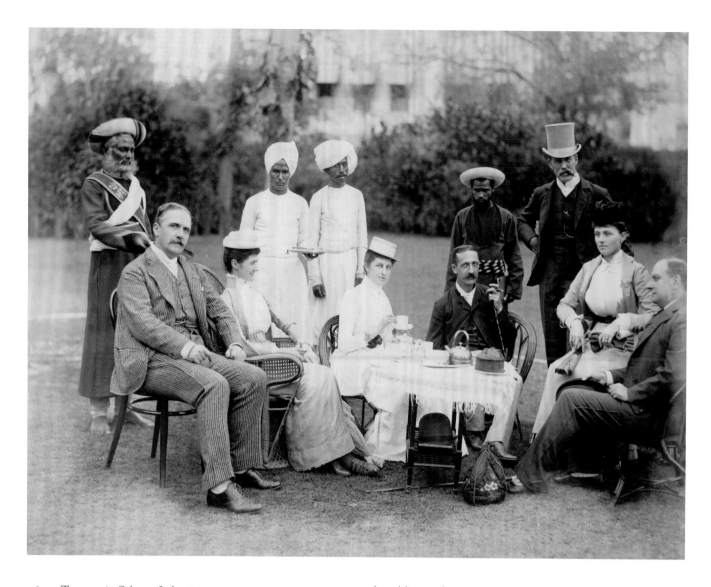

9.8 Tea party in Calcutta, India, circa 1890
Photograph
21.6 x 28 cm

This photograph of an elegant tea party with well-dressed guests and polite servants hovering in anticipation ignores the reality of the suffering endured by the Indian plantation workers who produced the beverage that is being consumed.

toward the tea industry. In Dowding's view, if the tea plantations could not function in a morally responsible fashion, they should not be permitted to function at all: "If you cannot open out Assam without this frightful waste of life, you had better leave it unopened. It is not to be borne that the defense-less coolie is to be pushed hither and thither in the interest of the idle capital of England with absolute indifference (coolies being cheap) whether he lives or dies. A coolie is not a pawn but a living man with wife and children depending on him. He is not to be classed with livestock" (Dowding 1896).

Broad public awareness about the oppressive tea industry also grew due to the efforts of brave Indian journalists who journeyed to the Assam plantations and reported back about the morbidity, mortality, abysmal living arrangements, and

slave-like conditions on the tea gardens. Not only did leaders of the new Indian National Congress (founded in 1885) use criminal violence in Assam to expose the failure of the government to hold the planters accountable, condemnation of the "planters' *zulm*" (planters' oppression) also provided a vivid platform for a broader critique of the criminality of colonialism itself. The Congress party eventually turned the "coolie question" into a scandalous and chilling national issue that captivated and motivated the Indian masses. The abolition of Assam's indenture system was in no small part due to their interventions.

In 1915, in the middle of World War I, Mohandas Karamchand Gandhi returned to India from South Africa where he had launched his political career. After the war, Indians experienced severe economic hardship as taxes and inflation skyrocketed, prices for basic items rose dramatically, and food riots and armed insurrections spread across the country. In this context, Gandhi began what he called his "experiments with truth," launching small-scale nonviolent noncooperation movements, which involved peaceful marches, *swadeshi* (the boycott of foreign-made goods), civil disobedience, and courting of mass arrests. In August 1920 Gandhi launched his first all-India noncooperation movement, leading thousands of ordinary Indians in a mass campaign against colonial oppression. As people across the country participated in the protests, boycotts, and voluntary arrests, Gandhi announced: "Our triumph consists in thousands being led to the prisons like lambs to the slaughter house" (Gandhi 2001, 172).

Gandhi's personal charisma and political acumen turned the Indian National Congress into a truly mass-based party. His success at mobilizing the masses was partly enabled by his ability to martial the force and energy of preexisting peasant discontent and anti-imperial protest in localities across the subcontinent. Assam was one of the regions to which Gandhi and the Congress devoted particular attention (Pouchepadass 1999). On August 18, 1921, Gandhi arrived for a ten-day tour of Assam. Many tea workers traveled from near and far to see the Mahatma and thousands of onlookers burned bonfires of foreign cloth to demonstrate their support of his *swadeshi* campaign. Emboldened by their contact with nationalist leaders and rural Congress volunteers, the tea laborers of Assam increasingly struck work in the 1920s, demanding improved labor conditions and a reprieve from the daily misery of life under "Planter-raj" (planter rule). In May 1921, thousands of coolies abandoned their plantations in open revolt chanting "Gandhi Maharaj ki Jai," or "Victory to Gandhi!" (Guha 1977, 130).

Although Gandhi's noncooperation movement succeeded in expanding the role of Indians in the local Assamese governing bodies, it did little to directly alleviate the oppression of the tea workers. Pressure on the laborers in Assam grew as annual per capita consumption of tea in the United Kingdom increased from 5.9 pounds in 1900 to 9.6 pounds in 1931 (Gupta 2009). In the 1930s, the global effects of the Great Depression hit Indian tea workers with devastating force. Labor strikes and struggles directed at British capitalists and planters gave voice to peasant anger about the low pay, heavy workload, and physical abuses on the plantations. During World War II, when Britain lost its colonies in Southeast Asia, the empire leaned even more heavily on India's tea plantations to supply the market at home.

After a long and protracted struggle, India finally won its independence on August 15, 1947. In certain important respects, however, national freedom did not revolutionize the Assam tea industry or liberate its workers. Even after the British rulers left, British tea planters and agency houses continued to dominate the local economy with control of 500,000 acres of land and as many workers on its tea plantations. Even when Indian industrialists bought out the foreign capitalists in the ensuing decades, little was done to improve the health and working conditions of the tea laborers.

Today, Assam accounts for approximately 55 percent of India's $1.5 billion tea industry (there are an estimated 2.2 million tea workers throughout India). Although Assam's tea workers—most of them women—are technically protected by labor legislation, their standard of living remains abysmal, and most exist just above the poverty line. In March 2007 there

9.9   Rupert Garcia (United States, b. 1941)
Ceylon Tea: Product of European Exploitation! 1972
Color screen print
Image: 63.8 x 48 cm
COURTESY OF RENA BRANSTEN GALLERY, SAN FRANCISCO, CA

Rupert Garcia, a founder of the Chicano art movement, created this politically powerful print in 1972. He used the iconic image and red-and-yellow color scheme from the Lipton tea box as counterpoint to his written message.

were reports of as many as one hundred starvation deaths in a closed tea garden in West Bengal. The following month, a study published by the Regional Medical Research Center described the health conditions of Assam tea workers as "precarious," with the majority suffering from malnutrition and infectious diseases (Tea Workers Health 2009).

In 1932 Miss Agnes Repplier published a paean to the dangers and delights of tea drinking whimsically titled *To Think of Tea!* The book, a pleasurable history of tea in Europe, makes no mention of the painful conditions under which the intoxicating leaf was produced. As for the tea lovers of today, what do we think about when we think of tea? ☙

Not a modern witches' council but members of the Holy
and Undivided Trinity of Castle Rising, Norfolk, England, 1920s
Photograph

NOTES

Teatime (Hohenegger)

1. According to the Food and Agriculture Organization (FAO), the most recent and still unpublished figure for 2007 world tea production is 3.85 million metric tons.

2. This figure is an unofficial estimate, given to me in a personal communication with Food and Agriculture Organization (FAO) tea expert Kaison Chang.

Chapter 1 (Owyoung)

1. The epigraph is taken from Lu Yü, *Chajing* [Book of Tea], specifically the Baichuan xuehai edition of 1273 CE (ch. 1, pt. 1, 1a), a woodblock printed version of the late Southern Song dynasty (960–1279) that is reproduced in Zhang Hong-yong, comp., *Lu Yü Chajing congkan* [A Collection of Printings of the *Book of Tea* by Lu Yü] (Taoyüan: Chaxue wenxue chubanshe, 1985), 3–42. Unless otherwise indicated, all translations are mine.

2. This passage is from the *Chaling tujing* [Atlas of Chaling], a lost geographic record that is cited in Lu Yü ([1273] 1985, ch. 3, pt. 7, 8b).

3. For other translations, see Wilbur (1943, 382–92); Hsü (1980, 231–34; and Wilbur (1994, 510–13).

4. The *Shuowen jiezi* [Commentary on Literature and the Explanation of Words] of 121 CE was compiled by Xü Shen (30–124) and is cited in Chen Binfan (1999, 4).

5. This anecdote is found in the "Biography of Wei Yao," in *Wu zhih* [Annals of the State of Wu]; see Chen Binfan (1999, 4, 20).

6. Du Yü's *Chuanfu* [Ode to Tea] is cited in Chen and Zhu (1981, 204); and Chen Binfan (1999, 3). For a translation of the poem, see Hohenegger (2006, 3).

7. See "Biography of Lu Ye" in Fang (1974, 7: ch. 77, *lieh* ch. 47, 2027); and Lu Yü ([1273], 1985, ch. 3, pt. 7, 4b).

8. Shan Qianzhi (active ca. 439–454) was the author of *Wuxing ji* [Record of Wuxing], which is cited in Lu Yü ([1273] 1985, ch. 3, pt. 7, 8b).

9. Shan Qianzhi's *Wuxing tongji* [Complete Record of Wuxing] is cited in Chen and Zhu (1981, 206).

10. The *Nan Qi shu* [History of the Southern Qi] is cited in Chen and Zhu (1981, 206).

11. Liu Xiaozhuo (481–539), "Thanking Prince An of the Jin for Presenting Provisions," is cited in Lu Yü ([1273], 1985, ch. 3, pt. 7, 7b).

12. This now-lost story remains to us only as a citation in ancient works; in this case: Liu Yiching, *Shishuo xinyü* [New Account of Tales of the World], cited in Chen Zongmou (1997, 651).

13. Feng Yan compiled *Fengshi wenjian ji* [Record of Things Heard and Seen] in the late eighth century CE. It is cited in Chen and Zhu (1981, 211).

14. A line from the poem "Verses on Tea" in the *Lidai fabao chi* [Record of the Dharma Treasure through the Generations], written after 775 CE, cited in Broughton (1999, 113, 162, n. 12).

15. Meng Shen, *Shiliao bencao* [Nutritional Medicines in the Materia Medica], cited in Chen and Zhu (1981, 209).

16. They were: Shouzhou, Shuzhou, Guzhu, Qimen, Changming, and Yonghu—teas from Anhui, Anhui, Zhejiang, Hubei, Sichuan and Hunan provinces, respectively, as noted by Li Zhao (ca. 806–825) in *Tangguo shibu* [Supplemental History of the Tang Empire] of 825, cited in Chen and Zhu (1981, 214). See also Paul Smith (1991, 53, 65, 358, n. 17).

17. Su Yi (ninth–tenth centuries), *Shiliu tangpin* [Sixteen Qualities of Water], reproduced in Ruan (1999, 33–36).

18. For a full translation of the "Song of Tea," see Hohenegger (2006, 20–21) and Owyoung (2008a).

19. Twitchett (1963, 64, 276, n. 126); Paul Smith (1991, 56, 359, n. 30); Li Jifu, *Yüanho junxian tuzhi*, ch. 25, 338, cited in Chen Binfan (1999, 49).

20. *Beiyüan bielu* (1186, attributed to Zhao Ruli, active ca. 1163–1190), cited in Liao (1996, 12).

21. Cai Xiang, *Chalu* [Record of Tea], ca. 1049–1053, printed 1064, cited in Ruan (1999, 64–70, esp. 65).

22. Xiong Fan (active ca. twelfth century CE), *Xüanho Beiyüan gongcha lu*, cited in Liao (1996, 100–113, esp. 103–5).

23. Zhou Mi (1232–ca. 1308), *Wulin jiushi* [Old Customs of Hangzhou], ca. 1280 CE, cited in Bao Dingbo ([1793] 1966, *zi* 1, ch. 2, 20b–21a).

24. Cai Xiang, *Chalu* [Record of Tea], ca. 1049–1053, printed 1064, reproduced in Ruan (1999, 64–70); Zhao Ji (Emperor Song Huizong, 1082–1135), *Daguan chalun* [Treatise of Tea in the Daguan Reign Period, ca. 1107], reproduced in Ruan (1999, 89–97); and Liao (1996, 29–30).

25. Cai Xiang, *Chalu* [Record of Tea], ca. 1049–1053, printed 1064, reproduced in Ruan (1999, 67). Cf. Lin Ruixüan (2002, 47–53).

26. Zhao Ji (Emperor Song Huizong, 1082–1135), *Daguan chalun* [Treatise of Tea in the Daguan Reign Period], ca. 1107, reproduced in Ruan (1999, 91).

27. Zhou Mi (1232–ca. 1308), *Wulin jiushi* [Old Customs of Hangzhou], ca. 1280, reproduced in Bao ([1793] 1966, *zi* 1, ch. 2, 4b–5a).

28. Wu Zimu (fl. 1300 CE), *Mengliang lu* [Record of the Millet Dream], ch. 16, 1a–2a, reproduced in *Baibu congshu jicheng* (1965–1970).

29. Wang Zhen (active ca. 1295–1309), *Nongshu* [Book of Farming], ca. 1309, cited in Chen Binfan (1999, 296–97).

30. Ni Can (1301–1374), *Qinghi ge chüanji* [Complete Collection of the Pavilion of the Pure and Hidden]; and Song Lian (1310–1381), *History of the Yüan Dynasty*, cited in Chen Binfan (1999, 296–97, 299–300).

31. Xü Xianzhong (1483–1559), *Wuxing zhanggu ji* [Collection of Historical Records of Wuxing], 1560, cited in Chen and Zhu (1981, 296).

32. Ye Zichi (d. 1385?), *Caomu zi* [Herbs and Plants], 1378, cited in Chen and Zhu (1981, 287).

33. *Ming dazheng ji* and *Ming Taizu shilu*, cited in Chen Zongmou (1997, 34, 112, respectively).

34. Wang Shu (1416–1508), *Shen Ming chafa zouzhuang*, cited in Chen and Zhu (1981, 537).

35. Zhu Qüan, *Chapu* [Treatise on Tea], 1440, cited in Chen and Zhu (1981, 120–23.

36. Qiu Jün, *Daxüe yanyibu* [Supplementary Elaborations on Great Learning], 1487, cited in Chen and Zhu (1981, 542).

37. Wang Shu, *Shenming chafa zouzhuang* [Explanatory Memorial on Tea Regulations], cited in Chen and Zhu (1981, 537).

38. Brewed and infused tea grew out of an ancient popular practice called "soaked tea." In the Tang period *Book of Tea*, Lu Yü described a variety of teas "coarse, loose, powdered, and cake" that were either "chopped, simmered, roasted, or pounded," and then stored in a pottery bottle or jar into which hot water was poured; this was called "soaked tea" (*yancha*). See Shen and Zhu (1995, 114–15).

39. Wen Zhengming (1470–1559), *"Wang Yinjūn muzhi"* [Eulogy to Wang Lai], in *Wen Zhenming ji* (1987, ch. 29, 1504).

40. Zhu Zunli (1444–1513), preface to the *Huicha pian* [Gathering for Tea] by Shen Zhou (1427–1509), cited in Wu Zhihe (1996, 154–55).

41. Zhang Dai, "The Tea of Old Master Min," in Wu Hongyi (1979, 93–96); Spence (2007, 36–39).

The Way of Tea in Japan (Hohenegger)

1. For more information on early developments of *chanoyu*, see Murai Yasushiko's essay "The Development of *Chanoyu*: Before Rikyū" (Varley and Kumakura 1989, 3–32).

2. Originally the *shoin* was the library in a Zen temple. In time, this type of room became the prototypical Japanese room with tatami mats and sliding doors.

Chapter 2 (Hirota)

1. All translations are mine. The majority of them have been previously published in Hirota (1995). I refer the reader to this volume for further discussion of the authorship and the editions of the quoted works.

2. A portion of a classical *renga* sequence with annotation is included in Hirota (1995, 175–87). The influence of *renga* on modern *chanoyu* practices is also discussed.

3. For a concise discussion of the concept of the way of the arts in *Essays in Idleness*, see Yasuraoka (1982, 7–14).

Chapter 3 (Graham)

1. Up to the 1990s, most publications about *sencha* were intended for *sencha* practitioners. Notable recent Japanese exhibitions and scholarly studies include: Osaka Shiritsu Bijutsukan (1997), Aichi-ken Tōji Shiryōkan (2000), Sencha no Kigen to Hatten Shinpojium Soshiki Iinkai, ed. (2000), Iruma-shi Hakubutsukan (2001), Ōtsuki (2004), and Nomura Bijutsukan (2007).

2. Potters making wares for *chanoyu* have been so designated since initiation of the system in 1955. Jōzan, a Tokoname ware potter, specialized in making burnished, unglazed teapots (*kyūsu*) inspired by Yixing wares of China. He learned his art from his father, Jōzan II (1897–1961), and grandfather, Jōzan I (1868–1942), one of the earliest Japanese potters to make such wares. See Aichi-ken Tōji Shiryōkan (2007).

3. Because of biases against China lingering from the late nineteenth century, scholars have only recently acknowledged the impact of China's literati on the writings of ancient Japanese courtiers of the Heian period (794–1185), an era celebrated for its coalescence of indigenous literary and visual aesthetics (Smits 2007, 106–7, 119).

4. See McKelway (2002), who wrote an insightful article about this theme as treated by the Kano school painter Sansetsu (1589–1651). Sansetsu may have painted such themes as commissions for independent-minded Confucian scholars.

5. On the Ōbaku monks' encouragement of *sencha* production by Uji tea manufacturers, see Ōtsuki (2004, 260–62). On Ōbaku and *sencha*, see Graham (1998, 47–57). On Ōbaku monks and their temples in Japan, see Baroni (2002) and Graham (2007a, 52–60).

6. On the *sencha* gatherings of Chinzan and his friends in Edo, see Funasaka (2003).

7. Kenkadō had his fortune and business confiscated because his brewery exceeded government-mandated rice allotments during a time of poor harvests. Although he was eventually acquitted (his brewery manager was in fact responsible), he switched professions as a consequence of the scandalous allegations that had been leveled at him. For his biography, see Rosenfield (1999, 3: 48–51).

8. For a list of these, see Graham (1998, 225–28).

9. For further discussion of this album, see Graham (1998, 79–82). For illustrations of the complete album, see Shufunotomosha (1975, 9–11). The definitive scholarly work on art associated with Baisaō, it also includes reproductions of numerous portraits of him by his contemporaries and later admirers.

10. Illustrated in Graham (1998, fig. 15, 81).

11. For more on Mokubei, see Graham (1998, 127–32).

Chapter 4 (Tanimura)

I would like to thank the Congregation of the Missionary Sisters of the Heart of Jesus, Horinouchi Sōkyū and Morikawa Sōetsu (the head and the vice-head of Katagiri Sōen School, Sekishū-ryū), Nakagawa Kiyo'o (the head of the Sumiya Hozon Kai), Nakamura Toshinori (the professor of Kyoto University of Art and Design), Tanaka Sendō (the vice-president of the Dai Nihon Chadō Gakkai), Tani Akira (the chief curator of Nomura Art Museum) for their invaluable help on this project. Any errors are, of course, my own.

1. Unless otherwise indicated, all translations are mine.

2. This passage appears on the page of *Onna kuku no koe* (1787) that is reproduced in fig. 4.15.

The Tea Craze in the West (Hohenegger)

1. "An Exact Description of the Growth, Quality and Vertues of the Leaf Tea" by Thomas Garway, quoted in Needham (1986, 6: sec. 40, 565). According to Needham, the list of "vertues" derives from a Chinese book on tea from the Ming.

2. The date on record for the first Dutch tea import is 1610; yet, most likely, the Portuguese brought tea to the West before that but did not trade it beyond Portugal. This may explain why the Portuguese Catherine de Braganza was already a tea drinker when she married Charles II in 1662, while he was new to the practice.

3. To learn more about the role of the coffeehouses in seventeenth- and eighteenth-century English society, see Aytoun Ellis, *The Penny Universities: A History of the Coffee-Houses* (London: Secker & Warburg, 1956).

4. William Ukers (1935, 1: 41) comments: "and it may not be out of place to state that these unique gathering places [the coffee houses], each with its own more or less distinct clientele, whether of business men, professional men, or literati, came to be called 'coffee houses' instead of 'tea houses' because the public sale of the coffee beverage, in England, antedated the public sale of tea by a few years."

5. With their innovative lines, sleek design, and exceptional spread of sails, clippers revolutionized transatlantic navigation in the 1840s and astonished the world with their speed, which earned them the name "greyhounds of the seas." Aside from the China trade, clipper ships were also built for use in the California Gold Gush and the opium trade. The clipper ships themselves had a short life and were rendered obsolete by the invention of the steamer. For a brief account of the transition from East Indiaman to clipper to steamship, see Hohenegger (2006, 169–76).

6. Johann Böttger is often incorrectly cited as discovering the porcelain-making process. For more on this topic, see Martin Schönfeld, "Was There a Western Inventor of Porcelain?" *Technology and Culture*, October 1998, 39: 4, 716–27.

7. For more specific information on this topic, see Bowen's lucid essay: "Tea, Tribute and the East India Company, c. 1750–1775." In *Hanoverian Britain and Empire: Essays in Memory of Philip Lawson*, edited by Stephen Taylor, Richard Connors, and Clyve Jones (Woodbridge, Suffolk, England: Boydell, 1998).

Chapter 5 (Smith)

1. The reason that tea and similar beverages were thought to counteract the ill effects of sugar was that the bitterness of the beverage balanced the sweetness of sugar. Intense sweetness was believed to produce an excess of the humor "choler" in the body (Smith 1992).

The Conversation Piece (Trumble)

1. Oxford English Dictionary, s.v. *conversation*, n. 10: "A painting representing a group of figures, esp. members of a family, arranged as if in conversation in their customary surroundings."

Chapter 6 (Carson)

1. They occur in the entries of July–September 1710, June 4–8, and most of August 1712.

2. The phrase "dish of tea" refers to the practice of pouring the tea from a cup to a dish and then drinking it.

3. Details can be found on the Web site "Probing the Past" <http://chnm.gmu.edu/probate inventory>. The database was created to furnish Gunston Hall, the Virginia plantation house of George Mason (1725–1792). It is a project of the Center for History and New Media, George Mason University and Gunston Hall Plantation. The inventories range in date from 1741 to 1810.
4. Henry Fitzhugh, 1742, "1 brass tea kettle & lamp" valued at 16/-, and Mr. James Wardrope, Prince Georges, Maryland, 1760, "1 Dutch Tea Kettle lamp & stand" 17/6." Do Coffee Pott & lamp" 10/0.
5. The origin of this ware is disputed. Archaeologists working in rural South Carolina and Florida sites attribute it to enslaved African American potters. Those digging in Virginia favor Native Americans. See Ferguson (1992) and Singleton (1991, 155–75).
6. Alice Hanson Jones (1977) created a statistically accurate sample of 919 probate inventories from the colonies, all taken in 1774. Her questions of this evidence had to do with the economic basis that allowed Americans to think they might be able to finance a war. She was, however, well aware of other possible uses for these documents and published full transcripts.
7. The Virginia counties are Charlotte, Halifax, Southampton, Brunswick, Mecklenburg, Chesterfield, Fairfax, and Spotsylvania. For the Gunston Hall Probate Inventory Database see "Probing the Past" at <http://chnm.gmu.edu/probate inventory >.
8. The two silver pots were owned by merchants Samuel Neave and James Maccubin. Jones (1977, 1: 191, 206).

Chapter 7 (Merritt)
1. The Massachusetts Historical Society, American Antiquarian Society, the Old State House Museum, and Peabody Essex Museum all display vials of tea purported to be from the Boston Tea Party.
2. According to Richard Dillard (1925, 10–11), the "Patriotic Ladies" engraving only appeared at Edenton in 1830 when a traveling sailor found a copy in Minorca and brought it home, which in turn prompted the community to "remember" the incident. Dillard attempts to reconstruct a list of the petition signers.
3. Carole Shammas (1990, 84) indicates that colonists drank 0.5 to 0.8 pounds of tea annually, while Billy Smith (1981, 170) estimates that a laborer in the 1760s consumed only 0.2 pounds.
4. John Kidd, a Philadelphia merchant speculating on the "state of the Tea Trade of this Place" for his London agent, estimated that 37,315 pounds of tea were imported to Philadelphia alone in 1750, 43,403 pounds in 1751, and 52,507 pounds in 1752 (Kidd 1757).
5. In Boston, the legal tea trade was dominated by the interests of Governor Thomas Hutchinson and his extended family, particularly his sons Elisha and Thomas who acted as commissioners for the East India Company during 1773.
6. The full title of the Tea Act was: *An Act to allow a Drawback of the Duties of Customs on the Exportation of Tea to any of His Majesty's Colonies or Plantations in America; to increase the Deposit on Bohea Tea to be sold at the India Company's sales; and to impower the Commissioners of the Treasury to grant Licences to the East India Company to export Tea Duty-free* (London, 1773).

7. William Palmer of London to the Directors of the East India Company, May 19, 1773, in Drake (1884, 189). The East India Company hoped to introduce a wider variety of teas to American consumers, thus the first consignments amounted to 562,421 pounds of bohea, 22,546 pounds singlo, 5,285 pounds hyson, 2,392 pounds souchong, and 6,015 pounds congou teas (Drake 1884, 250–52.)
8. See John Morris to Corbyn Morris, Dec. 22, 1773, in Drake (1884, 342); Rogers (1974, 162). Despite a series of general meetings in March and April 1774, nothing else was done with the Company tea until October 1776, when it was hauled out of storage and sold to support the new State of South Carolina (Steedman 1967, 259).
9. "Postscript to *The Pennsylvania Gazette*, Dec. 24, 1773," in Etting (187[?], n.p.).
10. November 21, 1774, *The South Carolina Gazette*, quoted in Steedman (1967, 250–51). Steedman speculates that Charleston inhabitants also acted upon conflated fears of British taxation and a hatred of Catholicism, with the imposition of the Quebec Act in 1774 (p. 254).
11. See *Brig Peggy Stewart* (1774). Perhaps Stewart brought the crowd's anger upon himself, since he insisted on paying the tax duty on the tea, even though the "people would have been satisfied even with the Tea's being stored without paying the Duty" (Ringgold [1774] 1901, 253–54).

Tea and Empire (Hohenegger)
1. See "Poverty Starvation Stalk Bengal Tea Garden Workers." *Thaindian news.* <http://www.thaindian.com/newsportal/business/poverty-starvation-stalk-bengal-tea-garden-workers_10056300.html> (2008); see also the "Report on Hunger in Tea Plantations in North Bengal" (2004) prepared by the West Bengal Advisor to the Commissioners of the Supreme Court, available online at: <http://www.righttofoodindia.org/data/teagardenreport.doc>.
2. See the January 2, 2009, article in the Times of London: <http://www.timesonline.co.uk/tol/news/uk/article5429888.ece> (2009).

Chapter 9 (Kolsky)
1. In 2000 the tea market in the United Kingdom was valued at £707,000,000.
2. In brief, the Opium War began shortly after the Chinese government cracked down on the growing opium trade. After politely requesting Queen Victoria to cease exporting sin, the emperor ordered all foreign ships to surrender their opium chests and stop the trade. When they refused, he seized twenty thousand chests of illicit opium and detained members of the foreign community in Canton, prompting the British to launch attacks in defense of their right of "free trade." Britain would not cease its opium trade in China until 1911.
3. J. H. Williams, *Tea Estates and Their Management*, Oriental and India Office Collection, British Library, Mss Eur C796.

REFERENCES CITED

Addiss, Stephen, ed.
1986   *Japanese Quest for a New Vision: The Impact of Visiting Chinese Paint-ers, 1600–1900.* Lawrence: Spencer Museum of Art, University of Kansas.

Advertisement
1770   *Advertisement. Whereas an act was passed last session of Parliament, for repealing the act imposing a duty on paper, pain and glass.* New York, June 12. Broadside. Library Company of Philadelphia.

Aichi-ken Tōji Shiryōkan (Aichi Prefecture Ceramic Museum)
2000   *Sencha to yakimono: Edo, Meiji no Chūgoku shumi* [*Sencha* and Ceramics: The Taste for China in the Edo and Meiji Periods]. Seto-shi: Aichi-ken Tōji Shiryōkan.
2007   *Sencha tōgei no bi to dentō Ningen kokuhō Sandai Yamada Jōzan e no michi* [Tradition and Beauty of the Ceramic Art of *Sencha*: Living National Treasure Yamada Jōzan III and the Development of Tea Vessels]. Seto-shi: Aichi-ken Tōji Shiryōkan.

Andrews, Frank D.
1908   *The Tea-Burners of Cumberland County Who Burned a Cargo of Tea at Greenwich, New Jersey, December 22, 1774.* Vineland, N.J.: N.p.

Anjōshi Rekishi Hakubutsukan (Anjō City Historical Museum)
2007   *Sencha no sekai: Tokubetsuten Ishikawa Jōzan no kokoro* [The World of *Sencha*: Special Exhibition on the Spirit of Ishikawa Jōzan]. Anjō: Anjōshi Rekishi Hakubutsukan.

Anonymous
[1774?]   *A Sermon on Tea.* Lancaster, Penn.: Francis Bailey.

Appletons' Annual Cyclopaedia
1903   *Appletons' Annual Cyclopaedia and Register of Important Events: Embracing Political, Military, and Ecclesiastical Affairs; Public Documents; Biography, Statistics, Commerce, Finance, Literature, Science, Agriculture, and Mechanical Industry.* New York: D. Appleton and company.

Arima Nobuko et al., eds.
[1692] 1989   *E iri onna chōhōki.* Tokyo: Tōyoko Gakuen Josei Tanki Daigaku.

Asai Ryoi
[1682] 2002   *Tōkaidō meishō ki* [The Reports of the Tōkaidō Road]. Tokyo: Toshō Kankō Kai.

Auslander, Leora
1996   *Taste and Power: Furnishing Modern France.* Berkeley: University of California Press.

Baibu congshu jicheng
1965–1970   *Baibu congshu jicheng.* Taipei: Yiwen yinshu guan.

Baisaō and Norman Waddell
2008   *The Old Tea Seller: Baisaō: Life and Zen Poetry in 18th Century Kyoto.* Berkeley: Counterpoint.

Bao Dingbo, ed.
[1793] 1966   *Zhibuzu chai congshu.* Taipei: Yiwen shuguan.

Barka, Norman F.
2004   "Archaeology of a Colonial Pottery Factory: The Kilns and Ceramics of the 'Poor Potter' of Yorktown." In *Ceramics in America.* Hanover and London: Chipstone Foundation.

Baroni, Helen J.
2002   *Obaku Zen: The Emergence of the Third Sect of Zen in Tokugawa Japan.* Honolulu: University of Hawai'i Press.

Bartholomew, Terese Tse
1981   "A Study on the Shapes and Decorations of Yixing Teapots." In *Yixing Pottery,* 13–33. Hong Kong: Hong Kong Museum of Art.
1992   "The Art of Yixing." *Ceramics Monthly* (December): 38–45.
1998   "The first Annual Symposium for Western Potters, November, 1996." *La revue de la céramique et du verre,* supplement au no. 100 (May/June).

Beatty, Joseph M.
[1774] 1920   January 1774. "Letters of the Four Beatty Brothers of the Continental Army, 1774–1794." *Pennylvania Magazine of History and Biography* 44, no. 3 (July): 193–263.

Bello, David Anthony
2005   *Opium and the Limits of Empire: Drug Prohibition in the Chinese Interior, 1729–1850.* Cambridge, Mass.: Harvard University Asia Center and Harvard University Press.

Bengalee
1901   *Bengalee,* March 10 (Calcutta).

Bontekoe, Cornelis
1689   *Tractaat Van het Excellenste Kruyd Thee, Coffi, en Chocolate.* Amsterdam: N.p.

Booth, Benjamin
1774a   Benjamin Booth to James and Drinker, March 11, 1774. Philadelphia Tea Party Correspondence, 1773–1778. James and Drinker correspondence, transcribed by Francis R. Taylor, 1910. Historical Society of Pennsylvania, Philadelphia.
1774b   Benjamin Booth to James and Drinker, April 25, 1774. Philadelphia Tea Party Correspondence, 1773–1778. James and Drinker correspondence, transcribed by Francis R. Taylor, 1910. Historical Society of Pennsylvania, Philadelphia.

Boston Evening Post
1774   *Boston Evening Post,* July 25.

Bourdieu, Pierre
1984   *Distinction: A Social Critique of the Judgment of Taste.* Cambridge, Mass.: Harvard University Press.

Bowen, H. V.

1998   "Tea, Tribute and the East India Company, c. 1750–1775." In *Hanoverian Britain and Empire: Essays in Memory of Philip Lawson*, edited by Stephen Taylor, Richard Connors, and Clyve Jones. Woodbridge, Suffolk, England: Boydell.

Bridenbaugh, Carl, ed.

1948   *Gentleman's Progress: The Itinerrium of Dr. Alexander Hamilton, 1744.* Chapel Hill: The University of North Carolina Press for The Institute of Early American History and Culture.

Brig Peggy Stewart

1774   *The Brig Peggy Stewart*. Annapolis, October 18. Pamphlet. Library Company of Philadelphia.

Brook, Timothy

1998   *The Confusions of Pleasure: Commerce and Culture in Ming China.* Berkeley: University of California Press.

Broughton, Jeffrey L.

1999   *The Bodhidharma Anthology: The Earliest Records of Zen.* Berkeley: University of California Press.

Brown, Kendall H.

1997   *The Politics of Reclusion: Painting and Power in Momoyama Japan.* Honolulu: University of Hawai'i Press.

Bryson, Anna

1998   *From Courtesy to Civility: Changing Codes of Conduct in Early Modern England.* Oxford: Clarendon.

Byrd, William

1941   *The Secret Diary of William Byrd of Westover, 1709–1712.* Edited by Louis B. Wright and Marion Tinling. Richmond, Va.: Dietz.

Central Library

1978   *Mingren qŭanji ziliao suoyin* [Index of Biographical Materials of Ming Personages]. Taipei: Guoli Zhongyang tushuguan.

Chang, Lin-sheng

1982   "Sung Chien Ware: A Suggestion for a Revised Dating in the Light of Knowledge of the Tea Drinking Contests of the Northern Sung." *National Palace Museum Bulletin* 16, no. 6: 10.

Chaudhuri, K. N.

1978   *The Trading World of Asia and the English East India Company, 1660–1760.* Cambridge: Cambridge University Press.

Chen Binfan, ed.

1999   *Zhongguo cha wenhua jingtian* [Expressions of Chinese Tea Culture]. Beijing: Guangming ribao chubanshe.

Chen Zigui and Zhu Zizhen, eds.

1981   *Zhongguo chaye lishi ziliao xŭanji.* Beijing: Nongye chubanshe.

Chen Zongmou

1997   *Zhongguo chajing* Shanghai: Shanghai wenhua chubanshe.

Chikamatsu Monzaemon

1998   *Yari no Gonza kasane katabira.* In *Chikamatsu Monzaemon shū* 2. Shinpen Nihon koten bungaku zenshū 75: 583–637. Tokyo Shōgakukan.

Chiu-Duke, Josephine

2000   *To Rebuild the Empire: Lu Chih's Confucian Pragmatic Approach to the Mid-T'ang Predicament.* Albany: State University of New York.

Chotner, Deborah, and Julie Aronson

1992   *American Naïve Paintings.* Washshington, D.C.: National Gallery of Art; Cambridge: Cambridge University Press.

Connecticut Journal

1773   *Connecticut Journal*, December 31.

Cooper, Samuel

1773   Samuel Cooper to Benjamin Franklin, December 17, 1773. Benjamin Franklin Papers. American Philosophical Society, Philadelphia.

Cotton, Henry

1901   Henry Cotton to Lord Curzon, September 17, 1901. Private correspondence of Henry Cotton. British Library, Oriental and India Office Collection (OIOC), Mss Eur D1202/2.

Cowan, Brian

2005   *The Social Life of Coffee: The Emergence of the British Coffeehouse.* New Haven: Yale University Press.

2004   "Mr. Spectator and the Coffeehouse Public Sphere." *Eighteenth-Century Studies* 37, no. 3: 345–66.

Cunningham, Anne Rowe, ed.

[1903] 1969   *Letters and Diary of John Rowe, Boston Merchant, 1759–1762, 1764–1779.* Boston: W. B. Clarke; reprint New York: Arno.

Curzon, George

1901   "Curzon to the Secretary of State." Letter of August 28, 1901. British Library, Oriental and India Office Collection (OIOC), Mss Eur 235/1.

Dillard, Richard

1925   *The Historic Tea-Party of Edenton, October 25th, 1774, an Incident in North Carolina Connected with British Taxation.* N.p.

Ding Fubao, comp.

1969   *Chüan Han Sankuo Jin Nanbei chao shi* [The Complete Poetry of the Han, Three Kingdoms, Jin, and Northern and Southern Dynasties]. Taipei: Shijieh shuchü.

Doerflinger, Thomas

1983   "Philadelphia Merchants and the Logic of Moderation, 1760–1775." *William and Mary Quarterly*, 3rd ser., 40, no. 2 (April): 197–226.

Dowding, Charles

1896   "Dowding to the Secretary of State." Letter of September 23, 1896. British Library, Oriental and India Office Collection (OIOC), L/PJ/6/233, File 1431.

Drake, Francis S., intro.

1884   *Tea Leaves: Being a Collection of Letters and Documents Relating to the Shipment of Tea to the American Colonies in the Year 1773, by the East India Tea Company.* Boston: A. O. Crane.

Dufour, Philippe Sylvestre

1685   *Traités Nouveaux et Curieux Du Café Du Thee et Du Chocolate.* The Hague: Adrian Moetjens.

Eatwell, Ann

2008   "Tea à la Mode: The Fashion for Tea and the Tea Equipage in London and Paris." In *Boucher and Chardin: Masters of Modern Manners*, edited by Anne Dulau, 50–76. Glasgow: The Hunterian, University of Glasgow, in association with Paul Holberton.

Elliott, Charles Alfred

1885   "Conditions of Tea Laborers on the Tea Plantations in Assam." British Library, Oriental and India Office Collection (OIOC), L/PJ/6/233, File 1431.

Essex Gazette

1774   *Essex Gazette*, January 11 (Salem, Mass.).

Etting, Frank M.

187[?] *The Philadelphia Tea Party of 1773: A Chapter from the History of the Old State House*. Philadelphia: [E. Stern?].

Fairbank, John King

1987 *China Watch*. Cambridge: Harvard University Press.

Fa men si

1990 *Fa men si* [Famen Temple]. Xi'an Shi: Zhongguo Shanxi Lü you chu ban she.

Fang Xüanling, comp.

1974 *Yishu chuan* [Record of the Arts], *Jinshu* [History of the Chin Dynasty]. Beijing: Zhonghua Book Company.

Farish, Hunter Dickinson, ed.

1943 *Journal and Letters of Philip Vickers Fithian, 1773–1774: A Plantation Tutor of the Old Dominion*. Williamsburg, Va.: Colonial Williamsburg.

Feldbæk, Ole

1969 *India Trade under the Danish Flag, 1772–1808: European Enterprise and Anglo-Indian Remittance and Trade*. Copenhagen: Studentlitteratur.

Ferguson, Leland

1992 *Uncommon Ground: Archaeology and Early African America, 1650–1800*. Washington, D.C.: Smithsonian Institution.

Fister, Patricia

1988 *Japanese Women Artists, 1600–1900*. Lawrence: Spencer Museum of Art, University of Kansas.

Food and Agriculture Organization (FAO)

2008 "Current Situation and Medium-Term Outlook." Committee on Commodity Problems—Intergovernmental Group on Tea (CCP: TE 08/2).

Funasaka Fumiko

2003 "Tachi Ryūwan to *sencha* no shiyū" [The Advocates of *Sencha* in Edo: Tachi Ryūwan and His Friends]. *Nomura Bijutsukan kenkyū kiyō* 12: 1–28.

Galloway, John

[1774] 1901 John Galloway to Thomas Ringgold, Oct. 20, 1774. "Account of the Destruction of the Brigg 'Peggy Stewart' at Annapolis, 1774." *Pennsylvania Magazine of History and Biography* 25, no. 2: 248–254.

Galloway, Joseph

1770 Joseph Galloway to Benjamin Franklin, June 21, 1770. Benjamin Franklin Papers. American Philosophical Society, Philadelphia.

Gandhi, M. K.

2001 *Non-Violent Resistance*. North Chelmsford, Mass.: Courier Dover.

Ganev, Robin

2007 "Milkmaids, Ploughmen, and Sex in Eighteenth-Century Britain." *Journal of the History of Sexuality* 16, no. 1: 40–67.

Ganguli, Dwarkanath

[1872] 1972 *Slavery in the British Dominion*. Calcutta; reprint Calcutta: Jijnasa.

Gardella, Robert

1994 *Harvesting the Mountains: Fujian and the China Tea Trade, 1757–1937*. Berkeley: University of California Press.

Geinōshi Kenkyū Kai

1976 *Horinouchi monjinchō* [The List of Followers of Horinouchi House of the Omote Sen School]. Nihon shomin bunkashi shūsei 10: 715–30. Tokyo: San-ichi Shobō.

Gernet, Jacques

1996 *A History of Chinese Civilization*. Translated by J. R. Foster and Charles Hartman. Cambridge: Cambridge University Press.

Graham, Patricia J.

1983 "Yamamoto Baiitsu: His Life, Literati Pursuits, and Related Paintings." Ph.D. diss., University of Kansas.

1986 "Yamamoto Baiitsu no Chūgokuga kenkyū" [Yamamoto Baiitsu's Study of Chinese Painting]. *Kobijutsu* 80 (fall): 62–75.

1998 *Tea of the Sages: The Art of Sencha*. Honolulu: University of Hawai'i Press.

1999 "The Appreciation of Chinese Flower Baskets in Premodern Japan." In *Japanese Bamboo Baskets: Masterworks of Form and Texture*, edited by Joseph N. Newland, 60–83. Los Angeles: Cotsen Occasional Press.

2001 "China's Influence on Japanese Edo Period Paintings at the Indianapolis Museum of Art." *Orientations* (March): 78–92.

2002 "The Later Flourishing of Literati Painting in Edo-Period Japan." In *An Enduring Vision: 17th–20th Century Painting from the Gitter-Yelen Collection*, edited by Lisa Rotondo-McCord, 69–87. New Orleans: New Orleans Museum of Art.

2003 "*Karamono* for *Sencha*: Transformations in the Taste for Chinese Art." In *Japanese Tea Culture: Art, History, and Practice*, edited by Morgan Pitelka, 110–36. London: Routledge-Curzon.

2007a *Faith and Power in Japanese Buddhist Art, 1600–2005*. Honolulu: University of Hawai'i Press.

2007b "Ōtagaki Rengetsu and the Japanese Tea Ceremony." In *Black Robe, White Mist: The Art of the Japanese Buddhist Nun Ōtagaki Rengetsu*, edited by Melanie Eastburn et al., 63–68. Canberra: National Gallery of Australia.

Grousset, René

1970 *The Empire of the Steppes: A History of Central Asia*. New Brunswick, N.J.: Rutgers University.

Guha, Amalendu

1977 *Planter-Raj to Swaraj: Freedom Struggle and Electoral Politics in Assam, 1826–1947*. New Delhi: Indian Council of Historical Research.

Gupta, Bishnupriya

2009 "The History of the International Tea Market, 1850–1945." <http://eh.net/encyclopedia/article/gupta.tea>.

Guth, Christine

2006 "Meiji Response to *Bunjinga*." In *Challenging the Past and Present: The Metamorphosis of Nineteenth-Century Japanese Art*, edited by Ellen P. Conant, 177–96. Honolulu: University of Hawai'i Press.

Habermas, Jürgen

1989 *The Structural Transformation of the Public Sphere: An Inquiry into a Category of Bourgeois Society*. Cambridge, Mass.: MIT Press.

Hall, Catherine

1990 "The Sweet Delights of Home." In *A History of Private Life IV: From the Fires of Revolution to the Great War*, edited by M. Perrot, 47–94. Cambridge, Mass.: Belknap Press of Harvard University Press.

Hampden [pseud.]

1773 *The Alarm. Number V. My Dear Fellow Citizens*. New York, October 27. Broadside. American Antiquarian Society, Worcester, Massachusetts.

Hannah, A. C., and Donald Spence
1997   *The International Sugar Trade*. New York: John Wiley and Sons.

Hanway, Jonas
1767   *Letters on the Importance of the Rising Generation of the laboring part of our fellow-subjects....* London: A. Millar and T. Cadell; and C. Marsh and G. Woodfall.

Hawkes, David
1985   *Songs of the South: An Ancient Chinese Anthology of Poems by Qu Yuan and Other Poets.* London: Penguin.

Hickey, William
1913–1925   *Memoirs.* 4 vols. Edited by Alfred Spencer. London: Hurst and Blackett.

Hildyard, Robin
1999   *European Ceramics.* London: V and A.

Hirota, Dennis
1989   *Plain Words on the Pure Land Way: Sayings of the Wandering Monks of Medieval Japan.* (A translation of Ichigon Hōdan). Kyoto: Ryukoku University.
1995   *Wind in the Pines: Classic Writings of the Way of Tea as a Buddhist Path.* Fremont, Calif.: Asian Humanities.

Ho, Peng Yoke
2007   *Explorations in Daoism: Medicine and Alchemy in Literature.* New York: Rutledge.

Hochschild, Adam
2005   *Bury the Chains: Prophets and Rebels in the Fight to Free an Empire's Slaves.* Boston: Houghton Mifflin.

Hohenegger, Beatrice
2006   *Liquid Jade: The Story of Tea from East to West.* New York: St. Martin's.

Honour, Hugh
1961   *Chinoiserie: The Vision of Cathay.* London: John Murray.

Hsü Cho-yü
1980   *Han Agriculture: The Formation of Early Chinese Agrarian Economy (206 B.C. to A.D. 220).* Seattle: University of Washington Press.

Hsu Hong-yen et al., comps.
1986   *Oriental Materia Medica: A Concise Guide.* New Canaan: Keats.

Hutchinson, Thomas
1771   Thomas Hutchinson to Lord Hillsborough, August 25, 1771. Thomas Hutchinson Letter Books, transcription, vol. 27, 361. Massachusetts Historical Society, Boston.

Ihara Saikaku
[1682] 1996   *Kōshoku ichi-dai otoko* [The Life of an Amorous Man]. In *Ihara Saikaku shū 1.* Shinpen Nihon koten bungaku zenshū 66: 117–229. Tokyo: Shōgakukan.

International Tea Committee
1946   *Bulletin of Statistics.*

Iruma-shi Hakubutsukan (Iruma City Museum)
2001   *Tokubetsuten "sencha" denrai: Baisaō to bunjincha no jidai: Iruma shisei shikō* [Special Exhibition on the Introduction of *Sencha*: Baisaō and the Era of Literati Tea]. Saitama-ken Iruma-shi: Iruma-shi Hakubutsukan.

Itabashi Kuritsu Kyōdō Shiryōkan (Itabashi Ward Museum of Folklore)
1996   *Nagasaki Tōjin bōeki to senchadō* [The Nagasaki China Trade and the *Sencha* Tea Ceremony]. Tokyo: Itabashi Kuritsu Kyōdō Shiryōkan.

James and Drinker
1764   James and Drinker to Neate, Pigou, and Booth, November 6, 1764. James and Drinker Letter Book, 1764–1766. Henry Drinker Business Papers, 1756–1869. Historical Society of Pennsylvania, Philadelphia.
1773   James and Drinker to Thomas Hutchinson et al., December 17, 1773. Philadelphia Tea Party Correspondence 1773–1778. James and Drinker correspondence, transcribed by Francis R. Taylor, 1910. Historical Society of Pennsylvania, Philadelphia.

Jansen, Marius B.
1992   *China in the Tokugawa World.* Cambridge, Mass.: Harvard University Press.

Jarratt, Devereux
1952   "The Autobiography of the Reverend Devereux Jarratt, 1732–1763, with an Introduction and Notes by Douglas Adair." *The William and Mary Quarterly*, 3rd ser., IX, no. 3 (July).

Jha, K. C.
1996   *Aspects of Indentured Inland Emigration to North-East India, 1859–1918.* New Delhi: Indus Publishing.

Joichi Mariko
2007   "Muromachi suibokuga no [sencha]—bunjinzuyo o megutte" ["*Sencha*" in Muromachi Ink Painting: Discussing Literati Motifs]. *Nomura Bijutsukan Kenkyū kiyō* 16, *tokushū, sencha*: 54–81.

Jones, Alice Hanson
1977   *American Colonial Wealth: Documents and Methods.* 3 vols. New York: Arno.

Jordan, Philip
1934   "The Romance of Tea." *Fortnightly Review* 135 (February): 220, 222.

Kagotani Machiko
1995   *Shinshū bunka-shi no kenkyū.* Kyoto: Kyoto Jyoshi Daigaku.

Kamiya Sōtan
1977   *Sōtan Nikki* [Records of Tea Gatherings, 1586–1599]. *Sādo koten zenshū* 6: 133–382. Kyoto: Tankō Sha.

Kano Hiroyuki
2005   "The Philosophical Underpinnings of Eighteenth-century Kyoto Painting Circles." In *Tradition Unbound: Groundbreaking Painters of Eighteenth-century Kyoto*, edited by Matthew P. McKelway et al., 37–43. San Francisco: Asian Art Museum of San Francisco.

Karetzky, Patricia
1995   *Court Art of the Tang.* Lanham: University Press of America.

Karlgren, Bernhard.
1946   "Legends and Cults in Ancient China." *Bulletin of the Museum of Far Eastern Antiquities*, no. 18: 199–365.

Katō Etsuko
2004   *The Tea Ceremony and Women's Empowerment in Modern Japan: Bodies Re-presenting the Past.* London: Routledge Curzon.

Kidd, John
1752   John Kidd to Rawlinson and Davison, August 27, 1752. John Kidd Letter Book, 1749–1763. Historical Society of Pennsylvania, Philadelphia.
1757   John Kidd to Rawlinson and Davison, January 28, 1757. John Kidd Letter Book, 1749–1763. Historical Society of Pennsylvania, Philadelphia.

Kleeman, Terry F.
1998   *Great Perfection: Religion and Ethnicity in a Chinese Millennial Kingdom.* Honolulu: University of Hawai'i Press.

Kōshin
1975   "Kōshin Gegaki" [Memo Left by Kōshin, 1662–1663]. *Sadō koten zenshū* (Tankō Sha, Kyoto), 10: 67–98.

Kumar, Dharma, ed.
1983   *The Cambridge Economic History of India*. Cambridge: Cambridge University Press.

Kusumi Soan
[1701] 1975   "Chawa shigetsu shū" [Record of Fujimura Yōken's Conversation]. *Sadō koten zenshū* (Tankō Sha, Kyoto), 10: 199–266.

Labaree, Benjamin Woods
1966   *The Boston Tea Party*. London: Oxford University Press.

Le Corbeiller, Clare, and Alice Cooney Frelinghuysen
2003   *Chinese Export Porcelain*. New York: Metropolitan Museum of Art.

Lexington Resolves
1773   December 13, 1773. Lexington (Mass.) local records, 1765–1784, folio vol. 1: 28–33. American Antiquarian Society, Worcester, Massachusetts.

Liang, Zi
1994   *Zhongguo Tang Song chadao*. Xi'an: Shaanxi renmin chubanshe.

Liao Baoxiu
1996   *Songdai chichafa yü chachi zhi yanjiu*. Taipei: Guoli Gugong bowu yüan.

Lin Ruixüan
2002   *Duocha Shizuo*. Taipei: Wuling chubanshe.

Lin Yutang
1937   "On Tea and Friendship." In *The Importance of Living*. New York: Reynal and Hitchcock.

Lincoln Resolutions
1773   Lincoln, MA, Resolutions, December 27, 1773. U.S. Revolution Collection, 1754–1928, box 1, folder 3, 1754–1773. American Antiquarian Society, Worcester, Massachusetts.

Littlefield, Daniel
1991   *Rice and Slaves: Ethnicity and the Slave Trade in Colonial South Carolina*. Urbana: University of Illinois.

Liu Yiching
1972   *Shishuo xinyü* [New Account of Tales of the World]. Taipei: Taiwan Zhonghua shuchu.

Loyang qielan ji gouchen
1969   *Loyang qielan ji gouchen*. Taipei: Guangwen shuchü.

Lü Weixin and Cai Jiade, comps.
1995   *Cong Tangshi kan Tangren chadao shenghuo*. Taipei: Lu Yü chayi zhongxin chuban.

Lu Yü
[1273] 1985   *Chajing* [Book of Tea]. Baichuan xuehai edition. In *Lu Yü Chajing congkan* [A Collection of Printings of the *Book of Tea* by Lu Yü], compiled by Zhang Hong-yong, 3–42. Taoyüan: Chaxue wenxue chubanshe.

Macaulay, Thomas B.
1980   *The Works of Lord Macaulay*. 12 vols. New York: AMS.

MacDonald, Michelle Craig
Forthcoming   *Grounds for Debate: Coffee and Commerce in Early America*. Philadelphia: University of Pennsylvania Press.

Martin-Fugier, Anne
1990   "Bourgeois Rituals." In *A History of Private Life IV: From the Fires of Revolution to the Great War*, edited by M. Perrot, 261–338. Cambridge, Mass.: Belknap Press of Harvard University Press.

Matson, Cathy
1998   *Merchants and Empire: Trading in Colonial New York*. Baltimore: Johns Hopkins University Press.

Matsuyama Genshō An, ed.
1974   *Sadō shiso densho*. Chanoyu koten sōsho 1. Kyoto: Shibunkaku.

McKelway, Matthew P.
2002   "Autumn Moon and Lingering Snow: Kano Sansetsu's West Lake Screens." *Artibus Asiae* 62, no. 1: 33–80.

Mechanic [John Dickinson]
1773   *To the Tradesmen, Mechanics, etc.* Broadside. Historical Society of Pennsylvania, Philadelphia.

Meeting of the Committees
1774   *At a Meeting of the Committees, Annapolis, June 22, 1774.* Broadside. Historical Society of Pennsylvania, Philadelphia.

Meng Yüanlao
[1174] 1982   *Dongjing menghua lu zhu* [The Eastern Capital: A Dream of Splendors Past, 1174 CE]. Beijing: Xinhua shudian.

Merton, Thomas
1969   *Way of Chuang Tzu*. New York: New Directions.

Mintz, Sidney W.
1986   *Sweetness and Power: The Place of Sugar in Modern History*. New York: Penguin.
1994   "The Changing Roles of Food in the Study of Consumption." In *Consumption and the World of Goods*. New York: Routledge.

Mitter, Partha
1997   "Cartoons of the Raj." *History Today* 47, no. 9 (September).

Miyazaki Shūta
1996   "Meien zuroku no jidai" [The Era of Illustrated Records of Famous Utensils]. *Bungaku* 7, no. 3 (summer): 33–45.

Mote, F. W.
1999   *Imperial China 900–1800*. Cambridge, Mass.: Harvard University Press.

Mudge, Jean McClure
1986   *Chinese Export Porcelain in North America*. New York: Clarkson Potter.

Murase, Miyeko
2000   *Bridge of Dreams: The Mary Griggs Burke Collection of Japanese Art*. New York: The Metropolitan Museum of Art.

Nakagawa Kio'o
2002   "Kishi-ha to Sumiya no kōryū." *Sumiya Kenkyū* (Sukiya Hozon-Kai, Kyoto) 12: 29–41.

Nakamura Katsumaro
[1914] 1978   *Ii tairo sadō-dan*. Tokyo: Sōbunsha; reprint Tokyo: Daigaku Shuppan-kai.

Needham, Joseph, et al.
1986   *Science and Civilisation in China*. Vol. 6, part 1. Cambridge: Cambridge University Press.

Newcastle Magazine
1820   Anonymous letter, signed "W." *Newcastle Magazine* 1, no. 2: 149.

Newell, Thomas

[1773] 1878   Entry of December 16, 1773. "Diary for 1773 to the End of 1774 of Mr. Thomas Newell." *Proceedings of the Massachusetts Historical Society, 1876–1877.* Vol 15. Boston: Massachusetts Historical Society.

[1774] 1878   Entry of May 2, 1774. "Diary for 1773 to the End of 1774 of Mr. Thomas Newell." *Proceedings of the Massachusetts Historical Society, 1876–1877.* Vol 15. Boston: Massachusetts Historical Society.

New-York Journal

1773   *New-York Journal*, April 28.

Niemcewicz, Julian Ursyn

1965   *Under Their Vine and Fig Tree: Travels through America in 1787–1799, 1805 with Some Further Account of Life in New Jersey.* Translated and edited by Metchie J. E. Budka. Collections of the New Jersey Historical Society at Newark 14. Elizabeth, N.J.: Grassman.

Nihon Shigaku Kyōiku Kenkyūjo

1985   *Onna chōhōki—Otoko chōhōki.* Nihon Shigaku Kyōiku Kenkyūjo 122. Tokyo: Nihon Shigaku Kyōiku Kenkyūjo.

Niigata Prefectural Museum of Modern Art

1999   *Gift of the Tang Emperors: Hidden Treasures from the Famen Temple.* Nagaoka: Niigata Prefectural Museum of Modern Art.

Nomura Bijutsukan (Nomura Art Museum)

2007   *Nomura Bijutsukan kenkyū kiyō 16, tokushū, sencha* [Nomura Art Museum Research Bulletin 16, special issue on *sencha*].

Nomura Zuiten, ed.

1985   "Toji no tamoto" [Senior Ladies Sleeves]. *Tei-hon sekishū ryū* (Mitsumura Suiko Shoin, Kyoto) 2: 188–223.

Nunome Chōfū

2001   *Chakyo shōkai* [A Detailed Examination of the *Chajing*]. Tokyo: Tankosha.

Oaks, Robert F.

1977   "Philadelphia Merchants and the Origins of American Independence." *Proceedings of the American Philosophical Society* 121, no. 6 (December): 407–36.

Okakura Kakuzo

1906   *The Book of Tea.* New York: Fox Duffield.

Omori Ichiro, ed.

[1841] 1993   "Onna shorei ayanishiki." *Edo jidai josei seikatsu ezu daijiten* (Ōzora-sha, Tokyo) 4: 295.

[1836] 1993   "Shugyoku hyakunin-isshu ogura shiori." *Edo jidai josei seikasu ezu daijiten* (Ōzora-sha, Tokyo) 4: 295.

Omotesenke

2008   *Shin-pen Genpaku Sōtan Monjo* [New Version of the Documents of Genpaku Sōtan]. Kyoto: Omotesenke.

Onna daigaku

1980   *Onna daigaku* [Instruction for Girls]. Nihon Shisō Daikei 34: 202–5. Tokyo: Iwanami Shoten.

Osaka Shiritsu Bijutsukan (Osaka Municipal Museum)

1997   *Bunjin no akogare, seifū no kokoro sencha bi to sono katachi* [*Sencha*: Its Beauty and Spirit, Seeking after *Seifū*, the Purity of Mind Like a Bracing Breeze]. Osaka-shi: Osaka Shiritsu Bijutsukan.

Ōtsuki Mikio

2004   *Sencha bunka kō: Bunjincha no keifu* [Considering the Culture of *Sencha*: The Lineage of the Literati Way of Tea]. Kyoto-shi: Shibunkaku Shuppan.

Owyoung, Steven D.

2000   "The Connoisseurship of Tea: A Translation and Commentary on the 'P'in-ch'a' Section of the *Record of Superlative Things* by Wen Chen-heng (1585–1645)." *Kaikodo Journal*, 25–50.

2007   "A Story of the Qianlong Emperor and the Jade Tea Bowl." *Cha Dao* <http://tinyurl.com/33b4s3> (April 6).

2008a   "Lu T'ung and the 'Song of Tea': The Taoist Origins of the Seven Bowls." Parts 1 and 2. *Cha Dao* <http://tinyurl.com/5lxctd> (April 22 and 23).

2008b   "Lu Yü's Brazier: Taoist Elements in the T'ang Book of Tea." *Kaikodo Journal*, 232–52.

Oyudono no ue no nikki 1

1957   *Oyudono no ue no nikki 1.* Zuku gunsho ruijū hoi. Tokyo: Gunsho Ruijū Kansei Kai.

Oyudono no ue no nikki 2

1958   *Oyudono no ue no nikki 2.* Zuku gunsho ruijū hoi. Tokyo: Gunsho Ruijū Kansei Kai.

Pennsylvania Gazette

1770a   *Pennsylvania Gazette*, March 8.

1770b   *Pennsylvania Gazette*, September 20.

1770c   *Pennsylvania Gazette*, September 27.

1773   *Pennsylvania Gazette*, December 22.

1774   *Pennsylvania Gazette*, October 26.

Pennsylvania Journal

1767   *Pennsylvania Journal and Weekly Advertiser*, December 10.

Pigou and Booth

1773a   Pigou and Booth, New York, to James and Drinker, October 8, 1773. Philadelphia Tea Party Correspondence, 1773–1778. James and Drinker correspondence, transcribed by Francis. R. Taylor, 1910. Historical Society of Pennsylvania, Philadelphia.

1773b   Pigou and Booth, New York, to James and Drinker, October 18, 1773. Philadelphia Tea Party Correspondence, 1773–1778. James and Drinker correspondence, transcribed by Francis. R. Taylor, 1910. Historical Society of Pennsylvania, Philadelphia.

1773c   Pigou and Booth, New York, to James and Drinker, October 27, 1773, Philadelphia Tea Party Correspondence, 1773–1778, James and Drinker correspondence, transcribed by Francis. R. Taylor, 1910, Historical Society of Pennsylvania, Philadelphia.

1773d   Pigou and Booth, New York, to James and Drinker, November 10, 1773. Philadelphia Tea Party Correspondence, 1773–1778. James and Drinker correspondence, transcribed by Francis. R. Taylor, 1910. Historical Society of Pennsylvania, Philadelphia.

Pitelka, Morgan, ed.

2003   *Japanese Tea Culture: Art, History, and Practice.* London: Routledge-Curzon.

Plumb, J. H.

1982   "The New World of Children." In *Birth of a Consumer Society: The Commercialization of Eighteenth-Century England*, edited by Neil McKendrick, John Brewer, and J. H. Plumb, 286–315. Bloomington: Indiana University Press.

Portsmouth Resolves

1773   *Portsmouth Resolves Respecting Tea.* Portsmouth, New Hampshire, December 16. Broadside. Boston Public Library.

Pouchepadass, Jacques

1999   *Champaran and Gandhi: Planters, Peasants and Gandhian Politics.* New Delhi: Oxford University Press.

Qiu, Peipei

2005   *Basho and the Dao: The Zhuangzi and the Transformation of Haikai.* Honolulu: University of Hawai'i Press.

Ramsay, Allan
1763   *The Tea-Table Miscellany: or, a Collection of choice songs, Scots and English*. London: A. Millar.

Repplier, Agnes
1932   *To Think of Tea!* Boston: Houghton Mifflin.

Retford, Kate
2007   "From the Interior to Interiority: The Conversation Piece in Georgian England." *Journal of Design History* 20, no. 4: 291–307.

Richards, J. F.
1981   "The Indian Empire and Peasant Production of Opium in the Nineteenth Century." *Modern Asian Studies* 15, no. 1: 59–82.

Richardson, E. P.
1974   "Four American Political Prints." *The American Art Journal* 6, no. 2 (November): 36–44.

Rimer, J. Thomas et al.
1991   *Shisendō: Hall of the Poetry Immortals*. New York: Weatherhill.

Ringgold, Thomas
[1774] 1901   Thomas Ringgold to John Galloway, Oct. 25, 1774. "Account of the Destruction of the Brigg 'Peggy Stewart,'" at Annapolis 1774." *Pennsylvania Magazine of History and Biography* 25, no. 2: 248–54.

Roberts, Robert
1827   *The House Servant's Directory*. Boston: Munroe and Francis.

Rogers, George C., Jr.
1974   "The Charleston Tea Party: The Significance of December 3, 1773." *The South Carolina Historical Magazine* 75, no. 3: 153–68.

Rosenfield, John M.
1999   *Extraordinary Persons: Works by Eccentric, Nonconformist Japanese Artists of the Early Modern Era (1580–1868) in the Collection of Kimiko and John Powers*. 3 vols. Cambridge, Mass.: Harvard University Art Museums.

Roth, Rodris
1961   "Tea Drinking in Eighteenth-Century America: Its Etiquette and Equipage." In *Contributions from the Museum of History and Technology*. United States National Museum Bulletin 225. Washington, D.C.: Smithsonian Institution.

Rousmaniere, Nicole Coolidge
1996   "Defining Temmoku: Jian Ware Imported into Japan." In *Hare's Fur, Tortoiseshell, and Partridge Feathers: Chinese Brown- and Black-glazed Ceramics, 400–1400*, edited by Robert D. Mowry, 43–58. Cambridge, Mass.: Harvard University Art Museums.

Ruan Haogeng et al., comps.
1999   *Zhongguo gudai chaye chüanshu*. Hangzhou: Zhejiang sheying chubanshe.

Sage, Steven F.
1992   *Ancient Sichuan and the Unification of China*. Albany: State University of New York Press.

Sargent, William R.
1991   *The Copeland Collection: Chinese and Japanese Ceramics*. Salem: The Peabody Museum of Salem.

Seigle, Cecilia Segawa
2002   "Shinanomiiya Tsuneko: Portrait of a Court Lady." In *The Human Tradition in Modern Japan*, edited by Anne Walthall, 3–24. Lanham, Md.: SR.

Seikadō Bunkō Bijutsukan (Seikadō Bunko Art Museum)
1998   *Seikadōzō senchagu meihin ten* [Exhibition of *Sencha* Utensils from the Seikadō Collection]. Tokyo: Seikadō Bunkō

Sencha no Kigen to Hatten Shinpojium Soshiki Iinkai (The Association Committee for the Symposium on the Study of the Origin and Development of *Sencha*), ed.
2000   *Sencha no kigen to hatten shinpojium happyō ronbunshū* [Collected Papers Delivered at the Symposium on the Origin and Development of *Sencha*]. Shizuoka-shi: Sencha no Kigen to Hatten Shinpojium Soshiki Iinkai.

Shammas, Carole
1990   *The Pre-Industrial Consumer in England and America*. Oxford: Clarendon.

Sharma, Jayeeta
2002   "An European Tea 'Garden' and an Indian 'Frontier': The Discovery of Assam." *Centre of South Asian Studies Occasional Paper*, no. 6.

Shen Han and Zhu Zizhen
1995   *Zhongguo cha jiu wenhua shi*. Taipei: Wenjian chubanshe.

Shih Zunlaid, ed.
1999   *Taste Tea and Talk about Tea History and Culture of Chinese Tea*. Hangzhou: Zhejiang People's Fine Art Publishing.

Short, Thomas
1750   Discourses on tea, sugar, milk, made-wines, spirits, punch, tobacco &c: With plain and useful rules for gouty people. London: Longman.

Shufunotomosha
1975   *Baisaō shūsei* [Collected Records of Baisaō]. Tokyo: Shufunotomosha.

Sima Guang
1965   *The Chronicle of the Three Kingdoms*. Translated by Achilles Fang. Cambridge, Mass.: Harvard University Press.

Singleton, Theresa A.
1991   "The Archaeology of Slave Life." In *Before Freedom Came African American Life in the Antebellum South*. Charlottesville: The Museum of the Confederacy, Richmond, and the University Press of Virginia.

Smith, Billy
1981   "The Material Lives of Laboring Philadelphians, 1750–1800." *William and Mary Quarterly*, 3rd ser., 38, no. 2 (April): 164–202.

Smith, Paul J.
1991   *Taxing Heaven's Storehouse: Horses, Bureaucrats, and the Destruction of the Sichuan Tea Industry, 1074–1224*. Cambridge, Mass.: Harvard University Press.

Smith, Woodruff D.
1992   "Complications of the Commonplace: Tea, Sugar, and Imperialism." *Journal of Interdisciplinary History* 23, no. 2 (autumn 1992): 259–78.
2002   *Consumption and the Making of Respectability 1600–1800*. New York: Routledge.

Smits, Ivo
2007   "The Way of the Literati: Chinese Learning and Poetry in Mid-Heian Japan." In *Heian Japan: Centers and Peripheries*, edited by Mikael Adolphson, Edward Kamens, and Stacie Matsumoto, 105–28. Honolulu: University of Hawai'i Press.

Sons of Liberty of New York
1773   *The Association of the Sons of Liberty of New-York*, November 29. Broadside. New York Historical Society.

Spence, Jonathan D.
1991   *The Search for Modern China*. New York: W. W. Norton.
2007   *Return to Dragon Mountain: Memories of a Late Ming Man*. New York: Viking Peguin.

Steedman, Marguerite
1967   "Charlestown's Forgotten Tea Party." *The Georgia Review* 21, no. 2 (summer): 244–59.

Steinberg, David
2004   "Acquisition, Interrupted: Charles Wilson Peale's *Stewart Children* and the Labor of Conscience." Object Lessons. *Common-Place* 4, no. 3 (April). <http://www.common-place.org/vol-04/no-03/lessons/>.

Stiles, Ezra
1916   *Extracts from the Itineraries, 1753–1794*. New Haven: Yale University Press.

Sweeney, Erin Michaela
1998   "The Patriotic Ladies of Edenton, North Carolina: The Layers of Gray in a Black-and-White Print." *Journal of the American Historical Print Collectors Society* 23, no. 2 (autumn): 20–24.

Takai Kōichi
1991   *Tenpō-ki, shōnen shōjo no kyōyō keisei katei no kenkyū*. Tokyo: Kawade Shobō.

Tanihata Akio
1996   "Ii Naosuke no Chakai-ki." *Chanoyu Bunka Gaku* (Shibunkaku Shuppan, Kyoto), no. 3: 81–183.
2005   *Kuge sadō no kenkyū*. Kyoto: Shibunkaku Shuppan.

Tanimura Reiko
2001   *Ii Naosuke: Shūyō toshiteno chanoyu* [A Study of Ii Naosuke: Tea and the Cultivation of the Warrior in the Late Tokugawa Period]. Tokyo: Sōbunsha.
2004   "Tea of the Warrior in the Late Tokugawa Period." In *Japanese Tea Culture*, edited by Morgan Pitelka, 137–50. London: Curzon.

Taylor, Romeyn, trans.
1975   *Basic Annals of Ming T'ai-tsu*. San Francisco: Chinese Materials Center.

Tea Association of the United States of America
[1924]   *Celebration in Commemoration of the One Hundred and Fiftieth Anniversry of the New York Tea Party*. New York.

Tea Workers Health
2007   <http://www.bio-medicine.org/medicine-news/Tea-Workers-Health-Precarious--a-study-19754-1/> (accessed June 2009).

Thatcher, B. B. [Benjamin Bussey]
1835   *Traits of the Tea Party: being a memoir of George R. T. Hewes one of the last survivors; with a history of that transaction; reminiscences of the massacre, and the siege, and other stories of old times*. New York: Harper and Bros.

The Records of the Tea Gatherings by Itto
1969   "The Records of the Tea Gatherings by Itto." *Chanoyu* (Shibunkaku Shuppan, Kyoto), no. 1: 59–90.

Thomas, Peter D. G.
1987   *The Townshend Duties Crisis: The Second Phase of the American Revolution, 1767–1773*. Oxford: Clarendon.

Tinker, Hugh
1974   *A New System of Slavery: The Export of Indian Labour Overseas, 1830–1920*. London: Oxford University Press.

Trevelyan, George O.
[1864] 1992   *The Competition Wallah*. London: Macmillan; reprint New Delhi: HarperCollins.

Trocki, Carl A.
1999   *Opium, Empire, and the Global Political Economy*. London: Routledge.

Trumble, Angus
2007   "Mr. and Mrs. Hill." In *Paul Mellon's Legacy: A Passion for British Art. Masterpieces from the Yale Center for British Art*, edited by John Baskett et al., 249–50. New Haven: Yale University Press.

Tsao, Hsingyuan
2000   *Differences Preserved: Reconstructed Tombs from the Liao and Song Dynasties*. Portland, Ore.: Douglas F. Cooley Memorial Art Gallery, Reed College.

Tudor, John
1773   Entry of December 19, 1773. Diary, 1732–1793 (photocopy). John Tudor Paper, 1732–1793. Massachusetts Historical Society, Boston.

Twitchett, Denis C.
1963   *Financial Administration under the T'ang Dynasty*. Cambridge: Cambridge University Press.

Twitchett, Denis, and John K. Fairbank
1979   *The Cambridge History of China: Sui and T'ang China, 589–906*. Cambridge: Cambridge University Press.

Ukers, William H.
1935   *All About Tea*. Vols. I and II. New York: Tea and Coffee Trade Journal Co.; reprint New York: Hyperion Press, 1999.

Van Dyke, Paul A.
2005   *The Canton Trade: Life and Enterprise on the China Coast, 1700–1845*. Hong Kong: Hong Kong University Press.

Varley, Paul, and Kumakura Isao, eds.
1989   *Tea in Japan: Essays on the History of Chanoyu*. Honolulu: University of Hawai'i Press.

Wakeman, Frederic, Jr.
1975   *The Fall of Imperial China*. New York: The Free Press/Macmillan.

Watertown Resolutions
1774   Watertown, MA, Resolutions, January 3, 1774, U.S. Revolution Collection,, 1754–1928, box 1, folder 3, 1754–1773. American Antiquarian Society, Worcester, Massachusetts.

Watsky, Andrew M.
2006   "Locating 'China' in the Arts of Sixteenth-Century Japan." *Art History* 29, no. 4: 600–624.

Watson, Burton
1961   *Records of the Grand Historian of China*. Vol. 1. New York: Columbia University Press.
1976   *Poetry and Prose in Chinese by Japanese Writers of the Later Period*. Vol. 2 of *Japanese Literature in Chinese*. New York: Columbia University Press.
1990   *Kanshi: The Poetry of Ishikawa Jōzan and Other Edo-Period Poets*. San Francisco: North Point.

Wenwu
1974   "Changsha Mawangdui erh sanhao Hanmu fajüe jianbao" [Preliminary Excavation Report on the Han Tombs Numbers 2 and 3 at Mawangdui, Changsha]. *Wenwu*, no. 7: 45.
1989   *Zenghou Yi mu* [Tomb of Yi, Marquis of Zeng]. Vol. 1. Beijing: Wenwu chubanshe.

Wen Zhengming
1987   *Wen Zhenming ji* [Collected Writings of Wen Zhengming]. Shanghai: Shanghi guji chubanshe.

Wesley, John
1748   Letter to a Friend Concerning Tea. London, 1748. Cited in William Bates, "Tea Drinking." *Notes and Queries,* 5th ser., 12 (November 15, 1879): 390.

Wharton, Samuel
1901   "Observations upon the Consumption of Teas in North America, 1773." *Pennsylvania Magazine of History and Biography* 25: 139–41.

Wharton, Thomas
[1773] 1909   Thomas Wharton to Thomas Walpole, December 24, 1773. "Selections from the Letter-Books of Thomas Wharton, of Philadelphia, 1773–1783." *Pennsylvania Magazine of History and Biography* 33, no. 3: 321.

Wilbur, C. Martin
1943   *Slavery in China during the Former Han Dynasty 206 B.C.–A.D. 25.* Anthropological Series 34, 382–92. Chicago: The Field Museum of Natural History.
1994   "The Contract for a Youth." In *The Columbia Anthology of Traditional Chinese Literature*, edited by Victor H. Mair, 510–13. New York: Columbia University Press.

Wills, John E., Jr.
1993   "European Consumption and Asian Production in the Seventeenth and Eighteenth Centuries." In *Consumption and the World of Goods*, edited by John Brewer and Roy Porter, 133–47. London: Routledge.
1994   *Mountain of Fame: Portraits in Chinese History.* Princeton University Press.

Wilson, Richard L.
2001   *The Potter's Brush: The Kenzan Style in Japanese Ceramics.* Washington, D.C.: Freer Gallery of Art and Arthur M. Sackler Gallery, Smithsonian Institution in association with Merrell.

Wu Hongyi, comp.
1979   *Xianqing yiqü* [Matters of Leisure, Interests of Pleasure]. Taipei: Changqiao chubanshe.

Wu, Marshall P. S.
1998   "Black-glazed Jian Ware and Tea Drinking in the Song Dynasty." *Orientations* 29, no. 4: 22–31.

Wu Shan, ed.
1995   *Zhongguo gongyi meishu cidian* [Dictionary of Chinese Arts and Crafts]. Taipei: Xiungshi tushu.

Wu Zhihe
1996   *Mingren yincha shenghuo wenhua.* Taipei: Mingshi yanjiu xiaozu.

Xü Hairong, ed.
2000   *Zhongguo chashi tadian.* Beijing: Huaxia chubanshe.

Yasuraoka Kōsaku
1982   "On the Arts as Ways: Kenkō and Zeami." Translated by Dennis Hirota. *Chanoyu Quarterly,* no. 31: 71–74.

Yü Gongjie, ed.
1987   *Zhongguo di cha.* Beijing: Renmin chubanshe.

Zhang Hong-yong, comp.
1985   *Lu Yü Chajing congkan* [A Collection of Printings of the Book of Tea by Lu Yü]. Taoyüan: Chaxue wenxue chubanshe, 1985.

Zhang Linsheng
1978   "Jianjian yü Bei Song di doucha." *Gugong jikan* 13, no. 1: 79–90.

Zhen Yong-su et al., eds.
2002   *Tea: Bioactivity and Therapeutic Potential.* London: Taylor and Francis.

Zhou, Shiyong
1979   "Guanyü Changsha Mawangdui Hanmu zhongjian wen *jia* di kaozheng" [Evaluation of the Character *Jia* Found in the Han Tombs at Mawangdui, Changsha]. *Chaye tongxin,* no. 3, 65.
1992   "Zai tan Mawangdui Hanmu zhongjian wen *jia* di kaozheng" [Re-Evaluation of the Character *Jia* in the Han Tombs at Mawangdui, Changsha]. *Chaye tongxin,* no. 2, 200–203.

Zhu Zhongsheng
1985   *Bei Song cha zhi shengchan yü jingying* [Tea Production and Management during the Northern Song Dynasty]. Taipei: Xüesheng shujü.

INDEX

abolition. *See* slavery, in West Indian colonies
Acrelius, Israel, 158
Act of Grace (784), 39
aesthetic, of chill/withered, 82–84
ageya (teahouses), *115*. *See also* teahouses
    chaya v., 111
    tea ceremonies at, 117
Akaraku ware, *88*
American Colonies. *See* colonies
American Revolution, 16, 172, *173*, 183
    symbol for, *182*
antislavery movement, 144, 150–51
    sugar bowl of, *151*
anti-tea protests, 182. *See also* Boston Tea
      Party; prerevolutionary activism
Aoki Mokubei, 101–2
    death of, 102
    stoneware of, *102*
apprehension, of impermanence, 83
art, as Way, 80–82
    Shinkei on, 81
Articles of Association, 180
artistic mastery, 80–81
arts, of *za*, 84
Assam
    annexation of, 210
    Gandhi's tour of, 215
    indenture system in, 210–11, 214
    justice in, 213
    tea production in, 215
    working conditions in, 211–12
Assam tea, 16
    plantation of, *189*
    production of, 210–14
    wild growth of, 186
Azure Sea Tea Gathering. See Seiwan chakai

Bacerra, Ralph, *15*
Baiitsu. *See* Yamamoto Baiitsu
Baimudan tea, *20*
Baisaō, 99, *99*
    followers of, 100
    reverence for, 99
    tea cups of, 101
    tea stall of, 100
    tea utensils of, *101*
    teapot of, 100–101
bancha (green leaf tea), 90
Bashō, on *furyu*, 96
Berger, Daniel, *173*
Black Celebration tea, *21*
black tea, 12, *14*, 16–17. *See also* bohea tea
Blink Bonnie tea, *20*
Bodhidharma. *See* Daruma
Bodhisattva, 75
bohea tea, 12, *14*, *127*, 163–64. *See also* black tea

boiled tea, 14
Book of Tea (Lu Yü), 15, *36*, 38
Boston Harbor, 132
Boston Tea Party
    EIC and, 172
    as inspiration, 180
    Philadelphia and, 176–77, *178*
    significance of, 16
Bourdieu, Pierre, 138
brewed tea, 12, 38, 50, 54, 217n38
brothel, 111
Buddhism, 76. *See also* Mahayana Buddhist
      thought; Pure Land Buddhism;
      Zen Buddhism
Buddhist life, 78
Buddhist thought, on way of tea, 74
Byrd, William, 160–61

caffeine, 127
caked tea, *18*, *43*, 49, 57
calligraphy scrolls, 66
    by *tayu*, 113
Camellia sinensis
    assamica, 14
    growth of, 186
    importance of, 12
    sinensis, 14
Cang Jie, 31
ceramic production, 164–65
    unglazed earthenware, *166*
Ceylon (Sri Lanka), 187
chai preparation, 14
chaire (tea caddy), *64*
Chajing (Lu Yü), 15, *36*, 38
Chaling, 33–34. *See also* Tuling
chanoyu (Japanese tea ceremony), 16, 65, 74, 78,
      93, 99, *113*
    actions performed in, 76
    Confucian perspective on, 117–18
    criticism of, 67
    as demonstration, 74–75
    female participation in, 68, 108, *121*, 125
    linked verse and, 84
    origins of, 85–86
    perceived primacy of, 92–93
    poverty and, 79
    Raku tea bowls and, 88
    as religion, 106
    royal involvement in, 109–10
    schools of, 108
    Sen no Rikyū and, 86, 106
    sencha v., 95
    senchadō v., 67
    as social nicety, 121
    structural elements of, 104
    taught to women, 68, 108

    trivialization of, 125
    WWII and, 125
    Zen Buddhism and, 85–89
character traits, desired, 136–38
Charter Act (1833), 28
chaya (teahouse), 111, *112*. *See also* teahouses
    ageya v., 111
    as brothel, 111
child labor, *205*
chill/withered aesthetic, 82–84
China
    compelled openness of, 190
    England's failed embassy to, 148
    exoticism of, *139*, 140
    export porcelain from, *164*
    India v., 186
    Northern/Southern dynasties, 35
    on opium importation, 185
    as sole tea provider, *11*, 28–29, *186*
    tea plantations in, 194
    tea trade in, *11*, 192
Chinese
    commodity production of, 27
    porcelain manufacturing, 134, *164*, 199
    tea bowl, *82*
    view on tea of, 10
Chinese culture, tea as, 23
Chinese literati, in Japan, 95–99
Chinese tea practice, 16, *18*
Chinese water pipe, 199–200
chopsticks, 195
cinnabar, 37
class system, tea drinking within, 136. *See also*
      status differentiation
clay mining, 58
clay throwing, 58
coffee, tea and, 138, 170–71
coffeehouse, 129
    Byrd at, 160–61
    gossip at, 146
Collins, Richard, *156*
colonies
    disagreement on tea of, 175–76
    political response of, 174–83
    probate evidence from, 161–64, 166–71
    tea equipage in, 164
    tea use in, 158, 160, 175
    unrest amongst, 176
compressed tea, 14
Confucianism, 93
    chanoyu and, 117–18
    Edo period women and, 117–18
    influence of, 108
congo tea, 164
The Congregation of the Missionary Sisters
    of the Heart of Jesus, *124*

CONTRIBUTORS

Terese Tse Bartholomew is Curator Emeritus of Himalayan Art and Chinese Decorative Art at the Asian Art Museum of San Francisco, where she organized numerous exhibitions and installed the permanent galleries of Himalayan art and Chinese decorative arts at the museum's new location. Bartholomew began researching Yixing ware in 1977 and has curated several exhibitions on the subject. In addition to her many essays and articles, she is the author of the volume *Hidden Meanings in Chinese Art* (2006).

Barbara G. Carson served as Adjunct Associate Professor in the American Studies Program of the College of William and Mary until her retirement in 2006. Her research has focused on early American history, culture, and decorative arts, and her publications include *Ambitious Appetites: Dining Behavior and Patterns of Consumption in Federal Washington* (1990), *Interpreting the Historical Scene: Landscapes, Structures and Artifacts* (with Gary Carson, 1983), and *The Apparatus of Science at Harvard, 1760–1800* (with David P. Wheatland, 1968).

Patricia J. Graham, a former professor of Japanese art and culture and a museum curator, is presently an Adjunct Research Associate at the University of Kansas Center for East Asian Studies. Her publications include *Tea of the Sages, the Art of Sencha* (1998) and *Faith and Power in Japanese Buddhist Art, 1600–2005* (2007). She is currently completing another volume, *Buddhist-Inspired Art in Contemporary Japan: Intersections of Tradition and Imagination*, and has begun research on a book that will address attitudes toward nature and the environment in the arts of Japan.

Dennis Hirota is Professor of Shin Buddhist Studies at Ryukoku University in Kyoto. He is the head translator of *The Collected Works of Shinran* (1997) and has published numerous books and articles treating Japanese Pure Land Buddhist thought and Buddhist aesthetics. These include *Wind in the Pines: Classic Writings of the Way of Tea as a Buddhist Path* (1995), *Toward a Contemporary Understanding of Pure Land Buddhism* (2000), *Asura's Harp: Engagement with Language as Buddhist Path* (2006), and *Shinran: Shūkyō Gengo no Kakumeisha* (1998). Most recently, he has published articles treating the thought of Shinran and Heidegger.

Beatrice Hohenegger is an independent scholar and the author of *Liquid Jade: The Story of Tea from East to West* (2006). She has been researching the history and culture of tea for the last ten years, traveling to Europe and to Assam, India, the largest tea-growing region in the world. Her research interests focus on the sociopolitical and artistic significance of cross-cultural interchange. Fluent in English, French, Italian, and German, Beatrice holds an M.A. from the Department of History and Philosophy of the Università La Sapienza in Rome, Italy.

Elizabeth Kolsky is an Assistant Professor of History at Villanova University. Her research and teaching focus on colonization and decolonization in South Asia and the British Empire. She is the author of *Colonial Justice in British India: White Violence and the Rule of Law* (2009) and the co-editor of *Fringes of Empire: People, Place and Spaces in Colonial India* (2009), among other publications. She holds a B.A. in Middle Eastern and Asian Languages and Cultures and a Ph.D. in History, both from Columbia University.

Jane T. Merritt is Associate Professor of History at Old Dominion University in Norfolk, Virgina. She is the author of *At the Crossroads: Indians and Empires on a Mid-Atlantic Frontier, 1700–1763* (2003) and several articles about cultural encounters between Native Americans and Euro-Americans in early America. Her current research explores the eighteenth- and early nineteenth-century tea trade, tracing the development of colonial economic networks, consumer market behaviors, and revolutionary rhetoric, as well as the emergence of the United States as a commercial empire with direct trade to China.

Steven D. Owyoung is an art historian specializing in East Asia. In 2005 he retired as curator and head of the Department of Asian Arts at the Saint Louis Art Museum. In addition to his numerous reviews, essays, and articles, he has organized and contributed to many art exhibitions and catalogs, including the landmark exhibition *Nihonga, Transcending the Past: Japanese-Style Painting, 1868–1968*. He is a contributor to the forthcoming *Three Korean Classics of Tea*, a translation project headed by Brother Anthony of Taizé. Owyoung is currently finishing a study of Tang dynasty tea entitled *Ch'a-ching, The Book of Tea: An Introduction and Annotated Translation*.

Woodruff D. Smith is professor of history at the University of Massachusetts, Boston. His fields of research include modern German history, African history, imperialism, the history of social science, and the relationships among cultural, economic, and political history in the Atlantic world since the seventeenth century. He is the author of several books, including *Consumption and the Making of Respectability, 1600–1800* (2002) and *Politics and the Sciences of Culture in Germany, 1840–1920* (1991).

Reiko Tanimura received her doctoral degree from International Christian University, Tokyo in 1998. Her research focuses on the cultural and intellectual history of Japan. Her book *The Study of Ii Naosuke: Tea and Cultivation of the Warrior in the Late Tokugawa Period* (2001) is an analysis of the place of the tea ceremony (*chanoyu*) in the warrior culture and politics of mid-nineteenth-century Japan. It was awarded the Japan Association of Tea Ceremonies' prize for Scholarship Relating to the Tea Ceremony and Its Culture in 2001.

Angus Trumble is Senior Curator of Paintings and Sculpture at the Yale Center for British Art in New Haven, Connecticut. He has curated numerous exhibitions, including *Benjamin West and the Venetian Secret* (with Helen Cooper and Mark Aronson, 2008–2009); *The Worlds of Francis Wheatley* (with Cassandra Albinson, 2005); and *Love & Death: Art in the Age of Queen Victoria* (2001–2002). In addition to numerous essays, he is the author of *A Brief History of the Smile* (2004), and a regular contributor to *The Times Literary Supplement*.

John E. Wills Jr., received his Ph.D. from Harvard University. From 1965 until his retirement in 2004, he taught Chinese history and the history of the early modern world at the University of Southern California. His research into maritime China and its foreign connections, 1500–1800, led him to the sense of an interconnected world expressed in his books *1688: A Global History* (2001) and *The World from 1450 to 1700* (2009). He is the author of a survey of Chinese history, *Mountain of Fame: Portraits in Chinese History* (1994), two monographs on early Qing relations with Europeans, two edited volumes, and two chapters of the *Cambridge History of China*.

Karmarama Studios
Make Tea Not War, England, 2003
Poster
59.3 x 42 cm
PRIVATE COLLECTION

This poster was designed and issued by Karmarama Studios to encourage participation in the antiwar rally held in London on February 15, 2003, to protest the imminent invasion of Iraq. Millions of people—by some accounts as many as thirty million—took to the streets that weekend in eight hundred cities around the world.